THE SPANISH SOUTHWEST 1542 - 1794

AN ANNOTATED BIBLIOGRAPHY BY

HENRY R. WAGNER, LITT.D.

In Two Parts: Part II

ARNO PRESS
NEW YORK
1967

First Published by
THE QUIVIRA SOCIETY
1937
As Volume VII Parts I and II

•

Republished by
Arno Press
1967

•

Library of Congress Catalog Card
Number: 66-30073

•

Manufactured in the U.S.A.
Arno Press Inc.
New York

58. ATONDO Y ANTILLÓN: Isidro

Relacion De Servicios, Del Capitan Ayudante de Teniente de Maestre de Campo General, D. Ysidro de Atondo, Y Antillon, Almirante del Reyno de la California, y Governador de la Armada Real de su conversion.

Folio, 4 unnumbered pages, dated at the end, Mexico, March 23, 1686, then follow some manuscript notes by the secretary, Bustos, also dated Mexico, March 30.

Copy: AGI, 136-7-30.

Medina, no. 1790 of his *Biblioteca Hispano-Americana,* considers that this was printed in Spain, but I am unable to agree with him, as in the first place Atondo was in Mexico at the time, and in the second place the certification was by José de Bustos, the secretary of the virreinato.

Atondo refers to his services from August 1, 1658, until 1673, when he was appointed captain of the presidio of Sinaloa, and states that he served there for three years.

In December, 1679, he made a contract with the king through the viceroy for an expedition to California, of which he then gives a brief account, in which he states that he returned to Matanchel in April, 1685, under license of the viceroy.

In AGI, 136-7-22, there is a manuscript *relación de servicios* of Atondo of July 30, 1671.

In AGI, 1-1-2/31, are numerous letters and *testimonios* regarding Atondo's two expeditions to California, including the original contract entered into with him by the viceroy in November, 1678.

Father Francisco Kino accompanied the expedition, and there are several long letters from him regarding it in one of the *testimonios* in the same legajo and in 67-3-28.

An account from one of the documents in the archives was printed in Pacheco and Cárdenas.

RELACION
PVNTVAL DE LA ENTRADA
QVE HAN HECHO

LOS ESPAÑOLES ALMIRANTE D. ISIDRO DE ATONdo, y Antillõ en la Grande Isla de la California *este año de 1683 à 31 de Março*, sacada de carta de dicho Almirante de 20 y del Padre Eusebio Francisco Kino de la Cõpañia de Iesus de 22 de Abril, sus fechas en el puerto de la Paz

LA Isla de la California à sido desde la Conquista de la Nueva España empresa apetecible, por la gran riqueza de almas y perlas, que en su prolongado seno promete la opinion comun, y confirman muchas experiẽcias de los que han navegado por el. Ambos motivos llebaron à ella el primero al Adelantado de esta Nueva España el Marques del Valle D. Fernando Cortes Heroe de immortal nombre; que llamado poco tiempo despues de algunos temores de alteraciones q̃ en este Reyno como recien conquistado se presumieron, no pudo obrar lo que su gran valor, y fortuna prometian. Muchos grandes Capitanes continuaron la empreza despues de el en repetidas expediciones, cuias diligencias las frustraron varios acasos, ò desprevenciones sin aver tenido mas, que noticias de varias naciones, que la pueblan; y de grandes comederos de perlas, que ay en las Islas innumerables de su seno: y de algun ambar, que se encontrò en sus playas. Lo primero moviò à algunos sacerdotes, assi del Clero, como de las demas Familias Religiosas, a embarcarse, y entrar por este mar, a pescar almas; y lo segundo, no sin lo primero, à los q̃ a su costa armaron en diversos tiempos embarcaciones, y penetraron, segun sus relaciones, hasta casi treinta y cinco grados del Norte para descubrir sus grandes riquezas. Sus conatos fueron loables, pero por la mayor parte ineficaces las diligencias, y con poco provecho sus trabajos.

2. Yo discurro, que por no averse hasta aqui costeado à expensas solas de nuestro Catholico Monarca, (a quien tiene Dios señalado en la Iglesia por Atlante de la Fè, d[e] ella, para que estrive en sus Augustos ombros su peso, y se afiance en su Real zelo su promocion.) no ha tenido la Conquista el feliz sucesso, que se desea. *Este año de 1683 à 18 de Enero* saliò del Puerto de Chacala, que es del Reyno de la nueva Galicia Iurisdicion de la Iglesia de Guadalaxara, cõ dos navetas de buen porte, y vna balandra, para patachearlas, el Adelantado D. Isidro de Atondo. y Antillon muy bien prevenido de gente, municiones, y vituallas: despachado de el Excellentissimo Señor Marques de la Laguna Virrey, Capitan General desta Nueva España, que cum-

58a

Voyages De L'Empereur De La Chine Dans La Tartarie, Ausquels On A Joint une nouvelle découverte au Mexique.

A Paris, Chez Estienne Michallet, ruë S. Jacques, à l'Image S. Paul. M.DC.LXXXV. Avec Approbation.

12°, title, 3 unnumbered leaves of *epistre* to the King, and 110 numbered pages. At the end is the license, dated July 20, 1685.

The account was reproduced in the *Voyages au Nord*, III, 288-300, and an extract from it was published by Lockman in 1743 in volume I of the *Travels of the Jesuits*.

58b

A Relation Of the Invasion and Conquest Of Florida By The Spaniards, Under the Command of Fernando de Soto. Written in Portuguese by a Gentleman of the Town of Elvas. Now Englished. To which is Subjoyned Two Journeys of the present Emperour of China into Tartary in the Years 1682, and 1683. With some Discoveries made by the Spaniards in the Island of California, in the Year 1683.

London: Printed for John Lawrence, at the Angel in the Poultry over against the Compter. 1686.

12°, license leaf, title leaf, 6 preliminary leaves, and 272 pages. Some years ago Wilfrid M. Voynich, a dealer, turned up a copy with a canceled title to the second part.

58A. RELACION PVNTVAL

Relacion pvntval de la entrada qve han hecho los Españoles Almirante D. Isidro de Atondo, y Antilõ en la Grande Isla de la California este año de 1683 à 31 de Março, sacada de carta de dicho Almirante de 20 y del Padre Eusebio Frãcisco Kino de la Cõpañia de Iesus de 22 de Abril, sus fechas en el puerto de la Paz.

[Colophon:] Con Licencia. En Mexico: por la Viuda de Bernardo Calderon, en la Calle de S. Augustin.

4°, 4 unnumbered leaves with a running title.

Copies: G. R. G. Conway, Mexico city, and one other since discovered, both lacking the second and third leaves.

A comparison of what remains of this little account proves that the *Nouvelle Découverte* of 58a was translated from it. In view of the dates of the letters it seems to be a safe assumption that the *relación* was printed in the summer of 1683.

59. FLORENCIA: P. Francisco de

Vida Admirable, Y Mverte dichosa del Religioso P. Geronimo De Figveroa. Professo de la Compañia de Jesvs en la Provincia de Nueva-España. Misionero De quarenta años entre los Indios Taraumares, y Tepehuanes de la Sierra Madre: y despues Rector del Colegio Maximo, y Preposito de la Casa Professa de Mexico. [Jesuit device.] Con Licencia De Los Svperiores.

En Mexico: por Doña Maria de Benavides, Viuda de Juan de Ribera en el Empedradillo. Año de 1689.

4°, title, 3 unnumbered leaves of preliminaries, 40 numbered leaves, with the index on the verso of the last.

Preliminaries: 2 pages of dedication by Francisco de Florencia, the author, 2 pages of *pareceres,* and 3 pages of licenses, that of the government being dated December 1, 1689.

Copies: J, UT.

Father Figueroa was a native Mexican, born in 1604. He was one of the earliest missionaries to the Tarahumares and was employed in the missions there for nearly forty years. He finally returned to Mexico as rector of the Colegio Máximo. He died in the Casa Profesa in 1683.

This contains a long and interesting account of the missions in the north, mostly on the Rio Conchos.

60. BUSTOS: José de

Exmo. Señor. De la puntua execucion y debida cumplimiento â los ordenes expedidos por el Ex. Señor Conde de la Monclova . . .

Folio, 5 unnumbered leaves, verso of last blank, dated at the end, Mexico, 12th of January, 1690, and signed as above.

Copy: Medina, *La Imprenta en México,* no. 1468, describes this item from a copy in the Biblioteca Palafoxiana, probably the only one known.

According to Medina, this document is a report by Bustos, who at the time was secretary of the viceroyalty, on the results of the expedition made by Alonso de León to the bay of Espíritu Santo in 1689, when he came upon the site of La Salle's settlement.

The La Salle expedition made a great stir in Mexico and Spain, as was natural under the circumstances. The Spaniards considered that whatever the primary object might have been, the result was to take possession of a part of the province of Texas and set up fortifications there. As soon as they heard of it they immediately started expeditions by land and sea with the object, in the first place, of determining just where the party had landed. Their explorations began in 1686, but they did not discover the settlement until 1689, although the sea expedition in 1687 found the wrecks of La Salle's vessels in Matagorda bay.

A great quantity of material, mostly manuscript, is extant on these expeditions. Aside from the evidently brief account contained in the document that we are describing and the account published by Sigüenza in the *Trofeo de Justicia* in 1690, no others were printed at that time. Barcia, in his *Ensayo Cronológico,* however, gives a long account of the expeditions, no doubt taken from the original manuscripts. In 1857 Smith, in his *Colección de Varios Documentos,* published a short letter from Alonso de León himself, written apparently to a friend in Spain, giving an interesting account of his expedition of 1689.

In the *Texas Historical Quarterly* for 1899 there was published in facsimile, with a translation, a letter of Father Damian Massanet [or Manzanet, as it is spelled in the document] from the original in the library of the Texas Agricultural and Mechanical College.

In 1905, in the same Quarterly, there was published a translation of the *Derrotero* of León of the expedition of 1689, taken from a manuscript in the archives of Mexico.

In 1909 Genaro García published a book entitled, *Historia de Nueva León,* mostly taken from a book of manuscripts in his possession relating to León, and in this is inserted an account of the expedition of 1690, together with a shorter account of the preceding ones.

In 1916 Dr. H. E. Bolton, in *Spanish Exploration in the Southwest,* reprinted the translation of Father Massanet's letter from the *Texas Historical Quarterly* together with a reproduction of a map of the expedition of 1690, made by Don Carlos Sigüenza, from the original in the archives in Seville. Besides this he republished the *Derrotero* of the 1689 expedition from the same quarterly and a translation of another *Derrotero* of the 1690 expedition differing somewhat from that contained in García's *Historia de Nueva León.*

One of the most interesting problems connected with this expedition is the possible connection between La Salle and the Conde de Peñalosa. The Conde had been governor of New Mexico from 1661 to 1664, according to his own account, but after his return to Mexico he was arrested by the Inquisition, and after being imprisoned for some considerable time was sentenced to go out in an *auto de fe* on the 3d of February, 1668. Shortly after this he left Mexico and went to the Canary islands, and from there to England, where he attempted to interest the English court in a scheme to conquer New Mexico. Not receiving the continued necessary pecuniary assistance to enable him to stay there, he went to Paris in 1673 and proposed his schemes to the French court. Several memorials of his are extant in the French archives addressed to the Marquis de Seignelay, the first dated the 18th of January, 1682, the second, January, 1684, and the third, February, 1684. These three documents are reproduced in Margry, *Découvertes et établissements,* volume III.

In the first memorial Peñalosa proposed to plant a new French colony at the mouth of the Rio Bravo, from which point the conquest of Nueva Vizcaya would be an easy matter. In the second, he suggested going direct to Pánuco with an expedition, or undertaking a voyage up the Rio Bravo, which, according to Peñalosa, was the same as the Mississippi and had just been discovered by La Salle. In the third, he desired the command of an expedition to go to Pánuco, claiming that this would be an aid to that of La Salle which was at that time projected.

There is little doubt that the French court looked with great favor upon Peñalosa's schemes, and there is considerable evidence that an attempt was made to combine his scheme with that of La Salle. La Salle's expedition took place, but that of Peñalosa did not, and it is an open question whether that of La Salle was intended to take the place of both, or whether that of Peñalosa was simply abandoned for some reason now unknown. Dr. John Gilmary Shea discovered in New York among Buckingham Smith's papers a copy of a document entitled, *Relación del Descubrimiento del Pays y Ciudad de Quivira hecho por D. Diego Dionisio de Peñalosa* written by Fr. Nicolás de Freytas; and he printed it in 1882 together with a translation. Dr. Shea was aware of the documents published in Margry, and from a perusal of these documents he came to the conclusion that the French government combined the two projects of La Salle and Peñalosa and sent La Salle to commence operations in Texas, thus paving the way for Peñalosa's expedition. Dr. Shea was not aware of the fact that the *relación* which he printed was what might be called a fake document, having evidently been concocted by Peñalosa himself from the accounts of previous expeditions, chiefly those of Don Juan de Oñate. This fact was demonstrated by Captain C. Fernández Duro, who in the same year, 1882, in Madrid, published an *informe* on Peñalosa and his discoveries. This *informe* of Captain Fernández Duro contains a number of documents on Peñalosa which demonstrate his various activities during the period, among which will be found a number showing the early knowledge in Spain of Peñalosa's intrigues at the French court and the active measures which Spain took to combat them.

I had in my possession another memorial on Peñalosa, addressed to the French king, antedating any of those printed by Margry. In this Peñalosa proposes the conquest of New Mexico by means of an expedition from Canada which would proceed down the Ohio river to the Mississippi and then across the country. The date of it is uncertain, but it was probably written about 1675, and is perhaps the first effort which he made to enlist the support of the French crown in his schemes. In the Department of Marine in Paris there is a manuscript map of New Mexico which states that it is compiled from information from the Conde de Peñalosa and a written relation of Estevan de Perea. In some of Peñalosa's writings, and especially in the manuscript in my possession, he has a great deal to say about Teguayo; on this map Teguayo is shown, somewhat northwest of Santa Fe, in what is now the state of Colorado. The manuscript mentions also an expedition to Teguayo, and it is not at all impossible that he actually did make some such expedition. Teguayo was the Tewa country of New Mexico, comprising the pueblos of the northern Rio Grande region.

61. LE CLERCQ: P. Chrestian

Etablissement De La Foy Dans La Nouvelle France, Contenant L'Histoire des Colonies Françoises, & des Découvertes, qui s'y sont faites jusques à present. Avec Une Relation Exacte des Expeditions & Voyages entrepris pour la Découverte du Fleuve Mississipi jusques au Golphe de Mexique. Par Ordre Dv Roy. Sous la conduite du Sieur de la Salle, & de ses diverses avantures jusques à sa mort. Ensemble Les Victoires remportées en Canada sur les Anglois & Iroquois en 1690, par les Armes de Sa Majeste' sous le Commandement de Monsieur le Comte de Frontenac Gouverneur & Lieutenant General de la Nouvelle France. Par le P C.L.C. Tome Premier.

A Paris, Chez Amable Auroy, ruë Saint Jacques, attenant la Fontaine Saint Severin, à l'Image Saint Jerome. MDC.LXXXXI. Avec Privilege du Roy.

12°, title, 13 unnumbered preliminary leaves, 559 pages, and a map; Tome II: 458 pages [last misnumbered for 454], and 10 leaves of a catalogue of books.

Preliminaries: Dedication to Frontenac 13 pages, preface 4 pages, *Extrait du Privilege* 1 page, and 8 pages of table of chapters. There are two issues of the privilege page, one reading at the bottom: *Achevé d'imprimer pour la premiere le 20. Avril 1691,* with the catchword *Premier* at the foot of the page; and the other reading: *Achevé d'imprimer pour la premiere fois le 26. Juillet 1691,* without any catchword.

Map: Carte generalle de la Nouvelle France on est compris la Louisiane Gaspesie et le Nouueau Mexique auec les Isles Antilles. Dressée . . . 1691. I. Rouillard, delin. L. Boudan sculp. 48 x 34 cm.

The map is very rare and occurs only in a few copies. Dr. Wilberforce Eames states that the Rothschild copy of the book has an issue of the map dated 1692. Perhaps neither map belongs to the book, but from the title it was clearly intended to be issued with it, and also probably with the *Gaspesie.*

I have placed as the first issue the book with the above title, because the author's name appears only in the form of initials, thus following a general custom.

Dr. Wilberforce Eames has suggested a very plausible reason for the book's appearing with two colophons of different dates. Privileges for the *Gaspesie* and the *Nouvelle France* were both granted on the same date—30th of December, 1690,—in each case to last for eight consecutive years "to count from the day that the said book shall be printed for the first time." This would be a reason for giving the date of the first printing in the colophon. The *Gaspesie* was finished "for the first time the 20th of April, 1691," and the book ends with the words, "of this second mission which I reserve for the

Premier Etablissement de la Foi dans la Nouvelle France," thus indicating that the *Gaspesie* was printed first. On this theory the *Nouvelle France* finished printing "for the first time the 26th of July, 1691," without catchword. The publisher, to whom privileges for both books had been transferred by the author, changed the date from the 26th of July to the 20th of April to make it uniform with the privilege date of the *Gaspesie.*

61a

Premier Etablissement De La Foy Dans La Nouvelle France, Contenant La Publication de l'Evangile, l'Histoire des Colonies Françoises, & les fameuses decouvertes depuis le Fleuve de Saint Laurent, la Loüisiane & le Fleuve Colbert jusqu'au Golphe Mexique, archevées sous la conduite de feu Monsieur de la Salle. Par Ordre Dv Roy. Avec Les Victoires remportées en Canada par les armes de Sa Majeste' sur les Anglois & les Iroquois en 1690. Dedié à Monsieur le Comte De Frontenac, Gouverneur & Lieutenant General de la Nouvelle France. Par le Pere Chrestien Le Clercq Missionaire Recollet de la Province de Saint Antoine de Pade en Arthois, Gardien des Recollets de Lens. Tome I.

A Paris, Chez Amable Auroy, ruë Saint Jacques, attenant la Fontaine S. Severin à l'Image Saint Jerome. M.DC.XCI. Avec Privilege du Roy.

The same as the preceding, except for the title. Copies also occur with both issues of the privilege page.

61b

Histoire Des Colonies Françoises Et Les fameuses découvertes depuis le fleuve de S. Laurent, la

Loüisiane & le fleuve Colbert jusqu'au Golphe Mexique, achevées sous la conduite de feu Monsieur de la Salle. Avec Les Victoires remportées en Canada par les armes de sa Majesté sur les Anglois & les Iroquois en 1690. Tome Premier.

Imprimé à Paris, & se vend A Lyon, Chez Thomas Amaulry, ruë Merciere, au Mercure Galant. M.DC.XCII.

The same as the preceding, except for the title and the fact that in the only copy of which I know, that in the New York Public library, the table of eight pages follows the title in volume II, instead of being in volume I. This copy has the privilege page with the colophon, 26th of July.

It is generally stated that the book was suppressed at the time of publication. Harrisse, in his *Notes pour Servir a l'Histoire . . . de la Nouvelle France,* states that although the Jesuits made efforts to have the book suppressed they were unsuccessful. It has occurred to me that possibly failing in this, the Jesuits resorted to the method of buying up and destroying the book, a practice not altogether unknown. The appearance of an edition in 1692 with a different title, without the name of the author and purporting to be issued in Lyon, adds another element of mystery to the affair.

Le Clercq was not himself a member of the last expedition of La Salle, but inserted in his book an account by Father Anastase Douay, who did accompany the unfortunate explorer and witnessed his assassination. It appears to be the first published account of the ill-fated expedition. Later two other accounts were published, one by Tonty and the other by Joutel. While in Spain in 1923 I saw in the archives in Seville a manuscript relation of Cavelier addressed to Seignelay, which may possibly be the original written by La Salle's brother, which we know he wrote but which has disappeared.

62. SIGÜENZA Y GÓNGORA: Carlos de

Trofeo De La Jvsticia Española En El Castigo De La Alevosia Francesa Que Al Abrigo De La Armada de Barlovento, executaron los Lanzeros de la isla de Santo Domingo, en los que de aquella nacion ocupan sus costas. Debido todo à providentes ordenes del Ex.mo Señor D. Gaspar De Sandoval Cerda Silva Y Mendoza, Conde de Galve, Virrey de la Nueva-España. Escribelo D. Carlos de Siguenza Y Gongora Cosmographo, y Cathedratico de Mathematicas del Rey N.S. en la Academia Mexicana. [Sigüenza's own device.] En Mexico por los Herederos de la Viuda de Bernardo Calderon. Año de M.DC.XCI.

4°, title, 2 leaves of dedication, 1 leaf of index, 100 pages of text. Page [81] is occupied by a new title, *Epinicios Gratulatorios* . . ., followed by poems laudatory of the viceroy for the success of the expedition.

The dedication is addressed to the Condesa de Galve, the wife of the viceroy, and in it the author says that he is writing this at the order of the viceroy himself.

Copies: J, LC, UT, TWS, Y.

Eleven chapters of this book are devoted to the relations of the French and Spanish on the island of Santo Domingo. Chapter twelve deals with the expedition of La Salle and related affairs. The work is the only contemporary printed account of the events from the Spanish side, and, because of its very great rarity, has remained practically unknown. The text is now available in Francisco Salazar, *Obras de Carlos de Sigüenza y Góngora* (Sociedad de Bibliófilos Mexicanos, Mexico, 1928). Use of it was made by Irving A. Leonard in his work, *Don Carlos de Sigüenza y Góngora, a Mexican savant of the seventeenth century,* Berkeley, 1929.

TROFEO DE LA JVSTICIA ESPAÑOLA EN EL CASTIGO DE LA ALEVOSIA FRANCESA

QUE AL ABRIGO DE LA ARMADA de Barlovento, executaron los Lanzeros de la isla de Santo Domingo, en los que de aquella nacion ocupan sus costas.

Debido todo à providentes ordenes del Ex.mo Señor D. GASPAR DE SANDOVAL CERDA SILVA Y MENDOZA, Conde de Galve, Virrey de la Nueva-España.

ESCRIBELO

D. Carlos de Siguenza y Gongora

Cosmographo, y Cathedratico de Mathematicas del Rey N. S. en la Academia Mexicana.

En Mexico por los Herederos de la Viuda de Bernardo Calderon. Año de M. DC. XCI.

Alcedo, in his manuscript bibliography, cites the following: *Narración historica de los sucesos de la Armada Americana llamada de Barlovento desde finis del año de 1690 hasta principio del de 1691 victoria contra los franceses que ocupaban la costa del sur de la Isla Española conseguida por las tropas Españolasde la Isla . . . Mexico en casa de la Viuda y herederos de Bernardo Calderon 1691.* 4°.

This is not the only indication that Sigüenza printed two pieces in the same year on the same subject; and, indeed, Beristain says that there were two pieces printed, this and the *Trofeo.* Nevertheless I am of the opinion that only one was printed. I recently obtained in Mexico a copy of the *Trofeo.* Bound in with this at the end is the following in manuscript: *Relacion de lo svcedido a la Armada de Barlovento a fines del año passado, y principios de este de 1691. Victoria Que contra los Franceses, que ocupan la Costa del Norte de la Ysla de S^to^ Domingo tuvieron, con el ayuda de dicha Armada, los Lanzeros, y Milicia Española de aquella Ysla, abrasando el Puerto de Guarico, y otras Poblaciones. Debido todo al influxo, y providentissimos Ordenes del Exmo S^or^. D^n^. Gaspar de Sandoval, Cerda, Silva, y Mendoza, Conde de Galve, & meritissimo Virrey, Governador, y Capitan Genl. de esta Nueva-España.*

This manuscript consists of twenty-four small quarto leaves in a handwriting apparently of the early part of the eighteenth century, although it might possibly be contemporary. There is no indication as to who was the author, as it has no signature but only a rubric unknown to me.

A comparison of the title of this manuscript with those given by Alcedo and Beristain indicates that this is the lost pamphlet by Sigüenza, the wording being almost exactly that given by Alcedo. The narrative is different from that published in the *Trofeo,* being much more condensed and

EXPOSICION ASTRONOMICA DE EL COMETA,

Que el Año de 1680. por los meses de Noviembre, y Diziembre, y este Año de 1681. por los meses de Enero y Febrero, se ha visto en todo el mundo, y le ha observado en la Ciudad de Cadiz,

EL P. EUSEBIO FRANCISCO KINO

De la Compañia de JESVS.

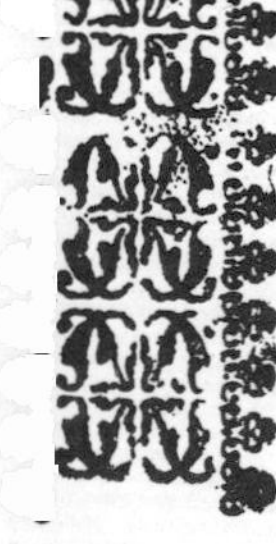

Con LICENCIA, en Mexico por Francisco Rodriguez Lupercio. 1681.

relating chiefly to the movements of the Armada. Nevertheless a comparison of different expressions indicates, from the use of almost the same words, that the manuscript is by the same author as the printed piece. The manuscript was probably written first, and it is, of course, possible that it was printed immediately after the expedition returned in the early part of March. Naturally this manuscript contains nothing about the movements of the French in Texas.

Sigüenza was a very prolific writer and left a number of printed works besides a large number of manuscripts, which, judging from the accounts that we have of them, consisted largely of unfinished works.

When the famous Father Eusebio Kino came to Mexico with a great reputation as an astronomer, Sigüenza says he treated him very well and lent him a number of his maps. Kino employed his time in writing a book, which he published in the latter part of 1681, with the following title: *Exposicion Astronomica De El Cometa, Que el Año de 1680. por los meses de Noviembre, y Diziembre, y este Año de 1681. por los meses de Enero y Febrero, se ha visto en todo el mundo, y le ha observado en la Ciudad de Cadiz, El P. Eusebio Francisco Kino De la Compañia de Jesvs.* [Virgin of Guadalupe.] *Con Licencia, en Mexico por Francisco Rodriguez Lupercio. 1681.*

4°, title, 7 unnumbered leaves of preliminaries, and 28 numbered leaves of text, together with a large astronomical map.

Kino says that he saw this comet in Cádiz on December 23, 1680, and that he sailed from there for Vera Cruz at the end of January, 1681. Although I do not find Sigüenza's name mentioned in the book, he took great offense at its publication, probably because of references to a book which he himself had previously published on the same comet, a book now lost. In consequence of this he wrote a very caustic reply, which was not published

LIBRA ASTRONOMICA, Y PHILOSOPHICA

EN QUE

D. Carlos de Siguenza y Gongora
Cosmographo, y Mathematico Regio en la Academia Mexicana,

EXAMINA

no ſolo lo que à ſu MANIFIESTO PHILOSOPHICO contra los Cometas opuſo el R. P. EUSEBIO FRANCISCO KINO de la Compañia de JESUS; ſino lo que el miſmo R. P. opinò, y pretendio haver demoſtrado en ſu EXPOSICION ASTRONOMICA del Cometa del año de 1681.

Sacala à luz D. SEBASTIAN DE GUZMAN Y CORDOVA, Fator, Veedor, Proveedor, Iuez Oficial de la Real Hazienda de ſu Mageſtad en la Caxa deſta Corte.

En Mexico: por los Herederos de la Viuda de Bernardo Cal deron
IXI. DC. XC.

until 1690, probably on account of the author's friendship with the leading Jesuits in Mexico.

62a

Libra Astronomica, Y Philosophica En Que D. Carlos de Siguenza y Gongora Cosmographo, y Mathematico Regio en la Academia Mexicana, Examina no solo lo que à su Manifiesto Philosophico contra los Cometas opuso el R. P. Eusebio Francisco Kino de la Compañia de Jesus; sino lo que el mismo R. P. opinò, y pretendio haver demostrado en su Exposicion Astronomica del Cometa del año de 1681. Sacala à luz D. Sebastian De Gvzman Y Cordova, Fator, Veedor, Proveedor, Iuez Oficial de la Real Hazienda de su Magestad en la Caxa desta Corte. [Sigüenza's own device.]

En Mexico: por los Herederos de la Viuda de BernardoCal deron IXI.DC.XC. [1690]

4°, leaf before title, title, 10 unnumbered leaves of preliminaries, and 188 pages numbered except the first.

Copies: C, J.

The dispute was a very pretty one and excited great interest in the circles of the savants of Mexico. Father Kino was still living in the Middle Ages and thought that comets presaged all kinds of horrible catastrophes, whereas Don Carlos ridiculed such an idea and explained that they were nothing but natural phenomena which had not the slightest influence on the affairs of men.

While not strictly pertinent to this work, I cannot refrain from giving a description of a long lost work of Sigüenza which recently came into my possession.

62b

Descripcion, Que De La Vaia De Santa Maria de Galve (antes Pansacola) de la Movila, y Rio de la

Paliçada, en la Costa Septentrional del seno Mexicano, hizo Don Carlos de Siguença y Gongora, Cosmographo del Rey nuestro Señor, y Cathedratico Jubilado de las Ciencias Mathematicas, en la Academia Mexicana, yendo para ello en compañia de Don Andrès de Pes, Cavallero de la Orden de Santiago, Almirante de la Real Armada de Barlovento, à cuyo cargo iba la Fragata Nuestra Señora de Guadalupe, y la Valandra San Joseph, por orden del Excelentissimo señor Conde de Galve, Virrey, Governador, y Capitan General de la Nueva España, Año de 1693.

Folio, 16 leaves numbered except the first, which contains a caption title only. At the end it is dated, May 15, 1693, and signed by the author.

Copy: My copy was sold to L. C. Harper and is now in the Jones collection; no other has been found.

It is probable that the work was published not when written, but more likely about 1719. The pamphlet contains an account of the expedition from Vera Cruz to Pensacola and the Mississippi by Admiral Pez in 1693. Sigüenza accompanied the expedition, and on his return made out this report, the original of which is still in existence in manuscript in the Ayer collection, forming part of an *expediente* which contains, besides Sigüenza's, the report of Admiral Pez of June 1, 1693, the account of the pilots, the instructions to Pez, and further communications from Sigüenza of June 1, 3, and 6, and the proceedings of the *Junta* in Mexico city, June 2.

The last positive notice which I have seen of this pamphlet is in Barcia's *Ensayo Cronológico,* where, on page 311, he states that a description of the bay of Pensacola by Sigüenza has recently been printed in 16 leaves and is therefore omitted. The only reason to suppose that it might have been printed about the time when it was written is because it was copied into Pulgar's manuscript history of Florida, where it appears as chapter II, with the title obviously copied from the above, or at least from a manuscript that was prepared for the press. Pulgar's history was written about 1700 but has never been published. Buckingham Smith found it in the Biblioteca Nacional in Madrid and had the chapter containing Sigüenza's work copied, undoubtedly with the intention of publishing it. The copy is now among Smith's papers in the New York Historical Society.

63. SIGÜENZA Y GÓNGORA: Carlos de

Mercurio Volante Con La Noticia de la recuperacion de las Provincias Del Nvevo Mexico Consegvida Por D. Diego De Vargas, Zapata, Y Luxan Ponze De Leon, Governador y Capitan General de aquel Reyno. Escriviola Por especial orden de el Excelentissimo Señor Conde De Galve Virrey, Governador, Y Capitan General De La Nueva-España, &c. Don Carlos De Sigvenza, Y Gongora, Cosmographo mayor de su Magestad en estos Reynos, y Cathedratico Iubilado de Mathematicas en la Academia Mexicana. [Sigüenza's own device.] Con licencia en Mexico:

En La Imprenta De Antuerpia de los Herederos de la Viuda de Bernardo Calderon, año de 1693.

4°, title, and 18 numbered leaves.
Copies: H, J, JCB, LC, UT.

Reprinted in 1900 by the Museo Nacional of Mexico as an appendix to volume II of the *Historia de la Nueva México* of Villagrá. Translated into English by Irving A. Leonard and published with a facsimile of the original by the Quivira Society in 1932 as volume III of its series.

MERCURIO VOLANTE

CON LA NOTICIA de la recuperacion de las PROVINCIAS DEL NVEVO MEXICO

CONSEGVIDA

Por D. DIEGO DE VARGAS, ZAPATA, YLUXAN PONZE DE LEON,

Governador y Capitan General de aquel Reyno.

ESCRIVIOLA

Por especial orden de el Excelentissimo Señor CONDE DE GALVE VIRREY, GOVERNADOR, Y CAPITAN GENERAL DE LA NUEVA-ESPAñA, &c.

DON CARLOS DE SIGVENZA, Y GONGORA, Cosmographo mayor de su Magestad en estos Reynos, y Cathedratico Iubilado de Mathematicas en la Academia Mexicana.

Con licencia en Mexico:
EN LA IMPRENTA DE ANTUERPIA
de los Herederos de la Viuda de Bernardo Calderon, año de 1693.

In the introduction to volume I of the 1900 edition, the editor speaks of the rarity of this piece, reprinted from a copy in the possession of Señor Agreda.

Sigüenza begins with a short description of the early expeditions to New Mexico, and continues with an equally short account of the conquest. Curiously enough, he says he does not describe the expeditions of Marcos de Niza or Coronado because, as they themselves said, they did not go exactly to New Mexico; and he begins his discoveries with Francisco Ruiz. After briefly referring to the revolution of 1680, he devotes the largest portion of his work to the expedition of Diego de Vargas in 1692, and gives a long account of his expedition to Zuñi and his final return to El Paso on the 20th of December of the same year.

All in all, Sigüenza was perhaps the most remarkable man born in Mexico during the viceregal period, and it is to be regretted that so many of his works have been lost; still, enough remain to show that he was a man of varied talent, of keen intelligence, and far ahead of his times. Andrade, in his bibliography of the seventeenth century, no. 1141, gives a very interesting account of his life, from which I extract a few short notices.

He was born in the city of Mexico, August 20, 1645, or possibly a few days earlier. On May 17, 1660, he entered the Jesuit order as a novice, but after seven years he was *despedido* in Puebla on the 3rd of August, 1667. Just what was meant by the word *despedido* is still in doubt among Mexican students. Father Cavo says that he left the Jesuits to comply with the wishes of his father. At some time he took sacred orders, just when or how is not known, but in July, 1672, he was appointed professor of mathematics in the university. In 1682 he was appointed chaplain of the Hospital de la Amor de Dios, where he lived until his death, August 22, 1700. During the riot in Mexico in 1692 when the palace was burned with all the archives, Sigüenza with a few friends succeeded in saving the *Actas de Cabildo.*

After his death, a nephew published one of his poems entitled, *Oriental Planeta Evangelico Epopeya Sacro-Panegyrica Al Apostol grande de las Indias S. Francisco Xavier . . . En Mexico . . . Año de 1700.*

4°, 5 unnumbered leaves of preliminaries, and 24 numbered pages.

In the dedication to this work, the nephew gives some account of his uncle and states that eleven of his works had been published during his lifetime.

64. ESCALANTE: P. Thomas de

Sermon Funebre, Que Predicò El P. Thomas De Escalante de la Compañia de Iesvs professo de quatro votos de ella. En las honrras de los Soldados difuntos Españoles, que de orden de su Magestad hizo celebrar en la Cassa Professa de la mesma Compañia de Jesus de Mexico el dia 15. de Febrero de esta Año de 1694. El Exmo. Señor D. Gaspar de Sandoval, Cerda, Silva, y Mendoza, Conde de Galve, Virrey, Governador, y Capitan General de la Nueva-España, y Presidente de su Real Chancilleria de Mexico. A Quien Humilde le dedica su Autor.

Con licencia en Mexico: en la Imprenta de Iuan Ioseph Guillena Carrascoso. Año de 1694.

4°, title, 18 leaves of dedication to the viceroy, 12 leaves of *sentir* and *aprobación,* 1 leaf of licenses, all unnumbered, 22 pages of sermon, all numbered except the last, followed by 17 unnumbered leaves of *Funebres Ecos.*

Copies: J, JCB.

The dedication is the only part of this pamphlet which contains any information of an historic nature. It is devoted largely to fulsome flattery of the viceroy, mentioning most of the events which had taken place during his government since 1690, simply to laud him and his various extraordinary qualities. He refers briefly to the sending of missionaries to Texas, Father Massanet, the English pirates on the coast of Sinaloa, and the reconquest of New Mexico by Diego de Vargas Zapata Luxán Ponce de León. To this latter event the author devotes several pages, quoting from a letter from Vargas dated January 20, 1694, giving an account of the capture of Santa Fe at the end of 1693. The author gives a considerable account of the expedition to Santo Domingo in 1690, and the inundation of Mexico in 1692 and 1693. He also refers at length to the foundation of new missions in Parral and Sinaloa, in the country of the Pimas, and the new missions in New Mexico. This dedication is dated May 1, 1694.

65. LÓPEZ: P. Eugenio

Satisfaccion pública y respuesta apologética al Gobernador de la Nueva Vizcaya, D. Juan Pardiñas, del Orden de Santiago, sobre los injustos cargos que hizo á los Jesuitas en el levantamiento de los Indios Tarahumares, Tepehuanes, Pimas y Conchos.

Impressa Año 1695, in folio.

Noted in Beristain, II, 178, from whom it was copied by Medina, *La Imprenta en México,* no. 1601.

66. DAMPIER: William

A New Voyage Round the World. Describing particularly, The Isthmus of America, several Coasts and Islands in the West Indies, the Isles of Cape Verd, the Passage by Terra del Fuego, the South

Sea Coasts of Chili, Peru, and Mexico; the Isle of Guam one of the Ladrones, Mindanao, and other Philippine and East-India Islands, near Cambodia, China, Formosa, Luconia, Celebes, &c. New Holland, Sumatra, Nicobar Isles; the Cape of Good Hope, and Santa Hellena Their Soils, Rivers, Harbours, Plants, Fruits, Animals, and Inhabitants. Their Customs, Religion, Government, Trade, &c. By William Dampier. Illustrated with Particular Maps and Draughts.

London, Printed for James Knapton, at the Crown in St. Paul's Church-yard. MDCXCVII.

8°, title, 4 unnumbered preliminary leaves, VI, 550 pages, and 1 unnumbered of errata, with 3 unnumbered pages of advertisements of books, 5 maps.

Preliminaries: Leaf of dedication to the Honorable Charles Montague, 2 leaves of preface, and 1 leaf of contents. The vi pages contain a resumé of Dampier's experiences down to 1681, and the book begins at April 17 of that year. Maps: Map of the World shewing the course of Mr. Dampier's voyages round it—from 1679 to 1691; Isthmus of Darien; Middle Part of America [shows California to the head of the Gulf]; East Indies; a plate containing four views of land and charts.

Reissued in 1697 with the errors corrected and therefore the errata omitted, the space being taken up with a catalogue of books. Also reissued in 1698, 1699, 1703, 1717, and 1729, the last forming volume 1 of the collection of voyages known as Dampier's Collection. In the later editions the title pages are the same as the first except that they read, "By Captain William Dampier The Second [Third] Edition Corrected."

The work was translated into French and Dutch and published in 1698, and into German in 1702.

Captain Swan was at the head of this expedition, which did not land in California; nevertheless Dampier has something to say about California and the Strait of Anian, on page 272 and elsewhere. They were on the Sinaloa coast in the winter of 1685-86, and left for the Ladrones in the spring.

67. TONTY: Henri

Dernieres Decouvertes Dans L'Amerique Septentrionale de M. De La Sale; Mises au jour par M. le Chevalier Tonti, Gouverneur du Fort Saint Loüis, aux Islinois.

A Paris Au Palais, Chez Jean Guignard, à l'entrée de la Grand' Salle, à l'Image saint Jean. M.DC.LXXXXVII. Avec Privilege du Roy.

12°, title, leaf of privilege, 333 pages, and 21 unnumbered of index and catalogue of books by the same publisher.

Leclerc, no. 2621, describes a copy in which pages 185-88 had been cancelled and printed on a single leaf with smaller type than used in the rest of the volume. There is some indication that a map was issued with the book, but no copy seems to be known that contains one.

Reprinted in the *Voyages au Nord*, volume v.

67a

An Account Of Monsieur de la Salle's Last Expedition and Discoveries In North America. Presented to the French King, and Published by the Chevalier Tonti, Governour of Fort St. Louis, in the Province of the Islinois. Made English from the Paris Original. Also The Adventures of the Sieur de Montauban, Captain of the French Buccaneers on the Coast of Guinea, in the year 1695.

London, printed for J. Tonson . . . 1698.

8°, title, 211 pages, and 44 pages for the adventures of Montauban.

Tonty did not accompany La Salle on his last expedition, and what he has to say about it is hearsay evidence. Nevertheless his contribution is important because it was, no doubt, derived from survivors of the expedition who managed to reach Illinois.

The work is made up from two manuscript accounts by Tonty, one written in Quebec and dated November 14, 1684, published in Margry, *Relations et Mémoires,* I, 571, and another written in 1693 and published also by Margry in a separate volume in 1867. This last was translated and published in French's *Historical Collections of Louisiana,* Part I, New York, 1846, from the original, and a translation was also inserted in Falconer's *Discovery of the Mississippi,* London, 1844.

Tonty had nothing to do with publishing the book,—at least he disavowed it.

68. VETANCURT: Fr. Augustín de

Chronica De La Provincia Del Santo Evangelio De Mexico. Quarta parte del Teatro Mexicano de los successos Religiosos. Compuesta Por El Reverendo Padre Fray Augustin de Vetancur, Mexicano, hijo de la misma Provincia, Difinidor actual, Ex-Lector de Theologia, Predicador Iubilado General, y su Chronista Appostolico, Vicario, y Cura Ministro, por su Magestad, de la Iglesia Parrochial de San Ioseph de los Naturales de Mexico. Dedicada Al Glorioso Patriarcha Esposo De La Que Es de Dios Esposa, Angel Custodio de la Ciudad Mystica Maria Santissima, Padre putativo de Christo nuestro Señor, Patron de la Nueva

España Señor San Ioseph. Con Licencia De Los Superiores.

En Mexico, por Doña Maria de Benavides Viuda de Iuan de Ribera. Año de 1697.

Folio, title, 5 unnumbered leaves of preliminaries, 136 numbered and 2 unnumbered pages, [new title] *Menologio Franciscano De Los Varones Mas Señalados,* and 156 numbered pages.

Preliminaries: 1 page of dedication, 2 pages of licenses, 2 pages of *aprobación,* 2 pages of *parecer,* 2 pages of prologue, and 1 page containing licenses of the government dated June 16, 1696, license of the archbishop dated June 18, 1696, and the errata. The 2 unnumbered pages of the first part contain the index continued from page 136. In the second part, pages 154-156 contain an alphabetical index of the illustrious members of the province.

The *Chrónica* is a prime authority for the history of New Mexico. I give the headings of some of the chapters: *De la Custodia de la conversión de S. Pablo de la Nueva Mexico,* page 94; *De la conversión de los Xumanos,* page 96; *De las casas que permanecen despues de el rebelión,* page 97; *De los pueblos amotinados,* page 99; *Del rebelión de los bárbaros, en la Nueva-México,* page 103; *De la entrada que se hizo a las Californias,* page 116; *De las entradas que se han hecho a la parte del Norte, de la Quibira y otras partes,* page 118.

69. SALVATIERRA: P. Juan María de

Copia De Qvatro Cartas De El Padre Juan Maria De Salvatierra de la Compañia de Jesvs, Missionero, que fue en la Taraumara, Visitador de las Missiones, de donde le sacò la obediencia para Rector de el Collegio de Guadalaxara, y de aqui para Rector, y Maestro de Novicios de el Collegio de Tepotzotlan, de donde salió siendo actual Rector para solicitar medios para la empressa de Californias, donde està oy dia. Las Dos Primeras Cartas Son A Los Excelentissimos Señores Virreyes de esta Nueva-España, cuyo zelo alentò â la empressa al Padre Juan Maria. Las Dos Vltimas, La Vna al Lic[do] Don Juan Cavallero, y Ossio Comissario de Corte: primer benefactor de las Californias, Natural de Santiago de Queretaro. La Otra Al Padre Maestro Juan de Ugarte Procurador de la Mission de Californias.

Con licencia en Mexico en la Imprenta de Juan Joseph Guillena Carrascoso, año de 1698.

Folio, title, verso blank, and 10 unnumbered leaves.
Copies: AGI, 61-4-23, WBS.

They were printed in *Documentos para la Historia de Mexico,* series II, volume I.

The first letter is dated November 28, 1697, the second the 26th of November, and the third and fourth, the 27th, all from Real de N. S. de Loreto in California. The third is particularly interesting as it contains an account of the voyage to California. The cross was planted at Loreto on October 23, and the first mass celebrated on October 25.

70. VETANCURT: Fr. Augustín de

Teatro Mexicano Descripcion Breve De Los Svcesos Exemplares, Históricos, Políticos, Militares, y Religiosos del nuevo mundo Occidental de las Indias, Dedicado Al Esposo de la que es del mismo Dios Esposa, Padre putativo del Hijo, que es Hijo del mismo Dios Christo, Dios, y hombre verdadero. Al que con el sudor de su rostro sustentó al que todo lo sustenta: Al que fue Angel de

Guarda de la Ciudad de Dios milagro de su Omnipotencia, y abismo de la gracia. Maria Señora Nuestra. Al Glorioso Patriarca De La Casa De Dios Señor S. Joseph. Dispuesto Por El R. P. Fr. Avgvstin De Vetancvrt, Mexicano, hijo de la misma Provincia, Difinidor actual, Ex-Lector de Theologia, Predicador Jubilado General, y su Chronista Apostolico, Vicario, y Cura Ministro, por su Magestad, de la Iglesia Parrochial de S. Joseph de los Naturales de Mexico. Con Licencia De Los Svperiores.

En Mexico por Doña Maria de Benavides Viuda de Iuan de Ribera. Año de 1698.

Folio, title, 5 unnumbered leaves of preliminaries, 66 and 168 numbered pages of text, and leaf of index.

Preliminaries: Leaf of dedication, leaf of licenses and errata, leaf to the curious reader, leaf of catalogue of printed authors and another of manuscripts. The license of the government is dated June 16, 1696, the same as of the *Crónica*. The errata include the Tratado de Mexico, which, in consequence, must have been added to this part of the work. It contains 56 numbered pages, having a caption title only.

71. SALVATIERRA: P. Juan María and PICOLO: P. Francisco María

Copia de cartas De Californias Escritas por el P. Juan Maria de Salvatierra y Francisco Maria Picolo, Su fecha de 9. de Julio deste año de 1699. Impressas Con Licencia del Excellentissimo Señor D. Joseph Sarmiento Valladares, Cavallero del Orden de Santiago, del Consejo de su Magestad, su Virrey, Lugar Theniente, Governador, y Capitan, Gl. desta Nueva España, y Presidente de la Real Audiencia, &c. Y Del Señor Doctor Don Manvel de Esclante Chantre desta Sancta Iglesia, Cathedratico jubilado de Prima de Sagrados Canones, en la Real Vniversidad desta Corte, Commissario Sub-delegado General de este Arçobispado, etc. [Vignette.]

En Mexico En la Imprenta de los Herederos de la Viuda de Bernardo Calderon, en la Calle de S. Agustin, año de 1699.

Folio, title, verso blank, 9 unnumbered leaves with the verso of the last blank.

Medina, *La Imprenta en México,* no. 1747, describes the book from an example in the Biblioteca Palafoxiana in Puebla, Mexico. No other copy seems to be known.

The principal letter of Salvatierra, dated July 9, 1699, was written from Loreto and is of the greatest interest. The other two of Salvatierra are without date. Father Picolo's letter is also from Loreto and dated July 2.

Mr. W. B. Stephens had a letter of Salvatierra to Juan de Ugarte, dated Loreto Concho, July 9, 1699, in which he relates what had taken place in the peninsula during May and June, 1699. It was printed separately, evidently before no. 71, and consists of 14 unnumbered folio pages. The verso of the last leaf is not blank, but is taken up by the last part of the letter, and the remainder of the page by an appeal of Ugarte for funds for the missions, with the word "Fin" in capitals at the bottom. The opening sentence of the letter reads, "Por Abril deste año de 99. remitiendo a la Nueva España la Lancha de S. Francisco Xavier escrevía Vr. la relacion de los ultimos meses desta Conquista Mariana . . ." The first sentence of the appeal for funds reads, "Otras Relaciones han venido, la fecha de Abril deste año de 99. que por ser largas, y costoso el imprimirlas, no se dan à la Estampa."

Evidently these other *relaciones* were printed afterward as no. 71, together with the letter of July 1, 1699. Whether this last letter was reprinted, or whether the appeal for funds by Ugarte was simply omitted and the other letters made to follow immediately after the first cannot be determined, as no copy of no. 71 is available for comparison.

72. SALINAS VARONA: Gregorio de

Relacion De Servicios Del Capitan De Cavallos Corazas D. Gregorio de Salinas Varona, residente en la Nueva-España.

Folio, 10 unnumbered pages, with a caption title, and dated at the end, Madrid, June 20, 1701.

Copy: AGI, 137-1-23.

After many years of service in Flanders, Salinas went to New Spain in 1687, going first to Tehuantepec to drive away a pirate, who, he says, had taken possession of the place. In December, 1689, he was sent to Texas with four missionaries from Santa Cruz de Querétaro, and suffered great hardships during the journey of nine months. On May 30, 1691, he was appointed captain of San Francisco de Monclova, and tells the story about rescuing some French at the Bahía de Espíritu Santo. He made two expeditions by sea to this bay from Vera Cruz, in 1690 and 1691. On the 3rd of May, 1693, under order of the viceroy, he undertook an expedition to Texas with twenty soldiers to carry supplies to the missionaries who were converting the Indians. After his return he was ordered, in August, to go after these missionaries and bring them back; he did bring them back because, as he says, the Tejas Indians threatened to kill them.

The *relación* contains a large amount of information about the northern provinces at this period.

The diary of Salinas and Don Manuel de Cárdenas [written by the latter] of their expedition in October and November, 1690, from Vera Cruz to Bahía San Bernardo, with a map of the bay, is in AGI, 61-6-21.

73. LOMBARDO: P. Natal

Arte de la Lengua Teguima vulgarmente llamada Opata. Compvesta por el P. Natal Lombardo de la Compañia de Jesvs, y Missionero de mas de veinte y seis años en la Provincia de Sonora. Le dedica al General D. Juan Fernandez de la Fuente, Capitan Vitalicio de el Real Presidio de San Phelipe y Santiago de Janos, y Theniente de Capitan General en aquellas fronteras por su Magestad. Con Licencia.

En Mexico por Miguel de Ribera, Impressor y Mercader de libros, año de 1702.

4°, title, 7 unnumbered leaves of preliminaries, and 252 numbered leaves.

Preliminaries: Dedication, opinion of P. Fran. Javier de Mora, Arizpe, December 24, 1701, opinion of Horacio Police, February 24, 1702, opinion of P. Juan Ventura Ferrer, February 25, 1702, license of the order, September 22, license of the government, July 17, and that of the ordinary, July 18.

Copies: Medina, *La Imprenta en México,* no. 2075, locates a copy in the Biblioteca Guadalajara. A copy was also sold at the Ramírez sale (no. 842), but I do not know where it is now to be found.

According to the preliminaries, Lombardo, who was a Jesuit missionary, was stationed in the *partido* of Aribelsi, and according to his associates, Police and Ventura

Ferrer, he was thoroughly acquainted with the Ópata language and had produced an entirely satisfactory work.

74. PICOLO: P. Francisco María

Informe Del Estado De La Nueva Christiandad de California, Que Pidio Por Auto, La Real Audiencia De Guadalaxara, Obedeciendo â la Real Cedula de N. Rey y Señor, D. Phelipe V. Fecha en Madrid, á 17. de Julio, de 1701. En Qve Ordena Sv Magestad, Se le Informe individualmente, à cerca de la Nueva Christiandad, del Progresso, Augmento, y Poblacion de aquel Nuevo Reyno. Dado, Y Respondido, à dicha Real Audiencia de Guadalaxara Por El P, Francisco Maria Picolo De La Compañia de Jesus, Uno de los primeros fundadores de dichas Missiones de California, en las quales ha vivido en compañia del Padre Rector Juan Maria De Salvatierra, estos cinco años que entraron en aquellas tierras.

[Mexico, Carrascoso, 1702.]

Folio, 16 pages numbered except the title.

The verso of the title is marked page 2, and this page, together with pages 3 and 4, contains a copy of the *cédula* of July 17, 1701; pages 5-16 contain Father Picolo's report in compliance with the *cédula,* dated at the end, Guadalaxara, February 10, 1702. Most authorities state that it was printed in Mexico in 1702, and Beristain, II, 425, states that it was printed by Carrascoso.

Copies: A, B, H, LAP, LC.

74a

Lettres Edifiantes Et Curieuses, ecrites des Missions Etrangeres par quelques Missionaires de la Compagnie de Jesus. V. Recueil.

A Paris: Chez Nicolas le Clerc, rue S. Jacquez, ...MDCCV. Avec Approbation et privilege du roy.

8°, title, 14 unnumbered preliminary leaves, 288 pages, 2 leaves, and a map.

This collection contains, on pages 248-287, a translation into French of Picolo's *Informe*. With this was produced the first issue of Kino's map.

Map: Passage Par Terre A La Californie Decouvert par le Rev. Pere Eusebe-François Kino Jesuite depuis 1698 jusqu'a 1701 ou l'on voit encore les Nouvelles Missions des PP. de la Compag^e^. de Jesus.

A manuscript of this map is to be found in the Archives of the Indies, which Dr. Bolton, who reproduced it in *Kino's Historical Memoir of Pimería Alta,* thinks is of later date than 1705, but it has some appearance of being earlier.

An extract from the *Informe* of Picolo was translated from the *Lettres Edifiantes* into English and together with the map appeared in *Philosophical Transactions* for November and December, 1708, usually found in the collection issued by Benjamin Mott in 1721, volume II, page 213. Kino's map has been reëngraved, but aside from the title only a few of the inscriptions are in English.

The *Informe* of Picolo and the map appeared again, together with a letter from M. de L'Isle, *Touchant la Californie,* in volume III of *Recueil de Voiages Au Nord, Contenant Divers Memoires Tres Utiles Au Commerce Et A La Navigation. Amsterdam: Chez Jean Frederic Bernard.* MDCCCXV.

12°, title, 340 pages, 2 folding maps.

Picolo's *Informe* appeared in German as no. 72 of Joseph Stöcklein's *Der Neue Welt-Bott,* part III, published in Augsburg in 1726. The Kino map is reproduced in part II, page 74, somewhat enlarged and with a little added at the bottom. It has a title,—Tabula Californiae

Anno 1702. Ex autoptica observatione delineata a R. P. Chino é S. J.

Part of the *Informe* of Picolo was translated into English again and appeared in London in 1743, together with Kino's map reëngraved, in *Travels Of The Jesuits, Into Various Parts of the World: Compiled from their Letters. Now first attempted in English. Intermix'd with an Account of the Manners, Government, Religion, &c. of the several Nations visited by those Fathers: With Extracts from other Travellers, and miscellaneous Notes. By Mr. Lockman. Illustrated with Maps and Sculptures. Vol. I. London: Printed for John Noon, at the White Hart near Mercer's Chapel, Cheapside.* MDCCXLIII.

8°, title, xxii, unnumbered leaf of contents, 487 pages, and 1 unnumbered of errata, and 2 maps; volume II, title, 4 pages, 2 unnumbered leaves of contents, 507 pages, and 1 unnumbered of errata, 2 maps, and 2 plates.

The Kino map is in volume I, page 395, and has the title and legends in English but most of the place names in Spanish. The account is on pages 395-408 of this volume.

Lockman's work was reissued in 1762 with a new title, with the addition of *A Concise Account of the Spanish Dominion in America.*

All the subsequent editions of the *Lettres Edifiantes* contain the *Informe*, as well as the translations into Spanish and Italian.

Beristain has a note that it was translated into Italian and published in Rome in 1706, but I have never seen any other record of such a book.

The *Informe* of Picolo has usually been considered the first printed account of California, and it certainly was the first to obtain any circulation, although only through the translations, as the original has always remained a very rare book. I have, however, described various pieces of earlier date.

The successful attempt of the famous Society of Jesus to reduce to some sort of civilization the barbarians of the peninsula and maintain its establishments in that inhospitable country must always be considered as one of its chief claims to glory. During the whole period of its occupation, some seventy years in all, rumors were persistent that the Jesuits had found in the peninsula some source of wealth, but when driven from it the truth was seen that poverty reigned supreme. The Jesuits had no gold or any other source of wealth. Throughout the period of their rule the missions had been sustained by money from Mexico and Spain, by the gifts of the pious, and not by the industry of the inhabitants. The Pious Fund, consisting of bequests and gifts of money and land, came, in time, to be a large undertaking, furnishing sufficient interest and profit to maintain the missions and even to extend them. At the expulsion of the Society the fund passed into the hands of the government, who pledged it for the future support of the missions, but after the struggle for independence the government's need for money was so great that the missions saw little of the income, and finally none at all. In later years the Catholic church in California set up a claim to the fund, which after years of litigation and arbitration was finally adjudged a valid one. The government of Mexico paid the award although it never ceased to claim that the decision was unjust.

75. LA VILLA DE SANTA FEÉ

La Villa de Santa Feé, Cabeçera de las Provincias de la Nueva Mexico, informa à V. S[a]. en el pleito que sigue contra Don Diego De Vargas, Zapata, Y Lvjan, Governador que fue de aquel Reyno, y Provincias, sobre diferentes excessos que el suso dicho, sus Ministros, y Criados executaron en el tiempo de su govierno, cantidades que percibiô para su manutencion, y no convirtiô en el fin â que se destinaron, que deve restituir á su Magestad, é interesados, y sobre que no buelva à governar dicho Reyno; proponiendo su informe en cinco puntos, que se expressaràn. [Vignette.]

[Mexico, 1703.]

Folio, 29 numbered leaves, signed, at the end, Ldo Christoval Moreno Avalos. The text begins on the verso of the title leaf, and the verso of the last leaf is blank.

Copies: AGI, according to Medina; J, JCB.

This document is devoted to a review of the legal proceedings in this case, the result of a suit brought in 1697 by the cabildo of Santa Fe against Vargas. Pedro Rodríguez Cubero had been appointed governor to succeed Vargas, who was very much disappointed because he had not been reappointed and he turned over the office to Cubero with considerable reluctance. Cubero took his *residencia* and as a result put Vargas in jail, where he remained until July, 1700. The main object of the suit of the cabildo apparently was to prevent the reappointment of Vargas as governor. He was accused of all kinds of crimes and misdemeanors, including graft, falsifying accounts, lack of prevision in the outbreak of 1696, bad treatment of the Indians, etc. Altogether he was charged with the embezzlement of 234,000 pesos, or, at least, he had not furnished proper vouchers for the expenditure of that amount. Nevertheless the auditors in Mexico had passed his vouchers, and one of the principal points of issue in this case was whether or not the *Audiencia* could review the work of the auditors. Finally, after an investigation, the king recognized the services of Vargas, created him Marqués de la Nava de Brazinas, and reappointed him governor of New Mexico, where he duly arrived and took possession on the 10th of November, 1703. On

A L
EXC.MO SEÑOR
CONDE DE FRIGILIANA,

DE EL CONSEJO DE ESTADO, y Gavinete de ſu Mageſtad (que Dios guarde) y ſu Preſidente en Xefe del Real, y S premo de Indias.

B. R. S. M.

FRAY ANDRES QUILES GALINDO, Lector Jubilado, y Procurador General de las Provincias de Indias, del Orden de San Franciſco.

Excmo. Señor.

HAVIENDO mi pequeñez merecido à la grandeza ſuperior de V. Exc. la ſingulariſſima honra de mandarme le ſirvieſſe; diziendole por eſcrito, lo que por ſu dignacion vna tarde me oyò hablar de la Situacion, y Climas; Montes, Rios, Coſtas, y Puertos en genero, y por mayor de los Reynos de las Indias; de Nueva-Eſpaña en eſpecie: por menor, y en individuo de

A lo

Vargas' return he compelled the cabildo to sign a statement, dated December 2, 1703, fully exonerating him, in which it is stated that the suit is still going on and that probably some more allegations will be filed in the case by the *procurador* of the city, one Joseph García Jurado. In other words, they were so far away that, notwithstanding their retraction of the charges, the suit would go on.

At the time this document was written Vargas had not been reappointed governor, but as it contains allegations in the case made in the fall of 1702, it appears likely that it was published early in 1703. Some documents regarding the case are in the Library of Congress.

Vargas himself, while on an expedition against the Apaches, contracted pneumonia, and died April 4, 1704, at Bernalillo.

76. QUILES GALINDO: Fr. Andrés

Al Exc^{mo}. Señor Conde De Frigiliana, De El Consejo De Estado, y Gavinete de su Magestad (que Dios guarde) y su Presidente en Xefe del Real, y Supremo de Indias. B. R. S. M. Fray Andres Qviles Galindo, Lector Jubilado, y Procurador General de las Provincias de Indias, del Orden de San Francisco.

[Madrid, 1707?]

4°, 19 numbered pages, with the title occupying the upper part of page 1.

Copy: J.

76a

Señor. Fray Andres Quiles Galindo, del orden de San Francisco . . . Pro Ministro Provincial, y Padre de su santa Provincia de Michoacan, y Procurador General en esta Corte de todas las de las Indias, puesto con el rendimiento que debe a los

Reales pies de V. Magestad, dize . . . [Madrid, 1714?]

Folio, 12 leaves.

Cited by Leclerc, *Bibliotheca Americana,* no. 1239. I have never seen a copy. Leclerc has a note, taken from the last mentioned work, that the first was printed in 1707; and I think it was almost certainly printed in Madrid. The earlier one contains a very interesting description of North America, or what was known as Nueva España, Florida, and Canada.

77. COOKE: Edward

A Voyage To The South Sea, And Around the World, Perform'd in the Years 1708, 1709, 1710, and 1711. Containing A Journal of all memorable Transactions during the said Voyage; the Winds, Currents, and Variation of the Compass; the taking of the Towns of Puna and Guayaquil, and several Prizes, one of which a rich Acapulco Ship. A Description of the American Coasts, from Tierra del Fuego in the South, to California in the North, (from the Coasting-Pilot, a Spanish Manuscript.) An Historical Account of all those Countries from the best Authors. With a new Map and Description of the mighty River of the Amazons. Wherein an Account is given of Mr. Alexander Selkirk, his Manner of living and taming some wild Beasts during the four Years and four Months he liv'd upon the uninhabited Island of Juan Fernandes. Illustrated with Cuts and Maps. By Capt. Edward Cooke.

London, Printed by H. M. for B. Lintot and R. Gosling in Fleet-Street, A. Bettesworth on London-

Bridge, and W. Innys in St. Paul's Church-Yard. MDCCXII.

8°, volume I, title, 11 leaves of preliminaries with the errata on the verso of the last, 456 pages, 5 unnumbered leaves of index, 1 leaf of advertisements, 2 maps, plan of Cusco, plan of Santiago, and 16 numbered plates of natural objects and natural history.

Volume II: title, 3 leaves of preliminaries with the errata on the verso of the last, xxiv, 328 pages, 4 unnumbered leaves of index, 5 maps, 2 plates, 3 folding tables. 4 leaves were cancelled and new ones in place thereof inserted in some copies.

According to an Ellis catalogue, no. 208, there was a second issue of the first volume in 11 preliminary leaves and 432 pages.

Reissued in 1718, with a new title, and again in 1726, but with only 2 plates.

The object of the expedition was to capture the Manila ship which usually reached Acapulco in early December, but this year she was late and, on December 20th, Cooke and Rogers decided not to wait any longer, but being delayed by calms and then by bad weather, the next day the Manila ship was sighted. She proved to be a comparatively small vessel and on the 22nd was captured after a short fight. It was then learned that the main Manila ship had probably not passed and three days later the *Bigonia,* of 900 tons and 60 guns, hove in sight. The battle began that night and continued nearly thirty-six hours, but the English shot made but little impression on the Spanish monster and they were fast getting the worst of it when they concluded the task was a hopeless one and in the night gave up the fight and returned to Puerto Seguro. Here the captured captain, a Frenchman, gave ransom, and the fleet, taking the prize, set sail for the Ladrones on January 12, 1710.

Cooke was second in command of the *Dutchess* in the joint expedition of Captains Rogers and Courtney which set out from Bristol in August, 1708. In December, 1709, while waiting at the end of the peninsula of California, Cooke went on shore at what he calls Puerto Seguro; and in volume 1, pages 335-344, he gives some account of the country, with two plates showing two natives and birds and fish. He was very much behind the times, because he says on page 401 that the Spanish have not yet made any conquests in California. On plate 14, page 331, will be found a drawing of Cape San Lucas, Puerto Seguro, and a figure of an Indian on a *balsa*. Cooke states that the Puerto was inhabited by about two hundred Indians. The map of the world showing the course of Captain Cooke was engraved by John Senex, and for all practical purposes, so far as the west coast of South and North America is concerned, is the same as Moll's map. They both show California as an island.

The second volume was not issued with the first, and is of very great rarity. Its publication seems to have been an afterthought induced by the expected appearance of Rogers' account of the voyage. It contains an elaborate description of the coast of the South sea, extending from page 109 to the end of the book. This has a separate title-page, at the bottom of which it is stated that the whole is translated and copied from the Spanish manuscript, *Coasting Pilot,* gathered from the experience and practice of that nation for two hundred years on those seas.

78. ROGERS: Woodes

A Cruising Voyage Round The World: First to the South-Seas, thence to the East-Indies, and homewards by the Cape of Good Hope. Begun in 1708, and finish'd in 1711. Containing A Journal of all the Remarkable Transactions; particularly, Of the Taking of Puna and Guiaquil, of the Acapulco

Ship, and other Prizes; An Account of Alexander Selkirk's living alone four Years and four Months in an Island; and A brief Description of several Countries in our Course noted for Trade, especially in the South-Sea. With Maps of all the Coast, from the best Spanish Manuscript Draughts. And an Introduction relating to the South-Sea Trade. By Captain Woodes Rogers, Commander in Chief on this Expedition, with the Ships Duke and Dutchess of Bristol.

London, Printed for A. Bell at the Cross-Keys and Bible in Cornhil, and B. Lintot at the Cross-Keys between the two Temple-Gates, Fleet-street. MDCC.XII.

8°, title, iii-xxi[1], 428 pages, map of the world, with the track of the *Duke* and *Dutchess* by Herman Moll; appendix containing description of the coast, etc., from Acapulco south, 56 pages, 7 leaves of alphabetical index of places, 4 maps forming a continuous chart of the coast from Acapulco to Ancon south of the Island of Chiloé, engraved by John Senex.

78a

A Cruising Voyage [the same title as the preceding] The Second Edition, Corrected.

London, Printed for Andrew Bell . . . M.DCC.XVIII.

8°, title, iii-xix, 428 pages, 57 pages, and 7 unnumbered pages of index, 5 maps.

78b

A Cruising Voyage [the same as the preceding] The Second Edition, Corrected.

London: Printed for Bernard Lintot . . . M.DCC.XXVI.

The same as the preceding, except with 2 plates. Description from Sabin, 72755.

78c

Voyage Autour Du Monde, Commencé en 1708 & fini en 1711. Par le Capitaine Woodes Rogers. Traduit De L'Anglois. Tome Premier. Où l'on a joint quelques Pièces curieuses touchant la Riviere des Amazones & la Guiane. [Vignette.]

A Amsterdam, Chez la Veuve De Paul Marret, dans le Beurs-straat à la Renommée. MDCCXVI.

12°, volume I: Engraved frontispiece, title, and 4 unnumbered leaves, 415 pages and 29 unnumbered pages, map, and 9 plates; volume II: Engraved frontispiece, title, 162 pages, 5 maps, and 5 plates; Supplement: Title, 75 pages, 24 unnumbered pages, and 4 maps; *Relation de la Riviere des Amazones,* etc., 255 pages and 24 unnumbered pages. The supplement is the translation of the appendix of the original.

78d

Voyage Autour Du Monde [A new title after Anglois].

A Amsterdam Chez l'Honoré et chatelan. MDCCXXIII.

12°, volume I: Engraved frontispiece, title and 4 unnumbered leaves, 359 pages, 27 unnumbered pages, map, and 7 plates; volume II: Engraved frontispiece, title, 288 pages, and 7 plates; Supplement same as in the preceding; title, 255 pages, and 24 unnumbered pages.

78e

Nieuwe Reize naa de Zuidzee, van daar naa Oost-Indien, en verder rondom de waereld. Begonnen in 1708, en geëyndigd in 1711.

Amsterdam: J. Oosterwyk & H. van de Gaete, 1715.

4°, engraved and printed titles, 2 unnumbered leaves, 14 pages, 438 pages, 4 unnumbered leaves, 4 plates, 5 maps.

Rogers was in command of the *Duke* in the joint Rogers-Courtney expedition. The ship spent some time cruising off Cape San Lucas waiting for the Manila galleon. Rogers gives his description of California on pages 312-318. Although he does not give any illustrations of the fish or of the birds, he saw just what Cooke saw, as they were both there at the same time.

At the end of the introduction is a memorandum to the effect that "since he [Rogers] advertised publishing his book the booksellers have thought it to their interest to hurry out the continuation of Cooke's voyage in which they have attempted at the views of several harbors and sights of land in the South Sea, which, though not done so effectively as I intended in mine, yet it has prevented my intention of engraving the harbors, which on second consideration, may at a proper time be better published separate, in a Coasting Pilot Book for that trade." Rogers actually made this promise good and did compile just such a book, although it was never published.

79. JOUTEL: Henry

Journal Historique Du Dernier Voyage que feu M. de la Sale fit dans le Golfe de Mexique, pour trouver l'embouchure, & le cours de la Riviere de Missicipi, nommée à present la Riviere de Saint Loüis, qui traverse la Louisiane. Où l'on voit l'Histoire tragique de sa mort, & plusieurs choses curieuses du nouveau monde. Par Monsieur Joutel, l'un des Compagnons de ce Voyage, redigé & mis en ordre par Monsieur De Michel.

A Paris, Chez Estienne Robinot, Libraire, Quay & attenant la Porte des Grands Augustins, à l'Ange Gardien. MDCCXIII. Avec Approbation & Privilege du Roy.

12°, title, leaves numbered iii-xxxiv, 386 numbered pages, and a map.

Preliminaries: Pages iii-xxxi *Au lecteur* by the publisher, and at the bottom of the last page the approbation; pages xxxii-xxxiv the privilege dated August 7, 1712, and the errata; pages 1-10 contain the preface of Michel, the editor of the *Journal*. Pages 382-386 contain the index.

Map: Carte Nouvelle de la Louisiane, et de la Riviere de Missisipi, découverte par feu M[r]. de la Salle, es années 1681 et 1686, dans l'Amérique Septentrionale, et de plusieurs autres Rivieres, jusqu'icy inconnuës, qui tombent dans la Baye de S[t]. Loüis; Dressée par le S[r]. Joutel, qui êtoit de ce Voyage. 1713.

In the publisher's introduction is the statement that this was printed from a manuscript which had fallen into his hands.

79a

A Journal Of the Last Voyage Perform'd by Monsr. de la Sale, To the Gulph of Mexico, To find out the Mouth of the Missisipi River; Containing, An Account of the Settlements he endeavour'd to make on the Coast of the aforesaid Bay, his unfortunate Death, and the Travels of his Companions for the Space of Eight Hundred Leagues across that Inland Country of America, now call'd Louisiana, (and given by the King of France to M. Crozat,) till they came into Canada. Written in French by Monsieur Joutel, A Commander in that Expedition; And Translated from the Edition just publish'd at Paris. With an exact Map of that vast Country, and a Copy of the Letters Patent granted by the K. of France to M. Crozat.

London: Printed for A. Bell. 1714.

8°, title, xxi, 9 unnumbered pages, 205 numbered, 5 unnumbered of index, and a map.

Map: A New Map of the Country of Louisiana and of y[e] River Missisipi in North America discouer'd by Mons. de la Salle in y[e] Years 1681 and 1686 as allso of several other Rivers before unknown and falling into y[e] Bay of S[t]. Lewis. By the S[r]. Joutel who perform'd that Voyage. 1713.

79b

Mr. Joutel's Journal of his Voyage to Mexico: His Travels Eight hundred Leagues through Forty Nations of Indians in Louvisiana to Canada. His Account of the great River Missasipi. To which is Added A Map of that Country; with a Description of the great Water-Falls in the River Misouris. Translated from the French publish'd at Paris.

London: Printed for Bernard Lintot. 1719.

The same as the preceding, except for the title.

79c

Diario Historico del ultimo viaje que hizo M. de la Sale para descubrir el Desembocadero y Curso del Missicipi. Contiene la historica trágica de su muerte y muchas cosas curiosas del nuevo mundo. Escrito en idioma Frances por M. T. Joutel, uno de los compañeros de M. La Sale en el viaje. Traducido al Español por el Coronel Jose Maria Tornel, Ministro de Mejico en los Estados Unidos. Et voluisse sat est.

Impreso en Nueva York por José Desnoues, año de 1831.

12°, title, and pages numbered 3-156.

Preliminaries: Preface of Tornel 3-6, *advertencias del impresor francés* 7-18, *prefacio de Mr. Michel* 19-22.

It is usually stated that Joutel complained about the publication of this book, saying that it was not authorized by him, and further, that it was not his work. Nevertheless, those who have compared this book with Joutel's state that it must have been taken from his narrative which still exists in the Department of Marine in Paris, and is published in full in Margry, *Relations et Mémoires Inédits,* III, 89-534.

Joutel accompanied La Salle on his last expedition, and it is generally considered that his account is the most trustworthy of all that have been published regarding this ill-fated expedition.

The journal of Joutel was published in the collection of sources compiled by B. F. French, *Historical Collections of Louisiana,* I, New York, 1846. Recently some remarkable La Salle documents were discovered in the Archives of the Indies at Seville. They were published in 1926 in the Bandelier sources edited by C. W. Hackett, *Historical Documents relating to New Mexico, Nueva Viscaya, and approaches thereto, to 1773,* II, 470-481.

80. RIVERA: Pedro de

Relacion De Servicios del Coronel Don Pedro de Ribera.

Folio, 3 unnumbered pages dated at the end, Madrid, August 1, 1713, and signed in manuscript, only by the *Relator*.

Copies: AGI, 136-7-39.

From a *testimonio* executed in Vera Cruz on March 4, 1711, it appears that Rivera, beginning as a simple soldier, had then served in the army in Europe, San Juan de Ulua, and the *flota,* more than thirty-four years, and in 1711 was governor *ad interim* of the presidio of Vera Cruz. At the end are some manuscript additions by the *Relator* dated February 15, 1721, stating that Rivera had aided in putting down a revolt in Tabasco and in dislodging some English corsairs from the Isla del Carmen.

81. MÉNDEZ: Joseph

Breve Memorial, Extracto, Y Declamacion, Que hazen los cien Soldados del Presidio de la Nueva-Mexico, Al Exmo. Señor D. Balthassar de Zuñiga, Guzman, Sotomayor, y Mendoza, Marquês de Valero, de Ayamonte, y Alenquèr, Gentil Hombre de la Camara de su Magestad, de su Consejo, y Junta de Guerra de Indias, Virrey, Governador, y Capitan General de esta Nueva-España, y Presidente de su Real Audiencia, y Chancilleria, Contra Los Excessos De D. Pedro de Otero Bermmudez, y D. Felis Martinez, en la Administracion de sus Cituados, y en que les han gravado en cantidades excessivas. Demuestrase, en la mesma especificacion de las partidas, su justicia, Paraque la pijsima proteccion de su Exa. ni permita el effecto de los perjucios aparatados, y con la restitucion de los ya experimentados, corrija, y dexe satisfechas sus vrgencias; cuyo conflicto, embargandoles hasta las vozes, libran en el guarismo; para que este, manifieste en la suma, las quexas, que ni en él cupieran, de sus operaciones. [Printer's devices.]

Con licencia en Mexico por los Herederos de la Viuda de Miguel de Rivera; en el Empedradillo, año de 1720.

Folio, title, and 8 leaves, of which the first five are numbered. At the end signed, Ldo. Joseph Méndez, Mexico, June 17, 1720. Attached is a certification that it is an exact copy of the original made in compliance with the decree of the viceroy granting the license to print it.

Copies: BM, WBS.

This lawsuit grew out of a complaint of the presidial soldiers of Santa Fe, in 1711, against Don Francisco Cuervo y Valdés. The soldiers gave Felix Martínez a power of attorney to prosecute the suit, and an order for 10,000 pesos to pay for it out of their wages.

In 1712 the soldiers gave another power to Don Pedro de Otero to collect their pay, and between Martínez and Otero the accounts were so juggled, such enormous expense was incurred, and so many accounts of one kind and another were presented, that the soldiers got nothing. As a result they brought a criminal suit against both Martínez and Otero, and this particular memorial is addressed to the viceroy, setting forth the facts in the case and asking some immediate relief.

The documents contain interesting information regarding the officials in New Mexico during the period 1710-20.

82. BARREYRO Y ÁLVAREZ: Francisco de

Relacion De Servicios De Don Francisco De Barreyro y Alvarez, Ingeniero Militar en el Reyno de la Nueva-España.

Folio, 4 unnumbered pages dated at the end, Madrid, April 23, 1722, and signed in manuscript only by the *Relator*.

Copy: AGI, 136-7-40.

Barreyro came to New Spain with Viceroy Marqués de Valero, and in 1717 was appointed *ingeniero militar* attached to the expedition of General Martín de Alarcón destined for Texas, where he states he assisted personally in the erection of the church at the mission of San Antonio. In 1720 he returned to Spain under a general order that all Spaniards in Mexico whose wives were in Spain should return to that country.

He evidently later returned to Mexico, as he accompanied Pedro de Rivera on his inspection of the frontier presidios, 1724-28, and made the maps of the frontier provinces now in AGI, 67-4-4, a description of which will be found under Rivera, *Diario,* 1736.

83. PEÑA: Br. Juan Antonio de la

Derrotero De La Expedicion En La Provincia De Los Texas, Nuevo Reyno De Philipinas, que de orden del Exc^{mo}. Señor Marquès de Valero, Vi-Rey, y Capitan General de esta Nueva-España passa à executar el Muy Illustre Señor D. Joseph De Azlor, Cavallero Mesnadero del Reyno de Aragõ, Marques De S. Miguel De Aguayo, Governador, y Capitan General de dichas Provincias de Texas, Nuevas Philipinas, y de esta de Coaguila, Nuevo Reyno de Estremadura, por el Rey N. S. (que Dios guarde) Que Escribe El B^{r}. D. Juan Antonio de la Peña. [Printer's devices.]

Con Licencia En Mexico: En La Imprenta Nueva Plantiniana de Juan Francisco de Ortega Bonilla; en la Calle de Tacuba. Año de 1722.

Folio, title, and 29 numbered leaves. Included in the foliation are 3 plans replacing folios 21, 24, and 27. Another plan is inserted, usually between folios 22 and 23.

Plans: Plan Del Presidio De N. S. Del Pilar, de los Adays . . .; Plan Del Presidio De N. S. De Los Dolores . . .; Plan Del Presidio De San Antonio De Bejar . . .; Presidio De N. S. De Loreto En La Bahia del Espiritu Santo . . .

They measure about 29x40 cms. and are copper plate engravings done by Sylverio, according to the inscriptions. The title as given above is printed on the back of each plan, followed by a general description of each fortification. In one of the copies which I have had, the description of the presidio of Loreto is printed on the face instead of on the back. The plans show not only the presidios but the relative location of the rivers, and contain, in addition, figures of animals and plants,—I presume those supposed to be characteristic of the country surrounding them.

Copies: BM, H, J, JCB, K, TWS, WBS, Y.

The original plans, or copies of them, are in AGI, 67-3-11, with the *autos* on the expedition. Accompanying them is a map in colors measuring 42½x60 cms., which was not published with the book. It is entitled, "Carta de la Bahia del Spiritu Santo de la Provincia de las Nuevas Filipinas que dexo observado el Marques de San Miguel de Aguayo en 10 de Abril de 1722." The title and description are written on the back. The copy formerly in my possession had a similar manuscript map, either the original or a contemporary copy. Mr. Streeter's copy also has the extra plate.

In the July, 1911, number of the *Quarterly* of the Texas State Historical Association there is an article by Eleanor Claire Buckley on this expedition. Miss Buckley collected all the documents she could find about it, mostly from the archives in Mexico. I do not know whether or not the legajo in the archives in Seville to which the manuscript plans are attached contains further information, as I am not aware that it has ever been critically examined. The printed document itself has never yet been translated into English in spite of the fact that it is one of the chief sources of Texas history and very nearly the earliest printed one.

The immediate cause of this expedition was the attack by the French, during the war, on the upper missions, forcing the missionaries of the six missions there to retire to San Antonio. The enterprise was entrusted to the command of the Marqués de San Miguel de Aguayo, who organized a large force for those days, in the course of a year and a half. He finally set out in November of 1720, returning to Coahuila in May, 1722. The account is largely in the form of a diary written by Juan Antonio de la Peña, who accompanied the expedition as chaplain of the battalion of San Miguel. On the return to Monclova, Peña wrote up the account, added a few observations, and signed it there on June 21, 1722. At the end there is a certification by Dr. Joseph Codallos y Rabal, who also accompanied the expedition, that the account is strictly true, and as a voucher of this he signed it on the 23d of June.

Among other manuscripts formerly in my possession was one referring to the sums of money donated to the Marqués de Aguayo, mostly in 1722-23, for the upkeep of the new missions and presidios which he had founded, the total being 115,451 pesos, a very respectable sum of money for those days.

Mr. T. W. Streeter owns a memorial of the Marqués dated July 14, 1730, in which he sets forth the services of his ancestors as well as those of his wife. She was a descendant of Francisco de Urdiñola, whose father-in-law was the discoverer of the famous mines of Mazapil. This property was still in the possession of the wife of the Marqués and from 1711 he resided there continuously, maintaining a private army. The memorial contains also a long account of the expedition to Texas, and brief statements of the large amounts of money which he had advanced for the founding and maintenance of the mission.

84. GONZÁLEZ BARCIA: Andrés

Ensayo Cronologico, Para La Historia General De La Florida. Contiene Los Descubrimientos, y principales sucesos, acaecidos en este Gran Reino, à los Españoles, Franceses, Suecos, Dinamarqueses, Ingleses, y otras Naciones, entre sì, y con los Indios: cuias Costumbres, Genios Idolatria, Govierno, Batallas, y Astucias, se refieren: y los Viages de algunos Capitanes, y Pilotos, por el Mar de el Norte, à buscar Paso à Oriente, ò union de aquella Tierra, con Asia. Desde El Año De 1512. Que Descubriò la Florida, Juan Ponce de Leon, hasta el de 1722. Escrito Por Don Gabriel De Cardenas Z Cano Dedicado Al Principe Nuestro Señor. [Vignette] Con Privilegio.

En Madrid. En la Oficina Real, y à Costa de Nicolas Rodriguez Franco, Impresor de Libros. Año de . . . [1723]. Se hallaràn en su Casa, en la Calle de el Poço, y en Palacio.

Folio, title in red and black, 19 unnumbered leaves of preliminaries, 366 numbered pages, leaf with a Latin inscription, 27 unnumbered leaves of index, and a leaf of genealogical table of the Condes de Canalejas between pages 150 and 151.

Preliminaries: Leaf of dedication dated July 25, 1723, 3 leaves of *censuras, approbación,* errata, privilege, and *tasa,* 15 leaves of introduction.

As is well known, the author of this work was Andrés González Barcia. To him Florida meant everything north of New Spain except the Pacific coast, so he naturally covers not only the Spanish colonies but the French and English. A large portion of the work is devoted to the history of Florida proper, and especially to the exploits of Pedro Menéndez de Avilés. Considerable accounts, however, are given of the expeditions of Cabeza de Vaca, Coronado, De Soto, Oñate, and La Salle.

A very valuable part of the work is the introduction, in which he cites many manuscripts that were then in his possession or in well-known libraries but are now lost.

85. MARTÍNEZ: Felix

Relacion De Servicios De Don Felix Martinez, Governador, y Capitan General que fue de la Villa de Santa Fè, en la Nueva-Mexico, y Capitan Vitalicio, que es del Castillo Presidial de ella.

Folio, 4 unnumbered pages dated at the end in MS, Madrid, September 28, 1723, and signed in MS by the *Relator*.

Copy: AGI, 136-7-40.

From a *testimonio* made in Mexico, July 17, 1717, it appears that Martínez was a native of Alicante in Spain and enlisted in Zacatecas in 1693 in the expedition destined for New Mexico. He remained there till July 27, 1697, when on account of sickness he was licensed by Governor Cubero to return to Mexico.

On January 5, 1704, he was appointed captain of horse at the presidio of New Mexico by Vargas, and was ratified in this by the successive governors, Francisco Cuervo, March 1, 1705, and the Marqués de la Peñuela, August 24, 1706.

Then follows an account of his difficulties with the governor, Juan Flores Mogollón, who tried to oust him.

He was appointed captain-general of the province of Santa Fe, October 5, 1715, took possession December 1, and served in that capacity till December 29, 1716, when he went to Mexico by order of the viceroy to answer the charges made against him by the governor.

He cites a letter of recommendation written by the authorities of Santa Fe on November 12, 1716.

86. OLIVÁN REBOLLEDO: Juan de

Informe Jvridico Al Rey Nuestro Señor D. Phelipe Quinto, (Qve Dios Gvarde) En Sv Real, Y Svpremo Consejo De Las Indias. Por Don Jvan De Olivan Rebolledo, Oidor de la Real Audiencia de Mexico, y Auditor General de Guerra del Reyno de Nueva-España. Para Qve Se Declare No Aver Lvgar la admission de las quexas, que por varios vecinos de Mexico se han dado en su contra, sobre aver condenado à dos Reos à que devengàran en vn Obrage, en caso de no tener con que pagar vn Robo que hizieron; y para que se le de satisfaccion por las injurias, que le han inferido los Autores de esta demanda. Hecho Por D. Juan Antonio De Ahvmada, Colegial actual en el Insigne Mayor de Santa Maria de todos Santos de Mexico, y Abogado de dicha Audiencia.

[Madrid, 1724.]

Folio, title, leaves numbered 2-48.
Copy: J.

This document is an answer to a complaint made to the Council in 1724 by various citizens in Mexico against the action of the *Audiencia,* and especially against Oliván Rebolledo, one of the *oidores,* for having sentenced to forced labor two men who had been convicted of a robbery. It was claimed that these men were pure-blood Spaniards, and that it was a miscarriage of justice to sentence them to such an infamous punishment. The case in itself is interesting enough, but its only connection with the subject matter of this book is to be found in the notices it contains about Oliván Rebolledo, and in a document published in the margin of folios 30-32.

Oliván Rebolledo, after serving for a long period as *oidor* in the *Audiencia* of Guadalajara, was promoted to a similar position in the *Audiencia* of Mexico and took possession of his new office some time in 1717. In the same month in which he took possession, a *Junta general* was held on the entry which the French had made from Mobile into the country of the Asinais, and their design to occupy this area as well as Coahuila and Nuevo León; and Don Juan was instructed to write the *consulta.* He was also detailed to make an investigation of the entire matter, and incidentally to examine St. Denis. The result of this investigation is to be found in an extensive *testimonio* made by him during that year and dated Mexico the 30th of December, 1717. The document is in AGI, 61-6-35, and is accompanied by a map which states that it was presented with his *informe* on the 18th of December, 1717, to the viceroy, in consequence of his reconnaissance of those provinces by order of the viceroy. Those shown are the northeastern provinces, including Texas.

Notwithstanding the fact that the statement on the map would seem to imply that Don Juan had made a personal visit to Texas, I have not been able to find any positive evidence to that effect.

As a result of this *Informe,* Don Juan was made governor of Texas on the 5th of June, 1719; and the document in full is printed on the margin of the *Informe,* folios 30-32. Not only was he appointed governor, but the document proceeds to erect the "Pais de los Texas" into a province under the name of the "Nuevas Philipinas," and to assign boundaries to it. As I do not recall ever having seen this document before, I translate the part showing the boundaries assigned: "On the east the Mississippi river, which runs from north to south and empties into the Gulf of Mexico; on the south the coast, which runs from the mouth of the said river to the Bravo of the north, which empties into the same gulf; on the west the banks of the river Medina from its source to its outlet to the sea; and the north, from the source of the said river to the point of the river Colorado of the Cadodachas and its incorporation into the Mississippi."

As some proof that Oliván was in Texas I cite the following: a letter of his of 1716 in the Library of Congress stating that he had been nominated to make an examination of Texas and Louisiana; a *consulta,* not dated but written in the summer of 1717, and another dated December 24, 1717, both now in the library of the University of Texas. In the first of these *consultas* he refers to a preceding letter which he had written in 1715 on the same subject, all based upon a resolution of the Council of the Indies of August 22, 1715, in which it was decided to establish a presidio and mission in Texas.

There is in the Huntington library another *consulta* of Oliván Rebolledo, formerly in my possession, on the subject of founding a port in California, written about 1719.

Don Juan never officiated as governor of Texas, for on the 23d of August, 1719, in view of the need for his services in Mexico, the viceroy relieved him of the duty and conferred the appointment on the Marqués de Aguayo.

87. SAENZ DE SAN ANTONIO: Fr. Mathias

Señor. Si El Pastor no escucha el quexido de la oveja; si el Padre no oye el llanto de sus hijos; si el Señor no atiende a el ay de sus Vassallos, no podrà compadecerse su obligacion amorosa en las necessidades, como con el vulgo dize San Bernardo, ojos que no vèn, corazon que no quiebra.

A los Reales, y piadosos de V. Magestad Catholica se ponen oy las vrgentes necessidades, que tienen los habitadores de las Nuevas Philipinas, Provincia de los Texas, . . .

Folio, 6 leaves numbered except the first, the verso of the last blank. At the end signed as above, Madrid, April 7, 1724.

Copies: AGI, Y. Medina, in *Biblioteca Hispano-Americana,* no. 2528, describes the copy in AGI, but I have not seen it.

Father Mathias certainly paints a rosy picture of Texas in this memorial. He was one of the fathers who went to Texas in 1716 with Fr. Antonio Margil de Jesus to found the six new missions in northeastern Texas. He enlarges on the marvelous fertility of the soil, and does not neglect to say that it is also rich in minerals, adding that there is no hill in which there might not be a treasure. Altogether he gives a most interesting description of the country, which also has the merit of being the first printed account, as the *Derrotero* of Peña deals with more prosaic matters.

Father Mathias went to Spain with the object of urging the colonization of Texas from Spain or the Canary islands, as he says that the creoles of America are not suitable for colonists. It is quite likely that as a result of his efforts the colonists from the Canary islands were sent to Texas a few years later.

88. SHELVOCKE: George

A Voyage Round The World By the Way of the Great South Sea, Perform'd in the Years 1719, 20, 21, 22, in the Speedwell of London, of 24 Guns and 100 Men, (under His Majesty's Commission to cruize on the Spaniards in the late War with the Spanish Crown) till she was cast away on the Island of Juan Fernandes, in May 1720; and afterwards continu'd in the Recovery, the Jesus Maria and Sacra Familia, Etc. By Capt. George Shelvocke, Commander of the Speedwell, Recovery, Etc. in this Expedition. [Vignette.]

London: Printed for J. Senex, at the Globe against St. Dunstan's Church, Fleetstreet; W. and J. Innys, at the Prince's-Arms in St. Paul's Churchyard; and J. Osborn and T. Longman, at the Ship in Pater-noster Row. MDCCXXVI.

8°, title, 3 leaves of dedication with the errata on the verso of the last, xxxii pages of preface, 2 unnumbered leaves of contents, 468 pages numbered except the first, map, and 4 plates, one of which is of two California men and one of two California women.

Map: A Correct Map of the World Describing Cap[t]. Shelvock's Voyage round [Two hemispheres].

88a

A Voyage Round The World, By the Way of the Great South Sea: Performed in a private Expedition during the War, which broke out with Spain, in the Year 1718. By Capt. George Shelvocke. The Second Edition, revised and republished By George Shelvocke, Esq. [Vignette.]

London: Printed for W. Innys and J. Richardson, M. & T. Longman, in Pater-noster-row. MDCCLVII.

8°, title, 2 leaves of dedication, 3 leaves of preface and contents, 476 pages, and a map and 4 plates, the same as those in the 1726 edition.

A copy of the 1726 edition, formerly belonging to me, contains a note in contemporary handwriting on the fly-leaf, stating that the book was written by George Shelvocke the younger, a son of the Captain, who went on the expedition with his father.

Shelvocke had a kind of independent position as captain of the *Speedwell* in the privateering expedition of John Clipperton in 1719-22. Pages 390-415 contain the account of California, Shelvocke in August, 1721, having landed at Puerto Seguro, the same place visited by Rogers and Cooke. This place, which he said was so named by Sir Thomas Cavendish, was two leagues northeast of Cape San Lucas. He thought that they washed some gold out of the sand,—at any rate they washed quite a little of something and took it to China, where it was lost. He gives a very interesting account of the natives.

On the map California appears as an island, although Shelvocke is uncertain about this. He judiciously adds that it makes no difference to the English anyway.

The whole history of this expedition is a curious commentary upon the morals of the times. The English had passed out of the freebooting stage, strictly speaking, and were now eager to cover their privateering exploits with a little more clothing than in the preceding century. Nevertheless William Betagh, who wrote another account of the expedition, but got no farther than Peru, says that Shelvocke kept on his tour of capture in the South seas after he knew that Spain and England were at peace.

89. ARRIAGA Y BRAMBILA: Juan Joseph de

Señor. Don Juan Joseph de Arriaga y Brambila, Governador, y Capitan General de el Nuevo Reyno de Leon en el de Nueva España, puesto à los Reales pies de V. Mag. con el rendimiento debido, dice...

Folio, 4 leaves with the résumé on the verso of the last, undated, but Medina says Madrid, 1728.

Copies: Medina, *Biblioteca Hispano-Americana,* no. 7039, locates a copy in AGI, but I could not find it.

Medina says that it was a request to be reinstated in the above employment.

90. PÉREZ DE ALMAZÁN: Fernando

Relacion De Los Meritos, Y Servicios De Don Fernando Perez De Almazan, Governador, y Capitan General, que fue, del Presidio de San Antonio de Bejar, de la Governacion de la Provincia de los Texas, y Nuevas Philipinas.

Folio, 4 unnumbered pages dated at the end, Madrid, October 17, 1729, and unsigned except the certification by the *Relator.*

Copy: AGI, 137-1-3.

From a *testimonio* made at San Antonio de Béjar, February 8, 1726, it appears that Pérez de Almazán was appointed governor of Texas on January 22, 1722.

In this he states that he assisted in the siege and capture of New Caledonia on the Isthmus of Darien, and that he afterward was *alcalde mayor* of Saltillo and Parras, and assisted in raising troops for the expedition to Texas by the Marqués de Aguayo. Then follows quite an account of his activities as governor of Texas, among others the rebuilding of the presidio of Pilar de los Adais, which had been burned, the erection of the missions of San Miguel de los Adais, Nuestra Señora de los Ais, and that of Nuestra Señora de Guadalupe de los Nacogdoches.

He built the wall, ramparts, warehouses, officers' and soldiers' houses of the presidio at San Antonio de Béjar, all of stone, at his own cost. This was certified to by his successor, Melchor de Mediavilla y Ascona, June 23, 1727, who also said that the presidio de los Adais had six bronze cannon and one hundred men. Pérez also cites a certificate by Pedro de Ribera, who had made a secret examination of the province.

91. REGLAMENTO

Reglamento Para Todos Los Presidios de las Provincias internas de esta Governacion, Con El Nvmero De Oficiales, y Soldados, que los ha de guarnecer: Sveldos, Que vnos, y otros avràn de gozar: Ordenanzas Para el mexor Govierno, y Disciplina Militar de Governadores, Oficiales, y Soldados; Prevenciones Para los que en ellas se comprehenden: Precios De los Viveres, y Vestuarios, conque à los Soldados se les assiste, y se les avrà de continuar. Hecho Por El Exc^{mo}. Señor Marquès de Casa-Fuerte, Vi-Rey, Governador, y Capitan General de estos Reynos. De Orden De Su Exc^{a}.

En Mexico, en la Imprenta Real de el Superior Govierno: De los Herederos de la Viuda de

Miguel de Rivera Calderon; en el Empedradillo. Año de 1729.

Folio, title, 32 unnumbered leaves. Sig.: A-Q, two leaves in each. Described from a copy in JCB. Dr. Nicolás León in Boletín 1 of his *Instituto Bibliográfico Mexicano,* no. 333, states that it ought to have 35 leaves and 1 leaf double folded. Mr. Streeter's copy has at the end after Q2 three unnumbered leaves of *cédulas,* dated Seville, July 31, 1731, and a large folding broadside of the different presidios, the distance of each from Mexico, and the salaries of the various officers and soldiers stationed at each one.

Copies: J, JCB, TWS.

This *Reglamento* was issued by Juan de Acuña, Marqués de Casa-Fuerte, viceroy, with the following introduction explanatory thereof. I translate from page one:

"Juan de Acuña, Marqués de Casa-Fuerte, etc., Virrey, etc. After having discovered that the interior presidios of this kingdom are without rules or orders which they should observe, or at least without those which are appropriate to the situation in which they are found and the operations for which they were instituted, I found no other remedy than to propose to his Majesty that an exact inspection of them should be made, seeking, in the method and in the person who should execute it, all the conditions which the zeal and diligence to secure the remedy could find, as well as measures against the abuses which occur in the presidios, and especially those prejudicial to the royal hacienda. The inspection was undertaken by Brigadier D. Pedro de Rivera under the approval of his Majesty; and having been employed in it nearly four years, traveling over the extensive regions in which the presidios are situated, inspecting them and giving due attention to what was going on and what he personally saw, he returned to Mexico . . ."

He then proceeds to say that he has established the *reglamento* which follows, which will be observed until confirmed or reformed by his Majesty.

It is the first *reglamento* of the presidios of which we have any notice, although undoubtedly there was some kind of a rule or order for them previously. As it continued in effect (with, of course, some changes) until 1772, and as it forms the basis of the presidio system, I insert some notice of its provisions.

Two of the old presidios were to be extinguished, two small companies moved to other places, and nineteen in all retained. The commandants generally had a salary of six hundred dollars a year and the soldiers from three hundred dollars to four hundred and twenty, depending on location. An elaborate system of prices of goods for soldiers was established, varying with the nearness of farms for supply of food and with the distance from Mexico for clothing, etc. The commandants were prohibited from using the soldiers in their private affairs or receiving money from any of the subalterns or soldiers under any pretext. Special rules were laid down for the treatment of Indians and also methods to follow when an expedition was made against them. In such cases the commandant was obliged to see that before starting, the proper religious exercises were held, and all gambling prohibited. The commandants were strictly prohibited from making war on any Indians during peace times and likewise from assisting any Indians to make war on others who were friendly and peaceful.

The presidios gave constant trouble, largely due to the continual scandals emanating from the cupidity of the officials. They were always being inspected, and on account of the expense incurred in maintaining them, regular efforts were made by the officials in Mexico to curtail their number or the number of the forces maintained at them. As time went on the ones in the interior became less necessary, in fact useless, and the frontier, which was removed to the Rio Grande, needed greater protection. I once had in my possession a document of importance which fully illustrates this point. It is entitled, "*Autos de Pezquiza secreta practicada por Don Fran. Benitez Murillo, Alcalde Mayor de la Villa de Leon, en virtud de orden de el Exmo. Sr. Virey de este Reino sobre el estado de los Precidios . . . que se hallan en la Cordillera de el Camino Real de Chiguagua.*" It begins with the order of the Conde de Fuen Clara to Benitez Murillo to make the investigation, and is followed by the sworn statements of several officials and citizens as to the utility of the various presidios and the recommendations they had to make about them. The investigation took place in August and September, 1745, and the consensus of opinion was that the existing presidios of Gallo, Cerro Gordo, Valle de San Bartholomé and Conchos, as well as Mapimi, were useless. At this time the frontier was peaceful for thirty or forty leagues beyond Chihuahua, the savages having disappeared and all the roads being traveled by pack trains and individuals without escort. The haciendas were populated with plenty of cattle, the Indians were found only seventy leagues or so beyond Chihuahua and Janos, and the inhabitants in those places were sufficient to restrain them. The document also set forth the opinion that one presidio on the road—on the Nazas, Rio Florido, or San Pedro—would be sufficient, but suggested that a new one should be founded at the junction of the Conchos and Rio Grande where there was a Franciscan mission and where the missionaries had had a great deal of trouble with the Indians.

This document throws vivid light on the conditions in the north at this period, showing the country in an extremely flourishing condition, but it contains the usual complaints about the actions of the presidio captains and soldiers, who, with no work to do, had taken to all kinds of bad behavior.

TANTO

QUE SE SACÓ DE VNA CARTA,

QUE

EL R. PADRE FR. ALONSO DE BENAVIDES,

CUSTODIO QUE FUE del Nuevo Mexico,

EMBIÓ A LOS RELIGIOſos de la Santa Cuſtodia de la Cõverſion de San Pablo de dicho Reyno, deſde Madrid, el año de 1631.

Daſe á la eſtampa à expenſas de vn afecto à la Religion.

92. BENAVIDES: Fr. Alonso de

Tanto Que Se Sacó De Vna Carta, Que El R. Padre Fr. Alonso De Benavides, Custodio Que Fue del Nuevo Mexico, Embió A Los Religiosos de la Santa Custodia de la Conversion de San Pablo de dicho Reyno, desde Madrid, el año de 1631. Dase á la estampa à expensas de vn afecto à la Religion.

[Colophon:] Con Licencia De Los Superiores. Impresso en Mexico: por Joseph Bernardo de Hogal, Ministro, ê Impressor del Real, y Apostolico Tribunal de la Santa Cruzada en toda esta Nueva-España, Año de 1730.

8°, leaf with engraving on the recto, title, verso blank, 2 unnumbered leaves of dedication, and 10 numbered pages, with the colophon at the end.

The engraving is a copper plate of La Ve. M^e^. Maria de Iesus de Agreda, Predicando â los Chichimecos del Nuebo-mexico. Antt de Castro f^t^. This inscription is underneath the figure.

Copies: J, JCB.

In the dedication the anonymous author, possibly the printer himself, makes the following statement: [Translation.] "Having determined to give to the perpetuity of print the letter which the venerable Mother María de Jesús de Agreda wrote to the missionary religious of New Mexico, it being my purpose that letters so worthy of being put on record should not live in the prison of a silent retirement, I have determined, et cetera, to dedicate to you . . ." The author then goes on to say, speaking of the order of Saint Francis, that in the archives of that *Custodia* the original existed. This is a plain indication that the letter was then printed for the first time, an indication which becomes practically a certainty when we read what Fray Rafael Verger says about the matter in the memorial which he wrote in 1772. This memorial is devoted to a

La V. M. Maria de Iesus de Agreda. Predicando
à los Chichimecos del Nuebo-mèxico. Antt. de Castro f.

laudatory description of the great work which the Franciscans had accomplished in New Spain for the benefit of the king and the church. He states positively that the letter which we are describing was first printed in 1730 from a manuscript which existed in the archives of the *Custodia* of New Mexico in Mexico city, and he enclosed with the memorial one of the printed copies of the edition in sixteen pages.

92a

Tanto, Que Se Sacó De Una Carta, Que El R. Padre Fr. Alonso De Benavides, Custodio Que Fue Del Nuevo Mexico, Embió A Los Religiosos de la Santa Custodia de la Conversion de San Pablo de dicho Reyno, desde Madrid, el año de 1631. Dase A La Estampa A Expensas De Un Afecto, Quien La Dedica A la Soberana Emperatriz de los Angeles, Madre Inmaculada del Divino Verbo Encarnado, Maria Santissima En Su Purissima Concepcion.

[Colophon:] Reimpresso en Mexico, por la Viuda de D. Joseph Bernardo de Hogal. Año de 1747.

8°, engraving, verso blank, title, verso blank, and 14 numbered pages with the colophon at the end.

The copper plate preceding the title is quite different from that in the 1730 edition, and instead of having the legend at the bottom this is printed on the two sides and the top. The plate was engraved by Ponze. The dedication is omitted in this edition.

Copies: J, JCB, WBS.

Medina, *La Imprenta en México,* no. 3810, in describing this edition states that there was a first colophon, as follows: Renóvese este impresion siendo Abad de dicha Congregacion el Lic. Don Gonzalo de la Cerda, año de

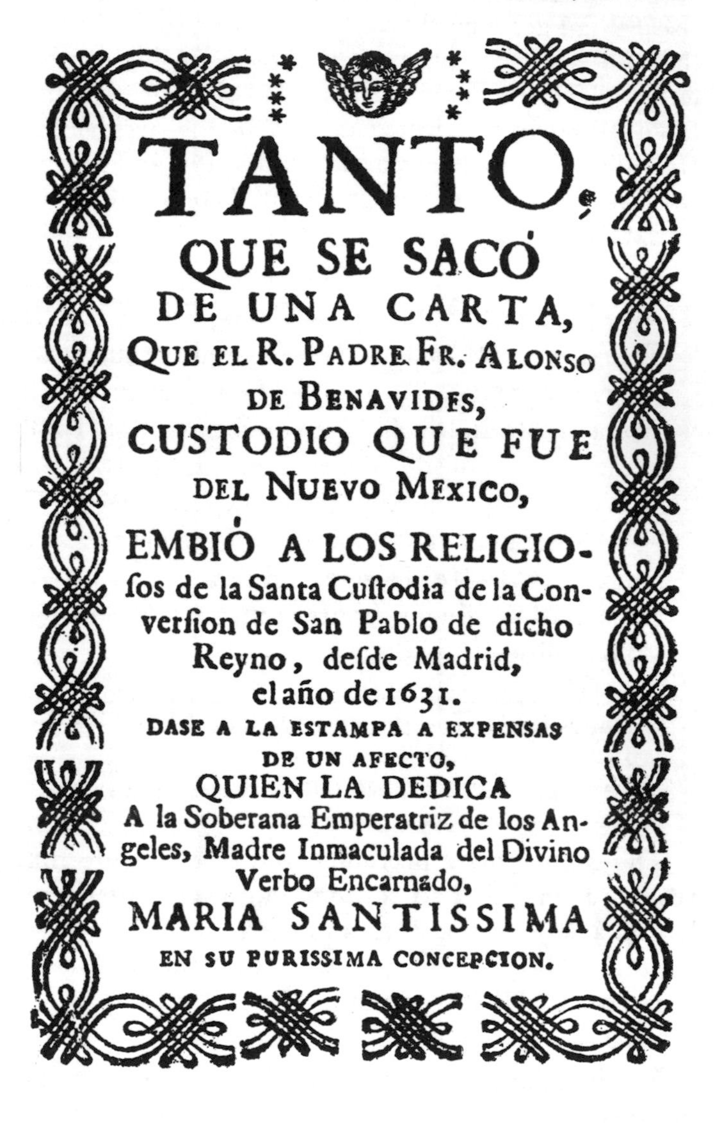
TANTO,
QUE SE SACÓ
DE UNA CARTA,
QUE EL R. PADRE FR. ALONSO
DE BENAVIDES,
CUSTODIO QUE FUE
DEL NUEVO MEXICO,
EMBIÓ A LOS RELIGIO-
ſos de la Santa Cuſtodia de la Con-
verſion de San Pablo de dicho
Reyno, deſde Madrid,
el año de 1631.
DASE A LA ESTAMPA A EXPENSAS
DE UN AFECTO,
QUIEN LA DEDICA
A la Soberana Emperatriz de los An-
geles, Madre Inmaculada del Divino
Verbo Encarnado,
MARIA SANTISSIMA
EN SU PURISSIMA CONCEPCION.

1650. As Medina did not locate any copy with this colophon, and he specifically stated that his own copy lacked it, to which I can certify because his copy was in my possession, I conclude that he got his *papeletas* mixed and that no edition exists with such a colophon. The first bibliographer to mention the letter as printed was Sanct Antonio, and his book was not published until after 1730, so no doubt he referred to that edition.

92b

Tanto, Que Se Sacó De Una Carta, que el R. P. Fr. Alonso de Benavides, Custodio, que fue del Nuevo Mexico, embiò à los Religiosos de la Santa Custodia de la Conversion dc San Pablo de dicho Reyno, desde Madrid, el año de 1631.

8°, leaf with engraving on the recto, and 16 numbered pages with the caption title only.

Copies: J, MNM, TWS, UT, WBS.

It is not known when this edition was printed, but it is usually referred to as having been printed in 1631, a manifest error. The copies usually have no leaf with the plate prefixed, but in the Museo Nacional in Mexico, in volume II of a small set of three volumes containing extracts of notices of manuscripts collected by José F. Ramírez, will be found a copy of this edition with the same copper plate engraving prefixed to it as that described with the edition of 1730. This would appear to indicate that it had been published between 1730 and 1747; but on the whole, Mr. George Parker Winship and I are inclined to agree that it was printed after 1747, probably about 1760, for it was a copy of this edition that Fr. Rafael Verger sent to Spain in 1772.

The text of these three editions is the same with the exception of differences in spelling, punctuation, and abbreviations.

Predicando á los Chichimecos del Nuebo Mexico.
La V.M. Maria de Iesus de Agreda

Paloú reprinted it in his life of Serra, 1787, and it appeared later with the life of Serra in 1852 attached to the edition of Clavijero's *Antigua ó Baja California.*

In the collection formed by Ramírez in the Museo Nacional in Mexico, the undated edition of this book is followed by a curious manuscript written by Padre Miguel Guerrero, a Jesuit, addressed to the Franciscans. It is a criticism of the alleged miracles of María de Jesús de Agreda, and the writer offers three reasons why he is unable to accept the tradition: First, no Indians had a king; second, what had become of the innumerable Indians who had been baptized in 1622 according to the account? third, how did it happen that no knowledge of these events reached Mexico city until 1628, and then something very different was related? He remarks that Father Zárate Salmerón went to New Mexico in 1618 and remained until 1626, but never once spoke of this large body of new Christians alleged to have been discovered in 1622. The manuscript is incomplete and there is no indication as to just when it was written, but certainly it was after 1730.

María Coronel, later known as María de Jesús de Agreda, was born April 2, 1602, in the little town of Agreda in old Castile. She entered a convent of the Descalzas, founded by her parents, in January, 1619. Her mother and sister entered at the same time, and on this occasion she took the name of María de Jesús. The convent afterward became famous as that of the Concepción Inmaculada de la Madre de Dios. In 1627 she was elected *presidente,* and with one or two short exceptions continued to rule the convent until her mystical death in 1651. Her body continued to live until May 4, 1666.

About 1635 she composed her famous book, the History of the Virgin, but it seems obvious that the church authorities were divided about the question of publishing

TANTO, QUE SE SACÓ DE UNA CARTA, que el R. P. Fr. Alonſo de Benavides, Cuſtodio, que fue del Nuevo Mexico, embiò à los Religioſos de la Santa Cuſtodia de la Converſion de San Pablo de dicho Reyno, deſde Madrid, el año de 1631.

CArisſimos, y amantiſsimos PP. Cuſtodio, y demàs Religioſos de N.S.P.S. Franciſco de la Cuſtodia Santa de la Conver-ſ[illegible] Pablo de los Reynos, y Provincias [illegible] Mexico: Infinitas gracias doy à la [illegible]geſtad [illegible] averme pueſto (aunque in-[illegible] el numero de la dichoſa ſuerte de VV. PP. pues merecen ſer tan favorecidos del Cielo, que los Ang[illegible], y N. P. San Franciſco les aſsiſten, y perſo[illegible], verdadera, y realmente llevan deſde la Villa de Agreda (que es raya de Caſtilla) à la bendita, y dichoſa Madre MARIA DE JESVS, de la Orden de la Concepcion Franciſcana Deſcalza, à que nos ayude con ſu preſencia, y predicacion en todas eſſas Provincias, y Barbaras Naciones. Bien ſe acuerdan VV. PP. que el año de 1628. aviendo ſido Prelado de VV. PP. y Siervo ſuyo, me determinè acaſo (ſi bien debiò de ſer particular mocion del Cielo) à paſſar à la Nueva-Eſpaña à dàr razon al Señor Virrey, y Reverendos Prelados de

it, and in 1645 her confessor compelled her to burn it together with other manuscripts which she had written. After her mystical death and her novitiate in the imitation of the Holy Virgin, her confessor urged her to rewrite the life and she completed it, as it is now known, in 1665. From the account of Ximénez Samaniego, in which he says the devils tried to prevent her from finishing the work as they similarly tried to prevent the completion of the first one, it seems apparent that there was some violent opposition in the church even at this time. Certainly we know that later such was the fact.

María de Jesús was subject to trances, but with it all seems to have been a level-headed woman of remarkable ability and character. Ximénez, who was provincial of the Franciscans in Burgos in whose jurisdiction the convent lay, wrote her life, and it is well worth reading as illustrating the development of mystical doctrines in the Catholic church. Ximénez knew her well and seems to have been a firm believer in her. Her life, written by him, was first published in Madrid about 1669 or 1670, to judge from the preliminaries of the edition that was published in Lisbon in 1681. This last is the earliest edition that I have seen, and here it is prefixed to the *Mística Ciudad de Dios,* forming three ponderous volumes.

In chapter XII Ximénez tells the story of her appearance to the Indians of New Mexico. At the end of this chapter he says that Benavides wrote a relation of these events from her statements and that she gave him a *Carta Exhortatoria* signed with her name. Benavides placed this in the archives of the *Custodia.* In 1668 the comisario general of the Franciscans sent *un tanto de ella* to Father Matheo de Heredia, the *procurador* of the Province in Madrid, "as a testimonial of what the order of San Francisco is continually doing in the New World for the conversion of the Indians against a certain competition which pretends to obscure their glory." Unexpectedly this fell into the hands of Ximénez. From this it appears likely that the miraculous visits of the nun had been kept secret, and indeed he elsewhere states this to be the fact, and it is probable that the first publication of these extraordinary visions is to be found in her life published by him. At any rate I have not been able to locate any earlier reference to her in this connection, the account published in Benavides' *Memorial* of 1630 being written obviously before he knew that she was the miraculous visitor. In that book the missionaries apparently thought the heavenly visitor must have been Mother Luisa de Carrión.

According to Ximénez Samaniego, the author of her life, the Lord in a vision showed her the whole world and the multitude of gentiles and heretics and told her that He was especially interested in the savages of New Mexico and other remote kingdoms there. So in a later ecstasy the Lord carried her to a remote pueblo of Indians where she preached to them in Spanish and they understood her and were converted. This was continued more than five hundred times and she converted the whole country, including the prince; and going to New Mexico, which was very distant, she recognized Franciscan fathers who were there, and told the Indians to seek the fathers to ask for aid and workers. All this she related to her confessor. The next important question was, did she pass in body or in spirit only; to which her answers were not very clear, but she finally thought an angel had passed in her form. Notwithstanding this, when other visits occurred later the prelates were persuaded that she passed in body and that only her humility prevented her from saying so.

After these visions had been going on for about six years, namely until about 1627 or 1628, her confessor sent a brief account of her wanderings to the archbishop-elect of Mexico, one Francisco Manso, and the archbishop wrote to Benavides in New Mexico to find out whether he had heard anything about these celestial visits. On Benavides' arrival in Mexico he conferred with the archbishop and the provincial of the order, giving them the information, no doubt that contained in his *Memorial,* and it was decided that Benavides should go to Spain, where he interviewed María de Jesús, who told him many circumstances connected with her visits to New Mexico, and said that she had seen Benavides himself, and gave him the letter previously referred to.

That the belief in the miraculous appearances of this nun to the Indians of New Mexico and other parts was widespread at one time in Mexico and Spain is apparent from the numerous references to her to be found in the documents of the seventeenth and eighteenth centuries, none, however, before 1670, the time of the appearance in print of her life. In Father Massanet's letter to Carlos Sigüenza, written in 1692, translated by Lilia A. Casís and printed in the April, 1899, number of the *Quarterly* of the Texas Historical Association, he says distinctly that he had come to the missions of Coahuila because of information regarding the appearances of this nun, information which he brought with him from Spain. In this letter he tells a tale about the governor of the Indians in one of the Texan villages asking him for a piece of blue baize to make a shroud in which to bury his mother. When Massanet asked him what he wanted a blue one for, he said it was because they had been frequently visited in times past by a very beautiful woman dressed in blue garments, who used to come down from the hills, and added that his mother, an aged woman, had seen her, as had other old people; to which the father adds, "From this it is easily seen that they referred to Mother María de Jesús de Agreda, as she moved very frequently in those regions, as she herself acknowledged to the father custodian of New Mexico, her last visit having been made in 1631, this last fact being evident from her own statement made to the said father custodian of New Mexico."

In the second part of the *Luz de Tierra Incógnita,* Juan Mateo Manje gives an account of the expedition which he made with Father Eusebio Kino in February, 1699. It seems that they had along with them an account of the expedition of Oñate to the Colorado river in 1604-05, and while on the Gila river they asked the old Indians if they remembered seeing a Spanish captain and soldiers and horses. The Indians said they had heard those now dead speak of it, but added voluntarily that there had come a woman, white and beautiful, dressed in white, gray, and blue down to her feet with a cloak which covered her head, who with a cross spoke to them in a language they did not understand. The nation of the Rio Colorado shot arrows into her on two occasions, leaving her for dead, but she came to life again and went off through the air to some unknown place, and in a few days she returned.

Two days before, Manje and Kino had heard the same thing, and wondered if it could not have been María de Jesús. Manje adds the wise remark that he does not see why the Indians could not understand her as, if God performed such a miracle as carrying her through the air from Spain, he would not have omitted to have her understood by the natives. However, he attributes this to forgetfulness, either natural or the work of the devil. From a later remark it seems that the Indians said she came from a house on the other side of the Colorado. Father Kino in his *Favores Celestiales,* as translated by Dr. Bolton, volume I, page 198, refers to Manje's opinion on this subject to the effect that the woman must have been María de Jesús, but seems a little skeptical and prefers to attribute the good customs of these natives to the fertilizing blood of the venerable father Francisco Xavier Saeta, of Caborca, who had been killed by the Pimas in 1695.

In 1772 Fr. Rafael Verger in his memorial on the work of the Franciscans in converting the Indians, gives quite an account of María de Jesús, mostly taken, however, from her letter and from Benavides.

Fr. José Antonio Pichardo, who, in 1808, succeeded Father Melchor Talamantes in charge of investigating the boundary between the United States and New Spain, wrote a disquisition on Quivira. In this he gives a long account of the nun and enters into an elaborate argument to justify his conviction of the truth of the story. At the time he quoted apparently all he could find on the subject, but the printed material was then very scarce. When he first began to write he had not seen the *Memorial* of Benavides, but obtained possession of one before he finished. He thought that the letter had been printed in Madrid in 1631 and also in Mexico about the same time, but his opinion was simply based upon the fact that the letter had been written in 1631. He entered into an argument with his deceased predecessor, Talamantes, who was a *Mercenario* and very skeptical about these miraculous appearances, having intimated that the Franciscans were trying to use her for some purposes of their own. There seems to be some truth in this theory, because the propaganda about her visits more or less coincided with the efforts of the Franciscans to make New Mexico a bishopric. This had been attempted in 1621, in 1631, and again about 1668 at the time the life of the nun was written.

Shortly after her death an attempt was made to have her beatified, but these efforts met with the most violent opposition. Some time about 1720-25 a regular center of propaganda was set up in Madrid with the same purpose in view, entitled *"Imprenta de la Causa de la Venerable*

Madre." From this press began to appear new editions of her life, and a number were printed between 1722 and 1757. Opposition to the beatification still continued, and I believe the cause is still pending in the Vatican. A short account of María de Jesús can be found in John Gilmary Shea's *Catholic Church in Colonial Days,* together with her portrait and a facsimile of her signature.

María de Jesús carried on an interesting correspondence with the king on various state matters, which is still extant, but her principal work was the *Mística Ciudad de Dios,* really a Life of the Virgin Mary. This is a ponderous work of the most mystical character, full of what might be called special revelations. It has been translated into many languages and a number of editions have appeared, but it was never translated into English until 1912. Fiscar Marison in that year published a translation of the first part of it, and completed it in 1914-15.

93. GONZÁLEZ: Fr. Fernando Alonso

Señor. Fray Fernando Alonso Gonzalez, Comissario General de las Provincias de los Reynos de la Nueva-España, de la Sagrada Religion de San Francisco, dize: . . .

[Madrid, 1731.]

Folio, 14 numbered pages, signed at the end as above.
Copies: BM, WBS.

This memorial is described by Medina, *La Imprenta en México,* no. 3178, and he assigns to it the year 1738 as the probable date of printing in Mexico. He is mistaken, however, because in the *Memorial Ajustado* presented in the same case in 1738 by Lic. Ramiro de Valenzuela, it is specifically stated that González presented his memorial in 1731. The *Memorial* shows that it was his intention to send it to the king by a vessel soon to leave for Spain.

In 1725 Bishop Crespo undertook a visit to New Mexico, but he went only as far as El Paso. The bishop claimed the right to exercise his episcopal rights in the province of New Mexico, and some opposition arose at this time. In 1730 he made another visit, and this time went as far as Santa Fe, where the *Custodio* presented a written objection. On Crespo's return, while at El Paso on September 25, he wrote a letter referring to the objections made by the Franciscans to his attempted exercise of episcopal rights, and incidentally made some very grave charges against them.

As a result of this visit and the documents presented in Madrid by Crespo, Fray González submitted this memorial, in which he answers point by point the various claims set up by the bishop, and refutes briefly the charges against the missionaries. The document contains a considerable history of New Mexico, and especially of the labors of the Franciscans in that province. In the last paragraph the writer suggests that New Mexico be erected into a bishopric, which he says had been attempted in the years 1621 and 1631.

93A. SECO: Fr. Francisco

Señor. Fray Francisco Seco del Orden de San Francisco, Lector Jubilado, y procurador general de las provincias de Indias de su sagrada religion, puesto a los reales pies de V. Magestad, dize:

[Madrid.]

Folio, eight numbered pages.

This memorial treats of the *visita* of Bishop Crespo to New Mexico in July, 1730, and his assumption of authority over the Franciscans in that province. It contains an extract of the previous history of New Mexico, but is largely devoted to a discussion of ecclesiastical rights.

He refers to the proceedings of Fray Fernando Alonso González and it appears to have been presented in Madrid in the latter part of 1731.

The only known copy of this unique document was formerly in the possession of Dr. F. W. Hodge, and is now in the Huntington Free library, Westchester Square, New York city.

94. PÉREZ VELARDE: Antonio

Relacion De Servicios De Don Antonio Perez Velarde, Theniente de Governador, y Capitan General del Reyno, y Provincias de la Nueva-Mexico en las de Nueva España.

Folio, 4 unnumbered pages dated at the end, Madrid, November 14, 1732, and unsigned except for the certification in manuscript by the *Relator*. Attached to this are two unnumbered printed pages of memorial by Pérez Velarde, undated, but evidently presented with the *Relación*.

Copy: AGI.

This memorial was probably printed in Madrid.

94a

Señor. Don Antonio Perez Velarde, Theniente de Capitan General de la Provincia de el Nuevo Mexico, à los pies de V. Mag. con el mayor rendimiento dize, . . .

Copy: AGI, 137-1-4.

From a *testimonio* made in Mexico, April 7, 1732, it appears that Pérez Velarde began his service in New Mexico in 1719. As evidence of his good services against the Apaches and the revolted Xemes he cites various certificates from Governors Bustamante and Cruzat, twenty Franciscans whose names will be found in the memorial, and Colonel Pedro de Rivera. He also refers to the rebellion of the Zia Indians in 1726.

95. BENITO DE ARROYO: Joseph

Relacion De Servicios De Don Joseph Benito de Arroyo, Capitan que fue de una de las Compañias del Batallòn de Infanteria Montada, que se formò para el desalojo de los Enemigos de la Provincia de Quaguila, Texas, y Nuevas Philipinas, en la Nueva España.

Folio, 3 unnumbered pages dated at the end, Madrid, June 18, 1733.

Copy: AGI, 137-1-25.

From a *testimonio* made in Mexico on March 30, 1730, it appears that Benito de Arroyo was appointed captain of mounted infantry by the Marqués de Aguayo and ratified in this by the viceroy, May 12, 1721. On January 25, 1723, he was appointed *teniente de governador* of Coahuila, and was left by the Marqués de Aguayo as captain of the presidio of Pilar de los Adais, where he remained two years in incessant labor in various expeditions back and forth from San Antonio to bring supplies to the garrison. He was licensed on account of consequent bad health, October 6, 1723.

96. FERNÁNDEZ DE CÓRDOVA: Juan

Relacion De Los Meritos, Y Servicios Del Maestro De Campo de Infanterìa Española Don Juan Fernandez de Cordova, Governador, y Capitan General, que fue de la Provincia de la Nueva Vizcaya.

Folio, 4 leaves numbered except the first, dated at the end in manuscript, Madrid, October 4, 1734.

Copy: AGI, 132-1-5.

Appointed governor of Nueva Vizcaya, May 7, 1702 [1722?], he founded a number of new towns, including Chihuahua and Batopilas. Some account is also given of the erection of mission churches in Chihuahua.

97. GONZÁLEZ CABRERA BUENO: Joseph

Navegacion Especvlativa, Y Practica, Con La Explicacion De Algvnos Instrvmentos, Qve Estan Mas En Vso En los Navegantes, con las Reglas necesarias para su verdadero vso; Tabla de las declinaciones del Sol, computadas al Meridiano de San Bernardino; el modo de navegar por la Geometria; por las Tablas de Rumbos; por la Arithmetica; por la Trigonometria; por el Quadrante de Reduccion; por los Senos Logarithmos; y comunes; con las Estampas, y Figuras pertenecientes à lo dicho, y otros Tratados curiosos. [Printer's device.] Compvesta Por El Almirante D. Ioseph Gonzalez Cabrera Bueno, Piloto mayor de la Carrera de Philipinas, y Natural de la Isla de Tenerife una de las Canarias. Qvien La Dedica Al M. Ill^tre^. Señor D. Fernando De Valdes, Y Tamon, Cavallero del Orden de Santiago, Brigadier de los Reales Exercitos de su Magestad, y de su Consejo, Governador, y Capitan General de las Islas Philipinas, y Presidente de su Real Audiencia, y Chancilleria, que en ellas riside. [Printer's device.]

Impresa en Manila en el Convento de Nuestra Señora de los Angeles de la Orden de Nr̃o. Seraphico Padre San Francisco Año de 1734.

Folio, title, 10 unnumbered leaves of preliminaries, 392 numbered pages, 2 unnumbered leaves of errata and index, and 13 plates of figures for astronomical calculations and measuring land.

Preliminaries: 2 leaves of dedication to Fernando de Valdés y Tamón, 2 leaves of *censura* by P. Pedro Murillo Velarde, 1 leaf of approbation, license of the government and license of the ordinary, dated June 17 and August 25, respectively, 1 leaf of prologue, 1½ leaves of introduction, and 2½ leaves of poetry.

Copies: B, A. Graiño of Madrid, LC, P.

The fifth part, beginning on page 292, contains the different routes in the Pacific, description of ports, etc., the route from Manila to Acapulco being described first. From this it appears that the course followed was, generally speaking, northeast to latitude 36° or 37° and longitude 40° [that is, 140 East] and then east to somewhere near Cape Mendocino, but turning southeast before reaching the coast. If land was not seen at 35°, by continuing in a southeast direction the first land seen would either be Cenizas or Cerros. If land was sighted at 35° or 35½°, they could run along in an easterly direction between the mainland and the islands, of which he states that there were seven large and three small ones. Th. coast at this point would be found full of trees, where spars could be obtained if necessary.

On pages 302-313 there is a description of the coast from Cape Mendocino south, copied from the *derrotero* of Francisco de Bolaños of 1603 with trifling changes. He places this cape in 41½°, Punta de los Reyes in 38½°, and gives a little description of the bay of San Francisco at this point. From his description it appears that at that period the middle *estero* could be entered, evidently by ship, and he says that, inside, friendly Indians and good water would be found. On page 303 he describes the bay of Monterey, placing Point Año Nuevo in 37½° and Point Pinos in 37°. Point Concepción he places in 35½°, and refers to the mountain which looked like an island,—obviously the one in Estero bay now called El Morro.

The description is positive proof that in 1734 the bay of San Francisco was not known to the Spaniards. What they called San Francisco was the small bay under Point

Reyes, of which the latitude is given as 38½°. Mr. J. T. Doyle has a note in *Noticias de la Nueva California,* II, 201, on this point, in which he copies the extract referring to the bay of San Francisco under Point Reyes, and from which he also deduces the obvious conclusion that the Spaniards did not know the present San Francisco bay. As a result of this discovery by him he published his *Memorandum as to the discovery of the bay of San Francisco. With introductory remarks by John T. Doyle, member of the American Antiquarian society. Read before the American Antiquarian society, at their annual meeting, October 21, 1873.* Worcester, Mass.: Printed by Charles Hamilton, 1874. 8°, 14 pages.

The first correct location of Drake's bay, or what was known to the Spaniards before 1770 as the bay of San Francisco, was made by Mr. H. H. Bancroft's assistant, Henry L. Oak, in the *Overland Monthly,* 1874.

98. RIVERA: Pedro de

Diario. Y Derrotero De Lo Caminado, Visto, Y Obcervado En El Discurso de la visita general de Precidios, situados en las Provincias Ynternas de Nueva España, Que De Orden De Su Magestad executó D. Pedro De Rivera, Brigadier De Los Reales Exercitos. Haviendo Transitado Por Los Reinos del Nuevo de Toledo, el de la Nueva Galicia, el de la Nueva Vizcaya, el de la Nueva Mexico, el de la Nueva Estremadura, el de las Nuevas Philipinas, el del Nuevo de Leon. Las Provincias, de Sonora, Ostimuri, Sinaloa, y Guasteca.

Ympresso en Guathemala, por Sebastian de Arebalo, año de 1736.

Folio, title, and 38 unnumbered leaves signed at the end, D. Pedro de Rivera.

There is no license to print, from which it appears probable that it was printed by the government.

Copies: A, B, H, IC, J, LC, TWS.

While acting as governor of Tlascala in 1724 Rivera received orders from the viceroy to go to Mexico, where he received instructions to make an inspection of the frontier presidios, and in accordance therewith left Mexico November 21. He passed by Zacatecas and Fresnillo to Nayarit and thence returned to Zacatecas.

Leaving Zacatecas again, May 21, 1725, he visited the Nueva Vizcaya presidios and reached Parral January 11, 1726. During the spring and summer he visited New Mexico, going to Sonora in October. His journey south extended to the presidio of Sinaloa, whence he retraced his steps and was back in Chihuahua, March 1, 1727. In June he left that place and proceeded by way of Gallo and the Laguna to Parras and Saltillo, and in August was in San Antonio, Texas.

After visiting the various presidios in that territory, he returned to Mexico by way of Monterey, Saltillo, and San Luis Potosi, reaching Mexico June 21, 1728.

The detailed reports still exist in the archives of Mexico and in Seville.

This is the most important printed document extant relating to the frontier provinces. Besides the route and the remarks on the character of the country traversed, the book contains condensed statements about the people, towns, resources, etc., of all of the provinces visited and a vast amount of scattered information on all manner of subjects,— missions, mines, officials, government, etc.

While Rivera was in Santa Fe he conducted an examination into the conduct of Governor Valverde and especially into the Villasur expedition. The *autos* are to be found in the Archivo General de la Nación, volume 37 of Provincias Internas.

Rivera had with him Francisco Alvarez y Barreyro, an engineer whom he detailed to draw up maps marking the boundaries of the various frontier provinces, and some six are still extant in AGI, 67-4-4, drawn in colors and accompanied by a descriptive account of the territory covered. A description will be found in Torres Lanzas, *Mapas, Planos, &, de México y Floridas,* published in 1900. Sr. Torres Lanzas was for many years the chief of the Archivo General de Indias.

No. 120—Plano Corográphico de el Nuevo Reyno de Toledo, Provincia de San Joseph de Nayarit, etc. Avril 4, 1725. 63x46½cms.

No. 121—Plano Corográphico é Hidrográphico de las Provincias de la Nueva Vizcaya y Culiacán, etc. Ag. 23, 1726. 77x57 cms.

No. 122—Plano Corográphico del Reyno y Provincia de el Nuevo Mexico, etc. Enero 12, 1727. 57½x40½ cms.

No. 123—Plano Corográphico y Hidrográphico de las tres Provincias de Sonora, Ostimuri y Sinaloa, etc. Junio 20, 1727. 46x41½ cms.

No. 124—Plano Corográphico de los dos Reinos el Nuevo de Extremadura ó Coaguila y el Nuevo de León, etc. Año 1729. 51x41½ cms.

98A. RODERO: Fr. Gaspar

Señor. El Padre Gaspar Rodero, de la Compañia de Jesus, Procurador General de Indias, en cumplimiento de lo mandado por V. Mag. sobre Californias, dice: Que para proceder con mayor claridad en el informe, que se le manda hacer, lo dividirà en quatro Puntos. En el primero harà descripcion de dichas Californias, que sirva de Mapa para el conocimiento del Paìs. En el segundo tratarà de lo acaecido sobre la Conquista de las referidas Californias, desde su descubrimiento, hasta el año de 1701. En el tercero expressarà los adelantamientos de esta Conquista, hasta el de 1733. Y en el quarto, finalmente, harà patente la rebelion, ò levantamiento, que sucediò el año de 1734. con lo demàs concerniente al mencionado assumpto, hasta el año pasado de 1736.

Folio, 12 pages, numbered except the first.

This hitherto unknown memorial has recently been acquired by the Huntington library. Although undated, it bears internal evidence that it was written about the end of the year 1737. In AGI, 67-3-29, there is a manuscript memorial by Rodero much the same as this, which was sent to the Council of the Indies, January 21, 1738, in compliance with an order of the same date from the secretary, apparently the order referred to in the beginning of the printed memorial. This, then, was probably printed at about the same time for distribution to members of the Council, as frequently happened in similar cases. The memorial is divided into four parts: the first contains a description of the country; the second and third, a short sketch of its history to 1701 and 1733, respectively; and the fourth, an account of the rising of the Indians in 1734 and the subsequent proceedings to 1736.

The document, although interesting, adds nothing to our knowledge of the history of the peninsula to that time, full accounts of which have been included in Venegas' *Noticia,* the *Apostólicos Afanes,* and Alegre's *Historia de la Compañia de Jesus en Nueva España;* but on the last page is printed a list of the persons who had contributed to the conquest and conservation of the Californias, with the amounts of their respective gifts, totalling, to 1720, some 548,000 pesos, a considerable part of which consisted of goods and supplies of various kinds.

99. ARLEGUI: Fr. Joseph

Chronica De La Provincia De N. S. P. S. Francisco De Zacatecas: Compuesta Por El M. R. P. Fr.

CHRONICA
DE LA PROVINCIA DE N.S.P.S.FRANCISCO DE ZACATECAS:

COMPUESTA
POR EL M. R. P. FR. JOSEPH ARLEGUI,
Lector Jubilado, Calificador del Sto. Officio, Examinador Synodal de los Obspados de Valladolid, y Durango, Padre Ex-Ministro Provincial, y Chronista de dicha Provincia:

LA QUE DEDICA
A N. S. P. S. FRANCISCO
DON JOSEPH DE ERREPARAZ,
Syndico General de dicha Provincia,
EN NOMBRE
DE NRÔ. RMO. P. FR. PEDRO NAVARRETE,
Predicador General, Calificador del Santo Officio, Padre de la Provincia de Santiago de Xalisco, ex-Ministro Provincial dos veces, y Padre de la del Santo Evangelio de Mexico, y Comissario General de todas las de la Nueva España, y Islas Philippinas.

CON LICENCIA DE LOS SUPERIORES.
En Mexico por JOSEPH BERNARDO DE HOGAL, Ministro, ê Impressor del Real, y Apostolico Tribunal de la Santa Cruzada en todo este Reyno.

Año de 1737.

Joseph Arlegui, Lector Jubilado, Calificador del Sto. Officio, Examinador Synodal de los Obispados de Valladolid, y Durango, Padre Ex-Ministro Provincial, y Chronista de dicha Provincia: La Que Dedica A N. S. P. S. Francisco Don Joseph De Erreparaz, Syndico General de dicha Provincia, En Nombre De Nrô. Rmo. P. Fr. Pedro Navarrete, Predicador General, Calificador del Santo Officio, Padre de la Provincia de Santiago de Xalisco, ex-Ministro Provincial dos veces, y Padre de la del Santo Evangelio de Mexico, y Comissario General de todas las de la Nueva España, y Islas Philippinas. Con Licencia De Los Superiores.

En Mexico por Joseph Bernardo De Hogal, Ministro, ê Impressor del Real, y Apostolico Tribunal de la Santa Cruzada en todo este Reyno. Año de 1737.

4°, title in red and black, 14 unnumbered leaves of preliminaries, 412 numbered pages of text, and 9 unnumbered leaves of index.

Preliminaries: 3 leaves of dedication by Erreparaz, 6 leaves of *pareceres,* 2 leaves of *sentir,* 1 leaf of licenses, that of the viceroy being dated September 12, 1736, and 2 leaves of prologue, *protesta,* and errata.

Copies: B, J, JCB, LC, NYP, TWS, UT.

Reprinted in Mexico in 1851 in 8°, xx [5] preliminary pages, and 488 pages. This contains some additions up to 1828 by Fr. Antonio Gálvez.

Arlegui, the author of this *Chrónica,* was a Franciscan who at the time of writing was living in San Luis Potosi. On November 6, 1734, he was selected by his province to undertake the task of writing a history of it in compliance

ARTE

DE LA LENGUA CAHITA
conforme à las Reglas de muchos
Peritos en ella.

Compueſto por un Padre de la Compañia de JESUS, Miſsionero de mas de treinta años en la Provincia de Cynaloa.

Eſta lo ſaca á luz, y humilde lo conſagra
al grande Apoſtol de la India Oriental,
y primer Apoſtol del Japon
SAN FRANCISCO XAVIER.

Año de

1737.

CON LICENCIA DE LOS SVPERIORES.
En Mexico en la Imprenta de D. Franciſco
Xavier Sanchez, en el puente de Palacio.

with an order given to all provinces by a general *capítulo* of the Franciscan order held in Milan June 15, 1729, to select a capable person to chronicle the history of each province. He finished writing it May 3, 1736.

The first convent in the province was founded in 1567, and it was first a *custodia* of the mother province of Santo Evangelio, but under a bull of Clement VIII of 1603 the *custodia* was erected into the province of San Francisco. The first part of the work relates to the discoveries from Zacatecas northward, including nearly all the mining towns in modern Durango and Chihuahua. We know from other sources that Franciscan missionaries accompanied Francisco de Ibarra in all his expeditions to the north, but we can hardly believe that the discoveries of the mines were due to the missionaries, as is stated by Arlegui. All the missions in Nuevo León were also founded by missionaries from this province, as well as some in Coahuila.

The book contains an account of the uprising of the Tepehuana Indians in 1617 and the Tarahumares in 1690. Pages 227-232 contain an account of the expedition to New Mexico of Fr. Agustín Rodríguez, with a short account of that of Antonio de Espejo.

100. BASILIO: P. Tomás

Arte De La Lengua Cahita conforme à las Reglas de muchos Peritos en ella. Compuesto por vn Padre de la Compañia de Jesus, Missionero de mas de treinta años en la Provincia de Cynaloa. Esta lo saca á luz, y humilde lo consagra al grande Apostol de la India Oriental, y primer Apostol del Japon San Francisco Xavier. Año de [Jesuit device] 1737. Con Licencia De Los Svperiores.

En Mexico en la Imprenta de D. Francisco Xavier Sanchez, en el puente de Palacio.

8°, title, 5 unnumbered preliminary leaves, 118 pages, and 26 unnumbered leaves of vocabulary. The last unnumbered leaf of the preliminaries is a leaf of errata with two stars for the signature.

Copies: BM, JCB, NYP.

There is no name of author, but in the dedication to the *Cathecismo,* which was probably issued with the *Arte,* it is stated that the author was P. Tomás Basilio.

The Tomás Basilio of this work must be the same individual who accompanied Father Andrés Pérez de Ribas in 1617 on the first mission to the Yaqui Indians. This man, an Italian, served thirty years or more as a missionary in Sinaloa and Sonora, long enough to have learned to write and speak the language fluently.

101. BASILIO: P. Tomás

Cathecismo De La Doctrina Christiana Traducido En Lengua Cahita. Compuesto Por Vn Padre De La Compañia De Jesus, Missionero En La Provincia De Cynaloa, La Qual Dedica Al Patriarcha Señor San Joseph. [Jesuit device.] Con Licencia De Los Superiores.

En Mexico: por Francisco Xavier Sanchez, en el puente de Palacio. Año de 1737.

8°, title, 3 pages of dedication, 12 pages of text, and 3 unnumbered pages at the end with borders enclosing religious poetry.

Copies: BM, NYP.

In the dedication it is stated that the author was P. Tomás Basilio. I think it very likely that this *Cathecismo* was issued with the *Arte,* as in the two copies known they are bound up together.

102. ESPINOSA: Fr. Isidro Felix de

El Peregrino Septentrional Atlante: Delineado En La Exemplarissima Vida Del Venerable Padre F.

Antonio Margil De Jesus, Fruto de la Floridissima Ciudad de Valencia, Hijo de su Seraphica Observante Provincia, Predicador Missionero, Notario Apostolico, Comissario del Santo Officio, Fundador, y ex Guardian de tres Colegios, Prefecto de las Missiones de Propaganda Fide en todas las Indias Occidentales, y aclamado de la piedad Por Nuevo Apostol De Guatemala: Dedicase Al Atlante De Mejor Cielo San Antonio De Padua: A expensas de los amartelados del V. Padre: Escribela El P. Fr. Isidro Felis De Espinosa, Predicador, y Missionero Apostolico, ex Guardian del Colegio de la Santa Cruz de Queretaro, su Chronista, y menor Hijo. Con Licencia De Los Superiores:

En Mexico por Joseph Bernardo De Hogal, Ministro, ê Impressor del Real, y Apostolico Tribunal de la Santa Cruzada en todo este Reyno, año de 1737.

4°, title in red and black, 18 unnumbered preliminary leaves, a copper plate engraving of Father Antonio preaching to the Indians, 456 numbered pages of text, and 4 unnumbered of index.

Preliminaries: 4 leaves of dedication by the author, 2 leaves of *aprobación* of Fr. Miguel de Aroche, 5 pages of *parecer* of Lucas del Rincón, 13 pages of *sentir* of Fr. Manuel Bravo de Acuña, 2 pages of licenses, that of the government being dated February 27, 1737, 3 pages of prologue, and 1 page of *protesta.*

Copies: A, B, GPH, H, J, JCB, LAP, S, TWS, UT.

102a

El Peregrino Septentrional Atlante: . . .

En Valencia: Por Joseph Thomàs Lucas, Im-

EL PEREGRINO

Pertenece a la Libreria del Colegio de la Sma Cruz de Queretaro

SEPTENTRIONAL ATLANTE:

DELINEADO

EN LA EXEMPLARISSIMA VIDA

DEL VENERABLE PADRE

F. ANTONIO MARGIL

DE JESUS,

Fruto de la Floridiſſima Ciudad de Valencia, Hijo de ſu Seraphica Obſervante Provincia, Predicador Miſſionero, Notario Apoſtolico, Comiſſario del Santo Officio, Fundador, y ex Guardian de tres Colegios, Prefecto de las Miſſiones de PROPAGANDA FIDE en todas las Indias Occidentales, y aclamado de la piedad

POR NUEVO APOSTOL DE GUATEMALA:

DEDICASE

AL ATLANTE DE MEJOR CIELO

SAN ANTONIO DE PADUA:

A expenſas de los amartelados del V. Padre:

ESCRIBELA

EL P. Fr. ISIDRO FELIS DE ESPINOSA,

Predicador, y Miſſionero Apoſtolico, ex Guardian del Colegio de la Santa Cruz de Queretaro, ſu Chroniſta, y menor Hijo.

CON LICENCIA DE LOS SUPERIORES:

En Mexico por JOSEPH BERNARDO DE HOGAL, Miniſtro, é Impreſſor del Real, y Apoſtolico Tribunal de la Santa Cruzada en todo eſte Reyno, año de 1737.

pressor del Ilustrissimo Señor Obispo de Teruel. Año de 1742. Vendese . . .

4°, title, plate of Margil de Jesús preaching to the Indians, 4 preliminary leaves, 411 pages of text, and 2 unnumbered leaves of index.

Copies: JCB, LC, TWS.

Father Antonio is particularly noted in Southwest history for his expedition to Texas in 1716 and the founding of the missions in northeast Texas. For some years previous he had been in charge of the organization of the College of Guadalupe in Zacatecas, and a guardian having been appointed in 1713, Father Antonio was free to make a missionary effort in the north. Several years were passed in Nuevo León and Coahuila, until in April, 1716, the Texas expedition set out from the missions on the Rio del Norte, the account of which will be found on pages 278-290. Espinosa accompanied Father Antonio on this expedition, and gives a touching account of the old man in an illness which overtook him. The French having invaded the province, the missionaries were obliged to abandon the missions in 1719. In 1722 Father Antonio returned from Texas to the College of Zacatecas, having been chosen guardian. He died in Mexico on August 6, 1726, at the age of seventy, after having spent fifty-three years in the priesthood. Principally engaged in missionary efforts among the Indians, his favorite field of labor was Guatemala, where he gained a high reputation for piety as well as great success as a missionary. After his death several funeral orations were printed in Mexico, and later in Guatemala and other places. None of them which I have seen contains any material facts in regard to the career of Margil in Texas.

Dr. H. E. Bolton discovered in the archives of the College of Guadalupe de Zacatecas a life of Father Antonio different from this of Espinosa. It is an unsigned manuscript of 300 pages, evidently original. The library of the College also contains a collection of relics and some of his original letters.

Shortly after his death the Franciscans initiated a movement looking towards his beatification. In 1792, in Rome, there was published in Latin a collection of letters from various religious and other bodies in favor of this movement. The library of Georgetown University contains the following work relating to this matter: *Notizie Della Vita, Virtu Doni E Miracoli Del Ven. Servo Di Dio Fr. Antonio Margil Di Gesù. Estrate dai processi compilati per la causa della sua beatificazione e canonizzazione e data alla luce dal P. Fr. Giuseppi Maria Gusman.* Roma 1836. 8°, viii, 216 pages.

The *causa* is, I believe, still pending before the papal court.

103. COS Y LOMBRAÑA: Francisco de

Relacion De Los Meritos, Y Servicios De Don Francisco De Cos y Lombraña, Theniente de Governador, y Capitan General, que ha sido de la Bahia del Espiritu Santo, Provincia de los Tejas, ò Nuevas Philipinas.

Folio, 2 unnumbered pages dated at the end, Madrid, March 4, 1738.

Copy: AGI, 137-1-7.

Cos began to serve as a soldier in 1724 at the presidio of Loreto in Texas. On May 12, 1735, he was appointed at Pilar as *teniente general* by the governor, Juan Antonio Bustillo y Cevallos, and served while the governor was absent in San Antonio. He also produced certificates of good conduct from Fray Juan Gregorio de la Campa Cos, vice-prefect of the Texas missions, and Fray Joseph González, missionary at Bahía de Espíritu Santo.

104. GARCÍA DE PRUNEDA: Luis

Relacion De Los Meritos de Don Luis Garcia de Pruneda, Theniente General, Governador, y Capitan General, que ha sido del Nuevo Reyno de Leon, Regidor Perpetuo, y Alcalde Provincial de la Ciudad de Monterrey, su Capital.

Folio, 4 unnumbered pages dated at the end, Madrid, March 15, 1738, and signed in manuscript by the *Relator*.

To this is added the item in 104a.

104a

Señor, Yo Juan Joseph Garcia Pintado, Escribano de su Magestad (que Dios guarde) y Notario publico de las Indias, y Receptor de la Curia Ecclesiastica en el Arzobispado de esta Corte, y Reyno de la Nueva España: Certifico, doy fè, y testimonio de verdad, que por el General Don Luis Garcia de Pruneda, . . .

Also folio, 4 unnumbered pages, certified to at the end in Mexico on February 25, 1737, and unquestionably printed in Mexico.

Copy: AGI, 103-5-21.

García de Pruneda was married to a daughter of Alonso de León, and the second document contains some account of his services. Don Luis García de Pruneda had been captain of the presidio of San Juan de Cadereita four years, and twice governor of Nuevo León. He recounts his services in pacifying the Indians, and says he founded the Franciscan mission of Guadalupe in Boca de Leones.

105. RIVERA: Pedro de

Relacion de servicios del Mariscal de Campo Don Pedro de Rivera Governador y Capitan General de las Provincias de Goathemala, y Presidente actual de la Audiencia Real de la Ciudad de Santiago de ella.

Folio, 3 leaves dated November 10, 1738.

Medina, *Biblioteca Hispano-Americana*, no. 3155, locates a copy in AGI.

106. VALENZUELA: Francisco Ramiro de

Memorial Ajustado, Que De Orden Del Consejo Supremo De Indias Se Ha Hecho Del Pleyto, Que Siguiò El Ill.mo S.or Don Benito Crespo, Obispo que fue de Durango. Y Lo Continua El Ill.mo S.or Don Martin de Elizacohea, su successor en dicho Obispado. Con La Religion De N. P. S. Francisco, de la Regular Observancia, y su Procurador General de las Indias. Sobre Visitar, y exercer los actos de la Jurisdiccion Diocesana en la Custodia del Nuevo Mexico en la Nueva España, poner Vicario Foraneo, y otras cosas.

Folio, title, a leaf of index, and 64 leaves of text. At the end it is signed thus—Madrid, 26 Sept. 1738, by Lic. Don Francisco Ramiro de Valenzuela. Before the title are the words, *Jesus, Maria, Y Joseph.*

Copies: BM, WBS. Formerly there was one in the Bancroft library, but it cannot now be located.

This document, which contains the record of an ecclesiastical quarrel over jurisdiction, contains much interesting history regarding New Mexico. On June 14, 1621, a *cédula* was issued erecting a bishopric in Durango, and on February 4, 1622, the division was made from that of Guadalajara, fixing the respective boundaries of the two bishoprics. Benito Crespo, who had been appointed bishop of Durango on March 22, 1723, started on a visit to New Mexico, November 20, 1725, but went no farther than El Paso del Norte, returning January 24, 1726. The Franciscans, who up to that time had been practically

higher price to the soldiers and others. He says that the captains managed to get all the money that was paid to the soldiers in exchange for goods. He then charges that, in order to get a position as a soldier, forty or fifty pesos had to be paid to the captain, and thus only boys and useless men enlisted. With such an inefficient force they never managed to get into a fight with the hostile Indians, who only laughed at them, so it was the custom to attack the friendly Indians and steal the girls and boys, who were then sold as slaves in the settled country, although this was absolutely prohibited by law. The location of the presidios was a pure matter of personal interest. He says that although the presidio of Sacramento had been founded in 1736, yet even in 1738 it had not actually found a location on account of the diverse interests which succeeded in getting different opinions sent to the viceroy, so that all was confusion.

He claims that the Indians who had been attached, at the time of the conquest, to the various haciendas, towns, and missions that had been founded, had largely run away, so that the entire country that was inhabited by Spaniards was surrounded on all sides by Indians who were bitterly hostile, making the country extremely unsafe, and that in consequence no advance was being made.

Villa Señor, in his *Theatro Americano,* volume II, page 311, refers to the various propositions made to colonize what was later known as Nuevo Santander, from which it seems four principal ones were made, one by Narciso Marquín de Montecuesta, one by Antonio Ladrón de Guevara, one by Joseph Xauregui, and the other by Joseph Escandón. After various *juntas,* Escandón was chosen as the one most likely to succeed. He made an *entrada* with 750 soldiers and a number of Indians from the Sierra Gorda. On his return he made a report, accompanied by a map, and proposed to found fourteen new towns. As a result a decree was issued on May 31, 1748, granting him the right to make the colonization.

Villa Señor, pages 311-319, prints the opinion of the *junta* in full.

The principal documents relating to this enterprise of Escandón are in volumes 53-56, *Historia,* Archivo General de la Nación, Mexico, and are cited in Bolton, *Guide to Materials . . . in Archives of Mexico,* page 38.

110. LADRÓN DE GUEVARA: Antonio

Noticias De Los Poblados De Que Se Componen El Nuevo Reyno De Leon, Provincia De Coaguila, Nueva-Estremadura, y la de Texas, Nuevas Philipinas: Despoblados que ay en sus cercanìas, y los Indios que las habitan, y causa de los pocos, ò ningunos aumentos. Dedicadas Al Excelentissimo Señor D. Pedro de Castro, Figueroa y Salazar, Duque de la Conquista, Marqués de Gracia Real, Cavallero del Avito de Santiago, Comendador de Castilseràs en la de Calatrava, Capitan General de los Exercitos de su Mag. Sargento Mayor, è Inspector del Regimiento de Guardias de Infanteria Españolas, Gentilhombre de Camera de Entrada de su Mag. Siciliana, de su Consejo Supremo, y del de Guerra, Cavallero del cèlebre Orden de S. Genaro, Virrey, Governador, y Capitan General de Nueva-España, y Presidente de su Real Audiencia, y Chancilleria. Por Don Antonio Ladron De Guevara, Vecino del Nuevo Reyno de Leon, como practico de lo que se contiene en este sucinto Papel.

Año de MDCCXXXIX. [Mexico.]

Folio, title, leaves numbered 2-18.

Copies: BM, H, J, JCB.

This, being addressed to the viceroy, contains, instead of the introduction addressed to the Conde de Montijo, 3 pages of fulsome flattery of the viceroy in which he says that he has already submitted to the Crown his scheme for colonizing Texas.

The rest of the memorial is almost word for word the same as the preceding number except that it contains some additional details relating to Martín de Zavala and Alonso de León.

111. GONZÁLEZ: P. Diego Pablo

Manual Para Administrar A Los Indios Del Idioma Cahita Los Santos Sacramentos, segun la reforma de NN. SS. PP. Paulo V. y Urbano VIII. Compuesto Por un Sacerdote de la Compañia de Jesvs, Missionero en las de la Provincia de Zynaloa. Sacalo A Luz La piedad del Alferez D. Sebastian Lopez de Guzman, y Ayala. Y lo Dedica, Al Gloriosissimo Patriarcha Señor S. Joseph.

Impresso en Mexico, con las licencias necessarias, en la Imprenta Real del Superior Gobierno de Doña Maria de Rivera, en el Empedradillo. Año de 1740.

8°, title, 12 unnumbered preliminary leaves, and pages numbered 1-163, followed by 5 unnumbered pages containing a prayer, a notice, an *oratio pro conversione infidelium,* two *alabados,* and errata.

Copies: BM, A. Graiño of Madrid, NYP.

According to Beristain, II, 42, González was the author of this work; and Medina, *La Imprenta en México,* no. 3556, thinks that the same information can be gained from the preliminaries. Father González, born in Spain, entered the Jesuit order in Mexico and spent many years as a missionary among the Cahita Indians.

MANUAL
PARA ADMINISTRAR A LOS INDIOS DEL IDIOMA CAHITA LOS SANTOS SACRAMENTOS,

ſegun la reforma de NN. SS.PP. Paulo V. y Urbano VIII.

COMPUESTO

Por un Sacerdote de la Compañia de JESUS, Miſsionero en las de la Provincia de Zynaloa.

SACALO A LUZ

La piedad del Alferez D. Sebaſtian Lopez de Guzman, y Ayala.

Y LO DEDICA,

Al Glorioſiſsimo Patriarcha Señor S. JOSEPH.

Impreſſo en Mexico, con las licencias neceſſa rias, en la Imprenta Real del Superior Gobierno de Doña Maria de Rivera, en el Empedradillo. Año de 1740.

112. SÁNCHEZ DE SARMIENTO: Joseph Gabriel

Señor. Don Joseph Gabriel Sanchez de Sarmiento, Sargento Mayor que fue de las Milicias del Valle de San Bertholomè en la Provincia de la Nueva Vizcaya, . . .

Folio, 4 unnumbered pages, probably dated at the end, Madrid, 1741.

Copy: Medina, *Biblioteca Hispano-Americana,* no. 7573, locates a copy in AGI, but I was unable to find it.

According to the account given by Medina of this document it was a solicitation for the appointment of colonel.

113. VERGARA: Agustín de

Manifiesto que saca a luz, el defensor de los bienes del Marques de Villapuente, en representacion de la Marquesa de las Torres, ambos difunctos, para el desagravio y Vindicacion de las imposturas, injurias, y agravios de D. Joseph Lorenz de Rada, con que á ofendido su buena memoria, en el pleyto, que sigue en la Real Audiencia, sobre Addiciones, aprecios y otros artículos, contra los inventarios, que se hizieron, por muerte del Marques de las Torres de Rada.

Dase noticia succintamente de los hechos ilustres de el Marques de Villapuente, los servicios á ambas Magestades, sus elogios, y el manantial innagotable de su caudal.

Tocase tambien la dedicacion, del de la Marquesa de las Torres, su piedad, y servicio al culto Santo de Dios.

Con licencia del Superior Govierno en la Puebla de los Angeles, en la Imprenta de la Viuda de Miguel de Ortega. Año de 1741.

Folio, 138 pages. Signed at the end by Dr. V. Augustin de Vergara.

Copies: WBS, and described by Medina, *La Imprenta en Puebla,* no. 432, from a copy in the Biblioteca Palafoxiana.

The Marqués de Villapuente died in Madrid, February 13, 1739. In 1735 the Marqués and his cousin, the Marquesa de las Torres de Rada, had executed a gift of a large amount of real property to the Jesuits which was the foundation of the trust estate known as the Pious Fund. A translation of the deed of gift was published during the arbitration proceedings in Washington some time about 1875, and the original can be found in "*Documentos relativos al piadoso fondo de Misiones* . . . Mexico, 1845.

I have not seen Vergara's *Manifiesto,* but it seems to be an answer in a suit brought by a nephew of the Marquesa de las Torres de Rada, one José Lorenz de Rada. This suit was going on in 1759 and even much later. The Marqués de Villapuente executed a power of attorney in the city of Mexico, April 30, 1737, to a Jesuit to make a will for him, and in virtue of this power such a will was made on the 8th of April, 1744, by Father Cristóbal de Escobar, provincial of the order. The Marqués had no sons but he left some relatives, probably nephews, and they proceeded to attack the testament. This suit had nothing to do with the California missions, the question at issue being the inventory of the estate of the Marqués de las Torres who had died in 1713 without direct heirs. See the Defensa Juridica of no. 136.

114. ANSALDO: P. Matheo

Empleos Apostolicos, y religiosas virtudes del fervoroso P. Joseph Xavier de Molina, professo de la

Compañia de Jesus, Visitador General de las Provincias de Missiones, y Ministro Doctrinero de la Reduccion de los Dolores, en la Pimerìa alta de la Provincia de Zonora, perteneciente â la Mexicana. Carta De el P. Provincial Matheo Ansaldo, de la mesma Compañia, a los Superiores de su Provincia de Mexico.

[Mexico, 1742.]

4°, 64 pages numbered except the first, which is occupied by the above title, the text beginning on the verso. At the end it is dated May 25, 1742.

Copies: BUG, L. C. Harper, H, J, JCB, S, WBS.

Father Molina was born in Antequera, Spain, and exercised the duties of priesthood in Spain for some time. When he first went to Sonora he was located at the mission of Nuestra Señora del Pópulo, but shortly afterward went to Dolores. While in Sonora he acted as *visitador* to the missions. The *Empleos Apostolicos* of Father Matheo Ansaldo contains an extremely interesting account of Father Molina's various travels, but has a singular fault, containing but one date, namely, the day of his death, April 21, 1741. The missionary was, however, at that time forty-seven years old, less three months, indicating that he had been born in 1694. How long he served in the missions of Pimería Alta it is impossible to judge, but probably only a very few years.

This letter is the only printed life, that I have seen, of any one of the Jesuit fathers who were located in Pimería Alta. The author, Matheo Ansaldo, was a kind of professional biographer of the Jesuits at this time. I once had a number of lives written by him, all of which seemed to have been printed solely for distribution among the members of the order. They are all of excessive scarcity in these days, and two or three of them are unknown to any bibliographer.

-:(✠):-

EMPLEOS APOSTOLICOS,

y religiosas virtudes del fervoroso *P. Joseph Xavièr de Molina*, professo de la Compañia de Jesus, Visitador General de las Provincias de Missiones, y Ministro Doctrinero de la Reduccion de los Dolores, en la Pimerìa alta de la Provincia de Zonora, perteneciente â la Mexicana.

CARTA

De el P. Provincial Matheo Ansaldo, de la mesma Compañia, a los Superiores de su Provincia de Mexico.

115. JURIDICA DEMOSTRACIÓN

Juridica Demostracion de la justicia que assiste a D. Joseph Lorenz de Rada. En el Pleyto, que sigue, como Heredero, y Successor del Maestre de Campo D. Francisco Lorenz de Rada, de el Orden de Santiago, Marques de las Torres de Rada, Chanciller, y Registrador Perpetuo de las Reales Audiencias de Mexico, Goathemala, Guadalaxara, Santo Domingo, y Manila.

Contra los Bienes y Herederos de Doña Gertrudis de la Peña, Viuda del Referido Marques, sobre que se declare por nula, de ningun valor, ni efecto la Adjudicacion, que fe le hizo por el Juzgado General de Bienes de Difuntos de este Reyno, del expressado Titulo, y Oficios, para en parte de pago de su Dote, y Tutelas de sus Hijos de primero Matrimonio, y que uno, y otro toca al mencionado D. Joseph, como Successor del Difunto Marques.

Con Licencia del Superior Gobierno. En Mexico, en su Imprenta Real, y del Nuevo Rezado de Doña Maria de Rivera. Año de 1742.

Folio, 246 pages, signed at the end, Lic. D. Joseph Hidalgo.
Copy: WBS.

See no. 113 for an account of this lawsuit.

116. RINALDINI: P. Benito

Arte De La Lengua Tepeguana, Con Vocabulario, Confessionario, Y Catechismo, En que se explican los Mysterios de Nuestra Santa Fè Catholica, Mandamientos de la Ley de Dios, y de Nuestra Santa Madre Iglesia. Por El P. Benito Rinaldini, De La Compañia De Jesus, Visitador de la

ARTE
DE LA LENGUA
TEPEGUANA,
CON
VOCABULARIO, CONFESSIONARIO,
Y CATECHISMO,

En que ſe explican los Myſterios de Nueſtra Santa Fè Catholica, Mandamientos de la Ley de Dios, y de Nueſtra Santa Madre Igleſia.

POR EL P. BENITO RINALDINI,
DE LA COMPAÑIA DE JESUS,

Viſitador de la Provincia Tepeguana, y Tarau-mara antigua.

Quien en nombre de todos los JESUITAS Miſſioneros de aquella ſu Provincia lo dedica

A LA MILAGROSA IMAGEN
DE MARIA SANTISSIMA
NUESTRA SEÑORA,

Que con la Advocacion de los MARTYRES ſe venera en la Miſſion del Zape, centro de los Tepeguanes.

Impreſſo en MEXICO (con las Licencias neceſſarias) por la Viuda de D. Joſeph Bernardo de Hogal: Calle de las Capuchinas. Año de 1743.

—Es de Tubutama año de 1778

Provincia Tepeguana, y Taraumara antigua. Quien en nombre de todos los Jesuitas Missioneros de aquella su Provincia lo dedica A La Milagrosa Imagen De Maria Santissima Nuestra Señora, Que con la Advocacion de los Martyres se venera en la Mission del Zape, centro de los Tepeguanes.

Impresso en Mexico (con las Licencias necessarias) por la Viuda de D. Joseph Bernardo de Hogal: Calle de las Capuchinas. Año de 1743.

4°, title, 7 unnumbered leaves of preliminaries, 72 numbered pages of *Arte,* 48 numbered pages of *compendio* [last misnumbered 43], 148 numbered pages of *vocabulario,* and 1 unnumbered leaf of errata.

Preliminaries: 2 leaves of dedication, 2 leaves of opinions and licenses, 3 leaves of introduction. The license of the government is dated January 14, 1743.

Copies: A, Bib. Guad, J.

This is the only work on the Tepehuana language written by any of the old missionaries.

Rinaldini was born in the province of Venetia, June 15, 1695, and entered the order December 7, 1712. In 1751 he was still alive, living at Guaxotitlán in Vizcaya.

117. ESPINOSA: Fr. Isidro Felix de

Chronica Apostolica, Y Seraphica De Todos Los Colegios De Propaganda Fide De Esta Nueva-España, De Missioneros Franciscanos Observantes: Erigidos Con Autoridad Pontificia, Y Regia, para la reformacion de los Fieles, y Conversion de los Gentiles. Consagrada A La Milagrosa Cruz De Piedra, que como titular se venera en su primer Colegio de Propaganda Fide de la muy Ilustre Ciudad de San-Tiago de Queretaro, sita en el Arzobispado de Mexico. Escrita Por El R. P. Fr.

Isidro Felis De Espinosa, Predicador, y Missionero Apostolico, Hijo, y ex-Guardian de dicho Colegio, Qualificador, y Revisor del Santo Officio, Chronista de la Santa Provincia de S. Pedro, y S. Pablo de Michoacan, y de todos los Colegios de Missioneros Apostolicos Observantes de esta Nueva-España. Parte Primera. Con Licencia En Mexico:

Por la Viuda de D. Joseph Bernardo de Hogal, Impressora del Real, y Apostolico Tribunal de la Santa Cruzada en todo este Reyno. Año de 1746.

Folio, title in red and black, 49 unnumbered leaves of preliminaries, 590 numbered pages, and 12 unnumbered leaves of two indexes and errata.

Preliminaries: 2 leaves of dedication by the author, 2 leaves of *censura* by Bartholomé Phelipe de Itta y Parra, 3 leaves of *parecer* of Dr. Eguiara y Eguren with licenses on the verso of the last leaf, 3 leaves of approbation of Fr. Joseph Torrubia with the license of the order on the verso of the last leaf, leaf of prologue and *protesta,* and 38 leaves of preface. Although the license of the government is dated July 5, 1745, the approbation of Torrubia, written in Spain, is dated June 10, 1747, and the license of Fogueras for the order is dated June 19, 1747. The approbation of Torrubia refers to an *información* taken by Fr. Francisco Xavier Ortiz, *visitador* to the Texas missions, taken in San Antonio, July 21, 1745, and adds that attached to this is the *expediente* of the College of Santa Cruz on the foundation of the new mission of San Xavier.

Copies: A, B, GPH, Har, J, JCB, LC, LAP, S, TWS, UT.

This is the standard history of the colleges of the *Propaganda Fide* of the Franciscans in New Spain, and contains, on pages 407-489, a history of the missions on the

Rio Grande and in Texas largely written from the personal experiences of Espinosa himself. He begins with the year 1688, when Father Massanet was at the mission of Santiago which he had founded in the valley of Candela, Coahuila. He then recounts the expedition of Captain Alonso de León, and later that of the Marqués de Aguayo. Naturally there is much on Father Antonio Margil de Jesús. Pages 260-286 contain a long account of Fr. Francisco Cassañas de Jesús María, who was one of the first missionaries in Texas, and who afterwards went to New Mexico in 1693, becoming missionary at the pueblo de San Diego de los Hemes (Giusiwa), where he was killed in the uprising of 1696.

Espinosa was the chronicler of the order and had already published several lives of illustrious Franciscans, notably that of Father Antonio Margil de Jesús in 1737. He also wrote a *Crónica* of the Franciscan province of San Pedro and San Pablo of Michoacán, published for the first time from the original manuscript in Mexico, 1899.

118. VILLA-SEÑOR Y SÁNCHEZ: Joseph Antonio

Theatro Americano, Descripcion General De Los Reynos, Y Provincias De La Nueva-España, Y Sus Jurisdicciones: Dedicala Al Rey Nuestro Señor El Señor D. Phelipe Quinto, Monarcha De Las Españas. Su Author D. Joseph Antonio De Villa-Señor, Y Sanchez, Contador General de la Real Contaduria de Azoguez, y Cosmographo de este Reyno. Quien La Escribió De Orden Del Excelentissimo Señor Conde De Fuen-Clara, Virrey Gobernador, y Capitan General de esta Nueva-España, y Presidente de su Real Audiencia, &c. Con Licencia En Mexico:

En la Imprenta de la Viuda de D. Joseph Bernardo de Hogal, Impressora del Real, y Apostolico Tribunal de la Santa Cruzada en todo este Reyno. Calle de las Capuchinas. Año de 1746.

Folio: volume I—title in red and black, engraved title, 8 unnumbered leaves of preliminaries, 382 numbered pages, 5 unnumbered leaves of index; volume II—title in red and black [dated 1748], engraved title [the same as in vol. I], 5 unnumbered leaves of preliminaries, 428 numbered pages, and 5 unnumbered leaves of index. In volume II two leaves are inserted between pages 232 and 233, which belong between the same pages in volume I.

Preliminaries: Vol. I—3 leaves of dedication dated January 7, 1745, leaf of *censura* of the Marqués de Altamira, 5 pages of opinion and licenses, 3 pages to the reader; vol. II—3 leaves of dedication, 2 leaves of *dictamen, sentir,* licenses, and errata.

Copies: A, B, BM, H, Har, HS, J, JCB, LC, LAP, NYH, NYP, TWS, UT, W.

This work was written in consequence of a royal *cédula* of July 19, 1740, directed to all the chief officials of the three viceroyalties to collect reports from all the *alcaldes mayores* and *justicias* of the subordinate jurisdictions by all means possible, notices of the number, and names of the different towns in their jurisdiction and of the nature, state, and progress of the missions. The viceroy of New Spain appointed Villa-Señor to take charge of collecting this information. In the *censura* the Marqués de Altamira says that notwithstanding the prohibition in the laws of the Indies against printing these matters, he has given advice about the remedy in his judicial opinion of the 6th of December, and on account of the public utility of this work he considers that it merits the license of the viceroy.

In volume II will be found the account of the frontier provinces. Pages 272-294 contain an account of California in which is Father Consag's journey to the Colorado in 1746. Pages 294-336 contain the account of Nuevo León, Coahuila, and Texas, with details about the La Salle expedition, and those of Alonso de León and St. Denis. Pages 383-409 contain an account of Sinaloa and Sonora; the remaining pages deal with New Mexico. The book is valuable for the many notices which it contains of the towns and mines in northern Mexico.

Winsor refers to an English translation issued in London in 1748, probably the book known as *The Statistical Account of Mexico.*

119. ESPINOSA: Fr. Isidro Felix de

Nuevas Empressas Del Peregrino Americano Septentrional Atlante, Descubiertas en lo que hizo quando vivia, y aun despues de su muerte ha manifestado El V. P. F. Antonio Margil De Jesus. Casos Admirables De nuevo averiguados, que no estàn en la Vida de este Siervo de Dios estampada en el año de 1737. y pueden dessear los afectos de esta Varon memorable. Dalos Recopilados Por Orden De Sus Prelados Superiores El P. F. Isidro Felis De Espinosa Predicador Apostolico de Propaganda Fide del Colegio de la Santa Cruz de la Ciudad de Queretaro, quien escribió su exemplarissima Vida: Y afectuosamente Consagra este Compendioso Resumen á la proteccion de la incorrupta Lengua del Thaumaturgo en los prodigios, San Antonio De Padua.

Impressas en Mexico, en la Imprenta Real del Superior Gobierno, y del Nuevo Rezado, de Doña Maria de Rivera, en el Empedradillo. Año 1747.

4°, title, 11 unnumbered preliminary leaves, and 46 numbered pages.

CARTA DEL P. FERNANDO CONSAG de la Compañia de JESUS, Visitador de las Missiones de Californias, à los Padres Superiores de esta Provincia de Nueva-España.

P. C.

YA que sola la California tuvo la dicha de logear en vida un tan insigne Operario, y Missionero, como fue el Padre Antonio Tempis, justo serà, que despues de su muerte, comunique à toda la Provincia el olor de sus virtudes, y la noticia de su Apostolico zelo; y assi aunque tan tarde, escribo esta Carta

Preliminaries: 2 leaves of dedication and *protesta,* 1 leaf of prologue, 7 leaves of *pareceres* with a license of the government at the end dated March 17, 1747, 1 leaf of licenses of the *provisor* and of Fr. Juan Fogueras.

Copies: B, L. C. Harper, J, JCB, LAP, S, UT, Y.

This supplement to the life of Father Antonio published by Espinosa in 1737 is nothing but a collection of duly authenticated miracles or near miracles performed by Father Antonio during his life, most of which occurred in Guatemala. The object of publishing them was to aid in the cause of the beatification of the zealous missionary, the king having authorized the collection of alms for that purpose.

120. CONSAG: P. Fernando

Carta Del P. Fernando Consag de la Compañia de Jesus, Visitador de las Missiones de Californias, à los Padres Superiores de esta Provincia de Nueva-España.

4°, 43 numbered pages. The first page has in the upper part a woodcut of two angels with the Jesuit insignia between, and in the center the above title, the text beginning below. At the end it is dated San Ignacio, October 1, 1748.

Copies: BM, L. C. Harper, H, JCB, P.

This is an account of the life of Father Antonio Tempis, who was born in Olmütz, a city of Moravia, June 25, 1703. In 1720 he entered the novitiate of the order and came to California as a missionary about 1735 or 1736, probably the latter year, as, at the time of his death, July 6, 1746, Consag said that he had been a missionary for ten years.

Father Tempis was stationed at the mission of Santiago where Fathers Tamaral and Carranco had been killed in 1734.

121. CÉDULA

El Rey. Don Juan Francisco de Guemes y Horcasitas, . . . mi Virrey . . . Por Fr. Francisco Xavier Ortiz, del Orden de San Francisco, y Comissario de las Missiones, que tiene a su cargo el Colegio de la Santa Cruz de Queretaro en la governacion de los Texas, ò Nuevas Philipinas; y que estando en San Antonio de Valero, fueron algunos Gentiles, y entre ellos quatro capitanes de las naciones Yoguanes, Deadoses, Mayeyas, y Rancheria Grande, pidiendo se les fundassen Missiones, a cuyo exemplo las Naciones de los Vidás, los Caòcos, los Lacopseles, los Anchoses, los Tupos, los Atias, los Apapax, los Tlacopseles, los Cancepnes, los Tancagues, los Hiscas, los Naudis, los Casos, los Tanico, los Quises, los Anatagua, los Atasacneus, los Pastates, los Geotes, los Atiasnogues, los Taguacanas, los Taguayas, y mas . . .

The king then orders the viceroy to send soldiers to found some missions and a *Hospicio* in San Xavier.

3 folio pages, dated at the end, Buen Retiro, diez y seis de Abril de mil setecientos y quarenta y ocho. Yo El Rey.

Copies: Museo Nacional, Mexico, in Tomo 1 of *Documentos Relativos a las Missiones de las Californias,* UT.

122. ALTAMIRANO: P. Pedro Ignacio

Informe Histórico, Canónico y Real, por las Missiones de la Compañia de Jesús de la Nueva España; en el expediente con el Ilmo. D. Pedro Sanchez de Tagle, Obispo de Durango, del Consejo de S. M. etc. Sobre si dicho Ilustrísimo Prelado puede o no señalar clérigo secular por Visitador de las Missiones de Sinoloa, Sonora y otras, que se dice comprehenderse en el Territorio de su Obispado.

Folio, 22 leaves, signed at the end by Altamirano.

Copy: Medina, *Biblioteca Hispano-Americana,* no. 1047, taken from *Catálogo de Obras Anónimas* of Uriarte.

Bishop Sánchez de Tagle took possession of his diocese August 27, 1749, and continued as Bishop of Durango until September 26, 1757. Consequently this lawsuit arose between those years. It is not known that Sánchez de Tagle made any *visita* to Sonora or Sinaloa, but the question of the right to make one was obviously decided in favor of the bishop, because Bishop Tamarón, who succeeded him, made an extended one from 1759 to 1763, and was in Sonora in 1760. It is not recorded that the Jesuits made any objection to Tamarón's exercising his rights as they had done before.

Altamirano was the representative of the Jesuits at the Court in Madrid, and it is probable that his *Informe* was printed there.

123 CATALOGUS

Catalogus Personarum, & Domiciliorum, in quibus sub A. R. P. Societatis Jesv Praeposito Generali XVI. P. Petro Zespedes Hispaniarvm Assistente. P. Joanne Antonio Balthazar Provinciæ Mexicanæ, Præposito Provinciali LXVI. Societas Jesv Mexicana pro Gloria Dei ex instituto laborat. Patribvs Conscriptis In habitis Almæ totius Provinciæ Comitijs dicataus, & consecratus.

Mexici: Ex Regalis, & Antiquioris Divi Ildephonsi Collegij Typographia. Anno M.DCC.LI.

Oblong 4°, title, and 34 unnumbered leaves, of which 4 are blank.

Copies: BM, J, JCB, Southwest Museum, UT.

(:✠:)

CARTA DEL P. PROVINCIAL Juan Antonio Balthassar, en que dà noticia de la exemplar vida, religiosas virtudes, y apostolicos trabajos del fervoroso Missionero el Venerable P. Francisco Maria Picolo.

P. C. &c.

A LOS VARONES esclarecidos, que se hicieron gloriosos con sus obras, les son las alabanzas muy debidas, y â ellas excita el Eclesiastico, diciendo: *Laudemus viros gloriosos, & parentes nostros.* (Eccl. 44. ℣. 1.) Y es cierto, que â sus heroycos hechos se hace grave injuria, quando se dexan sepultados en un perpetuo olvido, el qual no po-

A co

As far as I know this is the earliest catalogue of the Jesuits to be published in the Mexican province.

124. BALTHASAR: P. Juan Antonio

Carta Del P. Provincial Juan Antonio Balthassar, en que dà noticia de la exemplar vida, religiosas virtudes, y apostolicos trabajos del fervoroso Missionero el Venerable P. Francisco Maria Picolo. [Mexico, 1752.]

4°, 88 pages, dated at the end, Mexico, December 23, 1752, and signed Juan Antonio Balthasar. The title occupies the upper half of page 1.

Copies: A, Cw, H, J, JCB, UT, WBS.

Father Picolo, who was born at Palermo, Italy, March 24, 1654, came to Mexico, and soon after his arrival in 1682 or 1683 was sent to the Tarahumaras, where he remained fifteen years. While there he became interested in Christianizing the Californias, and soon after Father Salvatierra went to California Father Picolo followed him. In 1707 Picolo was appointed *visitador* of the province of Sonora. At this time a tremendous scandal had arisen in Sonora growing out of charges made against the missionaries that they were lacking in their obligations in the ministration and teaching of the Indians. The matter finally passed to the Inquisition, but Picolo obtained a great amount of evidence to prove that the missionaries were proceeding in the proper manner. In 1709 he was relieved and returned to California. In the month of November, 1716, Picolo made an expedition to the north. He died on February 22, 1719, seventy-four years, ten months, and twenty-eight days of age. He had been a missionary for forty-two years.

A letter of Father Picolo written in California, December 18, 1716, will be found in German as no. 173 of Stöcklein's *Die Neue Welt-Bott*.

Pages 75-80 contain an account of the life of Father Lorenzo Carranco and his death at the hands of the Indians; pages 81-88 give a brief notice of the life and death of Father Nicolás de Tamaral in the same manner.

Carranco was a Mexican born in Cholula, August 12, 1695, and entered the novitiate at Tepotzotlán, April 1720. About 1725 he went to Baja California and was assigned to Todos Santos, but very shortly was transferred to the new mission of Santiago among the Pericúes, where he was killed by these Indians in the uprising of October, 1734.

Born in Seville, February 24, 1686, Tamaral entered the novitiate of the order, October 3, 1704, and in 1717 went to California as a missionary. He founded the mission of the Purísima Concepción de Nuestra Señora, but from the lack of good land this was abandoned, and he founded San Joseph near Cape San Lucas among the Pericúes. He was also killed by the Indians in 1734, at the same time as Father Lorenzo Carranco.

These events are described at length in a journal by Father Sigismundo Taraval. He came to the peninsula in 1730 and wrote of events that he had witnessed. Marguerite Eyer Wilbur translated the work, and the Quivira Society published it in 1931 as volume II under the title, *The Indian Uprising in Lower California,* 1734-1737.

125. MENDOZA: Matheo Antonio de

Relacion De Servicios Del Coronel Don Matheo Antonio de Mendoza, Cavallero del Orden de Santiago, Governador, y Capitan General de la Provincia de la Nueva Vizcaya, en los Reynos de la America; por la que hace constar haver Servido á S. M. treinte y tres años, en distintos empléos, tanto en España, como en Indias; las Funciones en que se ha hallado; y encargos que ha obtenido, en atencion, y correspondencia â sus circunstancias, conducto, disinteres, zelo, y amor al Real Servicio, en que ha acreditado el valor de su Ilustre Sangre, y altas obligaciones de su Nacimiento.

Folio, 16 unnumbered leaves. At the end is a certificate of the *Commissario Real de Guerra,* Cádiz, February 25, 1752, from which it appears likely that it was printed at about that time and possibly in Cádiz.

Copy: AGI, 103-5-20.

Mendoza was one of the most active of all the officers who appeared on the frontier in the eighteenth century, and there are a large number of documents in the archives relating to his various campaigns against the Indians.

He went to America in 1742, and was appointed governor of Nueva Vizcaya on June 30, 1750, while he was in Madrid, but he did not take office until December, 1753. On July 31, 1759, he presented a memorial asking to be given a position in Europe. On May 8, 1760, the king wrote advising him that he would name his successor.

The document is accompanied by various manuscripts relating to the founding of Carrizal in 1758.

126. VILLAVICENCIO: P. Juan Joseph de

Vida, Y Virtudes De El Venerable, Y Apostolico Padre Juan de Ugarte De La Compañia De Jesus, Missionero de las Islas Californias, y uno de sus primeros Conquistadores. Escrita Por El P. Jvan Joseph de Villavicencio de la misma Compañia, Quien La Dedica A el Grande, y Admirable Apostol de el Oriente San Francisco Xavier.

Impressa, con las licencias necessarias, en Mexico, en la Imprenta del Real, y mas Antiguo Colegio de San Ildefonso. Año de 1752.

VIDA, Y VIRTUDES DE EL VENERABLE, Y APOSTOLICO PADRE JUAN DE UGARTE DE LA COMPAÑIA DE JESUS,

Missionero de las Islas Californias, y uno de sus primeros Conquistadores.

ESCRITA POR EL P. JUAN JOSEPH de Villavicencio de la misma Compañia,

QUIEN LA DEDICA A el Grande, y Admirable Apostol de el Oriente San Francisco Xavier.

Impressa, con las licencias necessarias, en Mexico, en la Imprenta del Real, y mas Antiguo Colegio de San Ildefonso. Año de 1752.

4°, title, 5 unnumbered preliminary leaves, 214 numbered pages, and 2 unnumbered of index.

Preliminaries: 3 pages of dedication, 2 of *pareceres,* 2 of licenses, and 3 of prologue. The license of the government is dated September 7, 1752.

Copies: A, BM, C, Cw, H, J, JCB, LC, S, UT.

Chapter 13 of this book contains an account of an expedition of Ugarte in 1705 to the south coast of California to comply with a *cédula* of the king to use every diligence to see if any port could be found in which the Philippine galleon could make a stop. Chapter 15 contains another account of an expedition of Father Ugarte to the north of the gulf to see whether or not California was an island.

Father Ugarte was born in Honduras, July 22, 1662. At Tepotzotlán he began his novitiate in the Company of Jesus, August 14, 1679. Here he became *Ministro del Noviciado,* and afterward went to Mexico to teach philosophy, and became rector of the college of San Gregorio. When Salvatierra undertook the work of evangelizing California, Father Ugarte became *procurador* of the missions in Mexico, and to his efforts in raising funds is due a large part of the credit of the success obtained by Father Salvatierra. On page 48 will be found the names of several of the early benefactors of the missions. In 1700 Ugarte went to California by way of Sonora. He never returned to the city of Mexico but died in California, December 29, 1730.

127. FARÍA: Francisco Xavier de

Vida. Y Heroycas Virtudes Del V[ble]. Padre Pedro De Velasco, Provincial, que fué, de la Compañia de Jesus, de Nueva-España. Por El P. Francisco Xavier de Faría de la misma Compañia de Jesus. [Jesuit device.] Con Licencia En Mexico:

APOSTOLICOS AFANES DE LA COMPAÑIA DE JESUS,

ESCRITOS

POR UN PADRE

DE LA

MISMA SAGRADA RELIGION

DE SU PROVINCIA

DE MEXICO.

CON LICENCIA.

Barcelona: Por PABLO NADAL Impressor, en la calle de la Canúda. Año 1754.

En la Imprenta de Doña Maria de Ribera. En el Empedradillo. Año de 1753.

4°, title, 6 unnumbered preliminary leaves, and 170 numbered pages.

Preliminaries: 2 pages of *pareceres,* 1 page of *aprobación,* 3 pages of licenses, 3 pages of *Calidad de la Obra,* 3 pages of index.

Copies: J, UT.

Father Velasco was one of the most prominent of the early Jesuits in Mexico. He was born in the city of Mexico in 1581, and in 1607 went to Sinaloa as a missionary, where he remained fourteen years, during which time he acquired three of the most difficult languages of the province. The rest of his life was spent in Mexico with the exception of a short period when he went to Rome as *procurador* of the province.

He was in Sinaloa during a very difficult period. The Indians were restless and gave a great deal of trouble, troubles which culminated finally in the rebellion of the Tepehuanes.

128. ORTEGA: P. José

Apostolicos Afanes De La Compañia De Jesus, Escritos Por Un Padre De La Misma Sagrada Religion De Su Provincia De Mexico. [Jesuit device.] Con Licencia.

Barcelona: Por Pablo Nadal Impressor, en la calle de la Canúda. Año 1754.

4°, title, 5 unnumbered preliminary leaves, 452 numbered pages, 4 unnumbered leaves of index, and 1 of errata.

Preliminaries: 3 pages of dedication, 2 pages of approbations, 1 page of errata dated Madrid, July 31, 1754, 1 page of *tasa* dated Madrid, August 1, 1754, 1 page of license of the order, and 2 pages of prologue.

Copies: A, B, Cw, H, Har, J, JCB, LC, LAP, NYH, S, UT.

Republished in Mexico in 1887 as the *Historia del Nayarit, Sonora, Sinaloa y Ambas Californias,* edited by Manuel de Olaguibel. In the introduction to this edition the author was identified as Father José Ortega, although this fact had been recognized long before.

The first part of this work, constituting book I, pages 1-223, contains an account of the reduction and conquest of the province of Nayarit. Book II, pages 224-343, treats of the beginning, progress, and decline of the spiritual conquest of the province of Pimería Alta to the death of Padre Eusebio Francisco Kino. Book III contains an account of the progress, various discoveries, and present state of Pimería Alta. In this last book, chapters IX to XI are occupied with the diary of the voyage which Father Consag made in the year 1751 from 27 2/3° to the north, between the Sierra Madre and the ocean.

In book II, chapter IV, the author states that having found a collection of the papers of Father Kino in which his voyages, enterprises, and discoveries are coördinated, it would be very convenient that his memoir should be conserved in a succinct relation in his history. Nevertheless what follows is not in the words of Father Kino, but is taken from his various manuscripts and is accompanied by data from other sources.

The work referred to by Father Ortega was, no doubt, Kino's *Favores Celestiales,* to which apparently Father Burriel also had access when he wrote his *Noticia de la California.* Father Burriel states distinctly that the manuscript work of Kino was in Spain; whereas Ortega, who was writing in Mexico about the same time, must have had access to another copy. In 1792 when Father Figueroa was searching the archives in Mexico for historical material to be forwarded to the Court at Madrid, he found in the archives of the extinguished province of the Jesuits in Mexico city what, from his description, was evidently the *Favores Celestiales* in the handwriting of Father Kino.

When Dr. Herbert E. Bolton was in Mexico searching the archives for historical material relating to the United States, he found the manuscript of the *Favores Celestiales,* probably the same copy as noted by Father Figueroa. Dr. Bolton had a copy of this manuscript made and translated, and in 1919 published it through the Arthur H. Clark Company of Cleveland as *Kino's Historical Memoir of Pimería Alta, 1683-1711.* In the introduction Dr. Bolton discusses Kino's writings and the references to them in various printed works, and gives a list of his writings.

Dr. Bolton in this work has also made use of the *Luz de Tierra Incógnita* . . . por el Capitán Juan Matheo Manje, published in *Publicaciones del Archivo General de la Nación,* tomo x, 1926. Two books of this are extant, *libro* I in the Biblioteca Nacional in Mexico, and *libro* II in the Archivo General in Mexico. The first part covers the history of the province of Sonora before Manje's day, and the second part covers his own experiences until 1721. The second part was printed in Mexico, 1856, in *Documentos para la Historia de México,* series IV, vol. I.

The *Favores Celestiales* has been printed in full from the text in the archives in Mexico in no. VIII of the *Publicaciones del Archivo General de la Nación,* Mexico, 1913-1922. Prefixed to the text is a biographical and bibliographical introduction by Dr. Emilio Bose, a monograph of very great merit. At the end of the book will be found a *Relación Diaria de la Entrada del Nordueste . . . desde 22 de Setiembre hasta 18 de Otubre de 1698.*

The later history of the Jesuits in Sonora is largely contained in the following work:

Historia De La Compañia De Jesus En Nueva-España, Que Estaba Escribiendo El P. Francisco Javier Alegre Al

Tiempo De Su Espulsion. Publicala Para Probar La Utilidad Que Prestará A La America Mexicana La Solicitada Reposicion De Dicha Compañia, Carlos Maria De Bustamante . . . Mexico. Imprenta de J. M. Lara, 1841.

4°, vol. I, vii, 4 pages of *prólogo*, 460 pages; vol. II, 1842, title, 3 preliminary leaves, 476 pages; vol. III, title, preliminary leaf, 309 pages; portraits of Alegre, Salvatierra, Velasco, and José María Morelos.

Bustamante afterward published a brief supplement of fourteen pages, which, however, is only a repetition of pages 325-338 of volume I.

Father Alegre's account reaches to the year 1763; the history is resumed in: *Continuacion de la historia de la Compañia de Jesus en Nueva España, del P. Francisco Javier Alegre. Por José Mariano Davila y Arrillaga.* Puebla, 1886-89. 2 vols.

129. RIAMBAU: Juan de

Por Don Francisco Joseph De Borja (num. 38.) Por Si; Y Como Padre; y Legitimo Administrador de Don Vicente Joachin de Borja, su hijo primogenito. (n.42.) Con Doña Mariana De Borja, Duquesa Que Fue De Bejar, (n.44.) Que murió Durante Este Pleyto, Y Como Su heredera la Mission de las Californias, y por este respecto el Padre Pedro Ignacio Altamirano, de la Compañia de Jesus, Procurador General de sus Provincias, en los Reynos de las Indias, (n.48.) Don Francisco Alfonso Pimentèl Vigil de Quiñones, Borja, y Centelles, Conde Duque de Benavente, (n.49.) Don Joseph Claudio de Gurrea y Aragon, Duque de Villahermosa, Conde de Luna, Marquès de Navarrès, de Cañizar, y San Felices (n.39.) Don Manuel Ossorio Velasco, y Borja, Marquès de Alcañizas, Conde Grajal, (n.50.) y don Joachin Antonio de Palafox, Marquès de Ariza. (n.47.) que ha salido al Pleyto, despues de la muerte de la Duquesa de Bejar. Sobre La Tenuta, Y Possession Del Ducado de Gandia, y sus Agregados, vacantes por muerte de Don Luis Ignacio de Borja, (n.43.) su ultimo posseedor.

Folio, title, and 39 numbered leaves, signed at the end, Doct. Don Juan de Riambau. At the beginning is a Jesuit device and the words, *Jesus Maria y Joseph.*

129a

Apendice A La Alegacion escrita por Don Francisco De Borja (num.38). [The rest of the title is the same as the preceding, except that it is transposed.]

Folio, title, and 16 numbered leaves, signed as the preceding. Copies: [both 129 and 129a.] H; Medina, *La Imprenta en México,* no. 8442, locates copies in the Biblioteca Colegio de Guanajuato.

These briefs in this famous lawsuit were written in Madrid in 1754, and were, no doubt, printed at the same time. There is no mention of California in either, except on the title pages.

130. VENEGAS: P. Miguel

El Apostol Mariano Representado En La Vida Del V. P. Juan Maria De Salvatierra, De La Compañia De Jesus, fervoroso Missionero en la Provincia de Nueva-España, y Conquistador Apostolico de las Californias. Escrita difusa, y eruditamente Por El P. Miguel Venegas, Professo de quatro Votos de la misma Compañia. Y reducida â breve compendio Por El P. Juan Antonio De Oviedo, Rector del Colegio de San Andrès de Mexico, y Calificador del Santo Oficio. Quien La

EL APOSTOL MARIANO
REPRESENTADO EN LA VIDA
DEL V.P. JUAN MARIA
DE SALVATIERRA,

DE LA COMPAÑIA DE JESUS,
fervoroſo Miſſionero en la Provincia de
Nueva-Eſpaña, y Conquiſtador Apoſtolico
de las Californias.

Eſcrita difuſa, y eruditamente
POR EL P. MIGUEL VENEGAS,
Profeſſo de quatro Votos de la miſma
Compañia.

Y reducida â breve compendio
POR EL P. JUAN ANTONIO
DE OVIEDO, Rector del Colegio de
San Andrès de Mexico, y Calificador del
Santo Oficio.

QUIEN LA DEDICA
A MARIA SANTISSIMA
Madre de Dios, Reyna de todos los Santos,
Señora de los Exercitos, y Conquiſtadora de
nuevos Reynos en ſu Sagrada Imagen
DE LORETO.

Con licencia en MEXICO: En la Imprenta de Doña Maria de
Ribera, Impreſſora del Nuevo Rezado. Año de 1754.

Dedica A Maria Santissima Madre de Dios, Reyna de todos los Santos, Señora de los Exercitos, y Conquistadora de nuevos Reynos en su Sagrada Imagen De Loreto. Con licencia en Mexico:

En la Imprenta de Doña Maria de Ribera, Impressora del Nuevo Rezado. Año de 1754.

4°, title, 4 unnumbered leaves of dedication, prologue and *protesta*, 1 leaf of licenses, dated Mexico, August 22, 23, and 29, 1753, 316 numbered pages of text, and 3 unnumbered leaves of index.

Copies: A, B, BM, C, H, HS, John Crerar library, LC, LAP, S, UT.

Father Salvatierra was an Italian, born in Milan of an Italian mother and a Spanish father. He was born on November 15, 1648; in 1666 he entered the Company of Jesus, and in 1675 arrived in Mexico, in company with Father Juan Baptista Zappa. After completing his studies in Mexico he was sent to the Sinaloa missions, and after ten years' service became *visitador* of the province.

The first thing that occurred was the uprising of the Pima Indians in 1690. According to Venegas, Salvatierra began to plan the conversion of California on the occasion when he met Father Kino in Sonora. His visit being concluded, he was appointed rector of the College of Guadalajara, and shortly after, rector of the College of Tepotzotlán. Here he took up in earnest his plan of converting California and had the good fortune to encounter Pedro Gil de la Sierpe, a man of means, who embraced the scheme with enthusiasm. Finally, together with Father Ugarte, he managed to raise sufficient money to undertake the expedition. In consequence he left for California early in 1697, leaving Father Ugarte in Mexico as *procurador*. Passing through Sinaloa, he finally arrived in California on October 19. In 1704 he was appointed provincial of the province of Mexico and was obliged to

✠

NOTICIA DE LA CALIFORNIA, Y DE SU CONQUISTA TEMPORAL, Y ESPIRITUAL HASTA EL TIEMPO PRESENTE.

SACADA

DE LA HISTORIA MANUSCRITA, FORMADA en Mexico año de 1739. por el Padre Miguèl Venegas, de la Compañia de Jesus; y de otras Noticias, y Relaciones antiguas, y modernas.

AÑADIDA

DE ALGUNOS MAPAS PARTICULARES y uno general de la America Septentrional, Assia Oriental, y Mar del Sùr intermedio, formados sobre las Memorias mas recientes, y exactas, que se publican juntamente.

DEDICADA

AL REY N.TRO SEÑOR

POR LA PROVINCIA DE NUEVA-ESPAÑA, de la Compañia de Jesus.

TOMO PRIMERO.

CON LICENCIA. En Madrid: En la Imprenta de la VIUDA DE MANUEL FERNANDEZ, y del Supremo Consejo de la Inquisicion. Año de M.D.CCLVII.

give up his personal labors in California for two years. In 1717 he received an order from the provincial to return to Mexico to hold a consultation regarding a new *cédula.* Although he was not in good health, he nevertheless undertook the journey, but becoming very ill in Guadalajara, could not proceed, and finally died there on the night of the 17th of July. Salvatierra had performed the labor of a pioneer missionary in a difficult province.

About one-half of the book is devoted to an account of Father Salvatierra's activities, and the other half to the usual account of his many virtues.

131. MONTERO Y QUESADA: Antonio

Relacion De Los Meritos, Y Servicios De Don Antonio Montero, y Quesada, Teniente que hà sido del Real Presidio de San Miguèl de Horcasitas, y Ayudante en el Govierno, y Capitania General de Sinaloa, y Sonora en el Reyno de la Nueva Galicia.

Folio, 3 unnumbered pages dated at the end, Madrid, August 20, 1755, and signed in manuscript by the *Relator.*

Copy: AGI, 137-1-14.

Don Antonio went to New Spain in 1749, and to Sinaloa with Don Diego Ortiz Parrilla, where, for three years, he was commandant of the presidio of San Miguel de Horcasitas, and served in several campaigns against the Seris.

132. VENEGAS: P. Miguel

Noticia De La California, Y De Su Conquista Temporal, Y Espiritual Hasta El Tiempo Presente. Sacada De La Historia Manuscrita, Formada en Mexico año de 1739. por el Padre Miguèl Venegas, de la Compañia de Jesus; y de otras Noticias, y Relaciones antiguas, y modernas. Añadida De

Algunos Mapas Particulares y uno general de la America Septentrional, Assia Oriental, y Mar del Sùr intermedio, formados sobre las Memorias mas recientes, y exactas, que se publìcan juntamente. Dedicada Al Rey N.tro Señor Por La Provincia De Nueva-España, de la Compañia de Jesus. Tomo Primero. Con Licencia.

En Madrid: En la Imprenta de la Viuda De Manuel Fernandez, y del Supremo Consejo de la Inquisicion. Año de M.D.CCLVII.

4°, title, 11 unnumbered leaves of preliminaries, 240 numbered pages, and a map.

Preliminaries: vol. I: 2 leaves of dedication signed Pedro Ignacio Altamirano; leaf of license of the order signed Gaspar Varona, Madrid, October 4, 1754; 3 pages of *pareceres;* 2 of license of the Real Consejo, Madrid, March 13, 1756, 3 pages of *aprobación,* a leaf of license and errata of vol. I, the last dated March 23, 1757; leaf of *tasa,* April 1, 1757, and index to vol. I; 2 leaves of prologue.

Map: Mapa De La California su Golfo, y Provincias fronteras en el Continente De Nueva España. The map is surrounded on the sides and bottom with engravings of animals, natives, etc.

Vol. II: title, leaf of *fee de erratas* dated March 24, 1757, and *tasa* dated April 1, 1757, 2 leaves of index, 564 numbered pages of text.

Vol. III: title, leaf of *fee de erratas* and *tasa* dated the 26th of March and April 1, 1757, 2 leaves of index, 436 numbered pages of text, and 3 maps, as follow:

Seno de California, . . . por el P.e Ferdinando Consag . . .

Carta de la Mar del Sur, ò Mar pacifico, entre el Equador, y 39½ de latitud Septentrional . . . (Anson's Map.)

Mapa De La America Septent.l. Asia Oriental Y Mar Del Sur, . . . sobre las Memorias mas recientes y exactas hasta el año de 1754.

Copies: A, B, C, Cw, H, Har, J, JCB, LC, LAP, NYP, Southwest Museum, UT. Besides these there are numerous other copies in circulation as it is one of the commonest of all the books listed in this work.

132a

A Natural and Civil History Of California: Containing An accurate Description of that Country, Its Soil, Mountains, Harbours, Lakes, Rivers, and Seas; its Animals, Vegetables, Minerals, and famous Fishery for Pearls. The Customs of the Inhabitants, Their Religion, Government, and Manner of Living, before their Conversion to the Christian Religion by the missionary Jesuits. Together With Accounts of the several Voyages and Attempts made for settling California, and taking actual Surveys of that Country, its Gulf, and Coast of the South-Sea. Illustrated With Copper Plates, and an accurate Map of the Country and the adjacent Seas. Translated from the original Spanish of Miguel Venegas, a Mexican Jesuit, published at Madrid 1758. In Two Volumes. Vol I.

London: Printed for James Rivington and James Fletcher, at the Oxford Theatre, in Pater-Noster-Row. 1759.

8°, title, 13 unnumbered pages of preface, 5 of contents, 455 pages, 2 plates, map; title, 5 unnumbered pages of contents, 1 blank page, 387 pages, 2 plates.

Map: An accurate Map of California, Drawn by the Society of Jesuits & dedicated to the King of Spain, 1757.

The map was engraved by J. Gibson, and has most of the inscriptions in Spanish, only a few being Anglicized.

A NATURAL and CIVIL

HISTORY

OF

CALIFORNIA:

CONTAINING

An accurate Description of that COUNTRY,

Its Soil, Mountains, Harbours, Lakes, Rivers, and Seas; its Animals, Vegetables, Minerals, and famous Fishery for Pearls.

THE

CUSTOMS of the INHABITANTS,

Their Religion, Government, and Manner of Living, before their Conversion to the Christian Religion by the missionary Jesuits.

TOGETHER WITH

Accounts of the several Voyages and Attempts made for settling California, and taking actual Surveys of that Country, its Gulf, and Coast of the South-Sea.

ILLUSTRATED WITH

Copper Plates, and an accurate Map of the Country and the adjacent Seas.

Translated from the original Spanish of MIGUEL VENEGAS, a Mexican Jesuit, published at Madrid 1758.

IN TWO VOLUMES.

VOL. I.

LONDON:

Printed for JAMES RIVINGTON and JAMES FLETCHER, at the Oxford Theatre, in Pater-Noster-Row. 1759.

Plates in volume I: Women of California and Men of California, two scenes on one plate, as a frontispiece, and the Cayote and Taye on another, at page 36. In volume II, the frontispiece has two scenes, the Manner of Curing the Sick in California, and Sorcerers of California, and at page 141 is represented the martyrdom of Father Carranco and Father Tamaral on the same plate.

As an illustration of the correctness of the translation I quote what is said of Drake, "who in the year 1577, being then on his second voyage round the world." The Spanish says, translated, "in the year 1577 having arrived at those coasts in the celebrated voyage on which he made the second turn around the world, after that of the ship Victoria [that is, Magellan's]."

132b

Histoire Naturelle Et Civile De La Californie, Contenant Une description exacte de ce Pays, de son Sol, de ses Montagnes, Lacs, Rivières & Mers, de ses Animaux, Végétaux, Minéraux, & de sa fameuse Pêcherie des Perles; les Mœurs de ses Habitans, leur Religion, leur Gouvernement, & leur façon de vivre avant leur conversion au Christianisme; un détail des différens Voyages, & Tentatives qu'on a faites pour s'y établir, & reconnoitre son Golfe & la Côte de la Mer du Sud. Enrichee de la Carte du Pays & des Mers adjacentes. Traduite de l'Anglois, par M. E . . . Tome Premier.

A Paris. Chez Durand, Libraire, rue Saint-Jacques à la Sagesse. M.DCC.LXVI. Avec Approbation & Privilége du Roi.

12°, half-title, title, preface [iii]-xxi, contents [xxii]-xxiv, 360 pages, map; half-title, title, [v]-viii, 375 pages; half-title, title, [v]-viii, 354 pages, and 1 leaf of approbation and privilege, dated December 6, 1766. Vols. II and III dated M.DCC.LXVII.

Map: Carte de la Californie levée par la Société des Jesuites. Dediée au Roy D'Espagne en 1757.

This is a rather precise translation made, according to Leclerc, by M. Eidous from the English edition. Appendix 6, containing the notice of the voyage of Henry Ellis, and appendix 7, containing the account of the construction of the map and the translation of De l'Isle's *Mémoire,* as well as the translation of the voyage of Admiral Fonte, were omitted. Only one map was reproduced, that of California, and the marginal figures which appear on the original were also omitted. Some of the inscriptions were changed to their French equivalents, but in the main most of the places appear with their original Spanish names.

The translator in his preface speaks very highly of this work, although he refers to the general system of the Jesuits which came in for world-wide criticism at this time.

132c

Naturliche und burgerliche Geschichte von Californien, nebst einer neuen Charte dieses Landes und der benachbarten Meere. Aus dem Englischen ubersetzt und herausgegeben von Johan Christoph Adelung . . . Erster Theil.

Lemgo, in der Meyerschen Buchhandlung, 1769 [and 1770.]

4°, title, *vorrede* pages [3]-8, *verzeichniss* 1 leaf, map, pages [11]-184; title, leaf of *verzeichniss,* pages [5]-198; title, leaf of *verzeichniss,* pages [5]-176.

Map: Carte De La California Levee par la Societe des Jesuits Dediee au Roy D'Espagne, en 1757.

This seems to be the map from the French edition, perhaps reëngraved. At any rate, it bears in the lower left-hand corner the following inscription: *I. D. Philippin geb: Sysangin p.*

132d

Natuurlyke En Burgerlyke Historie Van California. Behelzende Eene naauwkeurige Beschryving van dat Gewest, desselfs Grond, Bergen, Havens, Meiren, Rivieren en Zéen, Dieren, Gewassen, Mineralen en vermaarde Parel-Visscheryen. De Gewoontens van desselfs Inwoonders, hunnen Godsdienst, Regeering, en Levenswyze voor derzelver Bekeering tot den Christelyken Godsdienst door de Zendelingen der Jesuiten. Mitsgaders De Berichten van verscheidene Reizen en Tochten, tot Ternederzettingen derwaards gedaan; van de dadelyke Opneemingen dier Landstreek, derzelver Inham, en der Kust van de Zuyd-Zee. Opgehelderd Met Kopere Plaaten, en eene naauwkeurige Kaart van het Land en de naastgelegene Zéen. Uyt het oorsprongkelyk Spaans van Miguel Venegas, Jesuit te Mexico, te Madrid in 't Jaar 1758 uytgekomen, in 't Engels, en nu in 't Nederduyts vertaald door J.J.D. In Twee Boek-Deelen. Eerste Deel.
Te Haerlem, Gêdrukt by Johannes Enschedé, Stads-Drukker. 1761.

8°, title, 8 unnumbered leaves of *voorrede*, 2 of *inhoud*, 436 pages, plate, map; title, 2 unnumbered leaves of *inhoud*, 375 pages.

Map: Naauwkeurige Kaart van California, uytgegeven door de Maatschappy der Jesuiten, en opgedragen aam den Koning van Spanjen 1757.

The map is reëngraved with the legends in Dutch.

Plate: Women and Men of California, which is inserted between pages 64 and 65 of volume I. The illustration was copied from the frontispiece in the first volume of the English edition.

As is well known, the real author of this book was a learned Jesuit, Father Andrés Marcos Burriel. Aside from the documents quoted it is obvious that Burriel wrote the entire work, the identity of the original of Venegas having entirely disappeared. Buckingham Smith tells us, in a letter in the New York Historical Society written in 1851 to William Hunter from Mexico, that he had borrowed the original manuscript of Venegas from the College of San Gregorio. When he compared the document with the printed work he found that it bore very little resemblance to the original.

The preliminaries contain some interesting information regarding the book, and especially the prologue written by Burriel himself. At this time there was a decree in effect that no one should publish anything relating to America without the previous consent of the Council of the Indies, and inasmuch as this book contains more on Lower California than almost any other book that had been published in one hundred and fifty years, it seems strange that the Council should have permitted the publication. Nevertheless such was the case, and it passed through all the necessary channels before being printed. Burriel's name nowhere appears in connection with it, but it was sponsored by Father Altamirano, the *Procurador General de Indias* of the Jesuits of Madrid. At his solicitation the Council conceded a license to print it, after having submitted it to the *Real Academia de la Historia* and to the *Fiscal.* I have seen it asserted that the object of publishing this book was to counteract some assertions made in Anson's *Voyage Round the World,* originally printed in London in 1748, in which some aspersions were cast on the Jesuits, especially about their handling of the natives in the missions in California. There must have been some powerful reason which induced the government to allow the book to be printed.

I now present a translation of Burriel's prologue: "It has been four years since the greater portion of what this *Noticia de la California* contains was printed, and only the desire to make it less imperfect and more useful to the public has delayed its publication to the present time. At the end of the year 1749 there arrived in Madrid from Mexico a thick manuscript volume the title of which is, *Empressas Apostolicas de los Padres Missioneros de la Compañia de Jesus de la Provincia de Nueva-España, obradas en la Conquista de Californias, Etc. Historiadas por el P. Miguel Venegas, de la misma Compañia.* Having read it with care and examined the numerous documents relating to the California missions which are preserved in the *Procuraduria General de Indias* in Madrid, it soon appeared that the work of Father Venegas could not be published as it came. The Father himself, as he complained in his introduction, had not sufficient materials and notices to write it, and the work was concluded in Mexico on the 5th of August, 1739.

"Notwithstanding the fact that the work was very diffuse and scarcely treated of anything other than the enterprises of the Jesuits, there were lacking even on this subject many details, not to speak of other things lacking which properly could not be disregarded by curious readers. The work had to be undertaken anew, that of Father Venegas serving as the principal basis, and adding everything which the most active diligence could acquire; but the survey itself of the details as the work extended sufficed to indicate new shortages and vacant spots which could not be filled without new materials. In this way this *Noticia* was extended to 1750, and it seemed necessary to delay the publication until new documents to perfect it, which had been asked for from Mexico, should arrive. Added to this was the unexpected necessity of waiting to secure from Paris some maps and *memorias* with which it was necessary to treat, but these finally reached me at the end of the year 1753; and from Mexico after four years I have only received advice that they have sent as many papers as they could, although not all that were asked for, but these papers have not yet appeared. Contingencies where the distance is so great will always be the same, and prudence suggests that there should be published in Europe and sent to New Spain many printed examples of what today we know of California. In this manner it will be easily determined by many how much we do not know and what we desire to know; and what today we cannot perfect for the benefit of the public others in the future can finish with less work."

Volume I contains two parts,— a description of California and its inhabitants, and an account of the attempts to conquer California up to the time of the entrance of the Jesuit order. In the second part Father Burriel briefly sketches the early history of California from Gómara and Díaz del Castillo, and from Herrera and Torquemada for the later period to 1600. Subsequently he relies on unpublished original documents. The authorities for secular events are largely the printed works of the general historians, and for religious affairs the documents existing in the Jesuit archives. He did not seem to have been able to find in the archives of the government in Spain any of the original narratives of exploration which since have been found there.

Volume II contains the third part, relating the reduction of California by the Jesuits and occurrences up to 1754.

Volume III contains the appendices.

Appendix 1, López de Gómara, chapter 12 of the History of the Indies.

Appendix 2, Relation of the voyage of Sebastián Vizcaíno copied from Torquemada, book 5. In the introduction Burriel says that he wished to see the original relations of Vizcaíno, and especially the maps and plans of the voyage, but that in spite of the greatest search in the office of the secretary of the Supreme Council they could not be found.

Appendix 3, *Derrotero* of the voyage of Father Consag as far as the Colorado river, 1746, with a map of the Gulf of California and the coast newly discovered by Consag, 1747.

Appendix 4, Description of California from Woodes Rogers.

Appendix 5, Extract of notices of the voyage of Admiral George Anson and apology for the Jesuits, with a map of the coast between the Equator and 39½°, a copy of one found by Anson in the Philippine galleon.

Appendix 6, Notice of the relation of Henry Ellis and the different efforts of the English to discover the passage into the South sea.

Appendix 7, Account of the method of construction of the map of California and the general map of North America, with the translation of the memoir of De l'Isle of April 8, 1750, on the new discoveries to the north of the South sea, together with a translation of the letter of Admiral Bartholome de Fonte, with remarks by Burriel on both. Burriel could not accept De Fonte's story notwithstanding the powerful authority of De l'Isle and Buache, and to the question as to what was to be found in the fifty degrees on the map north of the river Gila and New Mexico he says, "I answer easily in a word, which if it has much shame for others costs me nothing, and I believe that it ought to cost nothing to any other well-meaning person. *Ignoro. Nescio. Yo no lo sè.*"

Throughout the work great attention is paid to the geography of the country, Father Burriel having obtained a large number of maps from which to study this, and in various footnotes many are cited. He was a great admirer of Father Kino and continually quotes from his manuscript, which he calls *Historia de las Missiones de la Compañia de Jesús de la Provincia de Sonora.* It is very probable that this manuscript is the one that we now know as the *Favores Celestiales.* Speaking of the expedition of Father Kino to the mouth of the Colorado river, Father Burriel states that this is referred to in the *relaciones* of Captain Juan Matheo Manje, printed in the French language, and adds, "although neither in that tongue nor in Spanish have I been able to obtain them."

Altogether the work is a most scholarly one, written in very lucid style and amply fortified by such authorities as he had. Although the author was a Jesuit, the work is written in a secular spirit, much different from the point of view usually taken by writers of other religious orders.

133. CATALOGUS

Catalogus Provinciæ Mexicanæ Societatis Jesu, in quo Singulorum Nomen, Cognomen, Patria, Aetas, atque Ingressus in eamdem continetur.

[Colophon:] Mexici: ex Regalis et Antiquioris Divi Ildefonsi Collegii Typis, Anno Domini 1758.

Oblong 4°, 13 unnumbered leaves, of which 3 have the verso blank. It is printed in four columns.

Copies: UT. Medina, *La Imprenta en México,* no. 4456, locates copies in the Biblioteca Palafoxiana and in his own collection.

According to Medina it seems that this was the first catalogue of the Society printed after that of 1751.

134. LÓPEZ: P. Juan Francisco

Carta De Edificacion, En Que El P Juan Francisco Lopez, Rector del Colegio Maximo de S. Pedro, y S. Pablo de la Sagrada Compañia de Jesus, participa â todos los Superiores, y Colegios de ella, La Fervorosa Vida, Y Religiosas Virtudes Del V. P. Joseph Maria Genovese, Natural de la Ciudad de Sicilia, Religioso professo de nuestra Sagrada Compañia, Missionero Apostolico, que fuè en las Missiones de Californias, nueve años Maestro de Novicios en el Colegio de Tepozotlàn, tres Rector en el de San Andrès, y tres en el Maximo de S. Pedro, y S. Pablo, donde falleciò con opinion comun de Santidad.

Impressa con las licencias necessarias en Mexico, en la Imprenta nueva de la Bibliotheca Mexicana. Año de 1758.

4°, title, and 35 numbered pages.
Copies: J, JCB.

In the whole 35 pages of this little book there is no mention of California; the author simply states that Father Genovese spent some years in missionary work in the California establishments.

135. GONZÁLEZ DE MENA Y VILLEGAS: Pedro

Por Don Manuel de la Puente. Regidor y Alguacil Mayor de la Villa de San Phelpe, de la Nueva España, por si y en representacion de sus primos hermanos residentes en estos Reynos. Con el Padre Ignacio Altamirano de la Compañia de Jesus, Procurador General de Indias, por la Provincia de la Nueva España y su Colegio de Mexico. Sobre que a dicho Don Juan Manuel de la Puente y Consortes se los declara universales herederos ab intestato del Marques de Villa-Puente, y por nulo el Poder para testar, que se dice otorgado por este en la Ciudad de Mexico a 20 de Abril de 1737, y el Testamento que en su virtud se supone hecho en 8 Abril de 1744, por el Padre Christobal de Escobar, Provincial, que era de dicha Provincia de Mexico.

Folio, 30 leaves, and signed at the end by Lic. D. Pedro González de Mena y Villegas, Valladolid, September 21, 1759.

Copies: Medina, *Biblioteca Hispano-Americana,* no. 7951, where he describes a copy in the library of the College of Guanajuato, Mexico.

See no. 113 for some particulars about the origin of this litigation. Not having seen a copy of this memorial it is impossible for me to give any account of its contents beyond what can be made out from the beginning of the allegation.

136. QUIJANO: Miguel

Defensa jurídica de las Missiones de California como herederas de Doña Gertrudis de la Peña, viuda de el Maestre de Campo D. Francisco Lorens de Rada, Caballero del Orden de Sant-Iago, Marqués de las Torres de Rada, gran Chanciller de esta Real Audiencia, y de las de Guatemala, Guadalaxara, Santo Domingo y Philipinas. En el pleyto que contra los bienes de dicha Doña Gertrudis siguen los Herederos ab intestato del referido D. Francisco en demanda de cantidad de pesos, que pagados la dote y demas derechos de Doña Gertrudis, dicen sobró del caudal de su difunto Tio, y en que quieren se verifique su herencia.

Con licencia en Mexico: En la Imprenta del Real y mas antiguo Colegio de San Ildefonso, Año de 1759.

Folio, title, and 156 pages. At end is "Sentencia de el Real y Supremo Consejo de Indias," dated Madrid, 16th April, 1749, signed Don Antonio de Salazar y Castillo. 3 unnumbered pages.

Copies: BM, WBS.

This document was written in Mexico and presented to the *Audiencia,* and was therefore probably printed in Mexico. It was signed by Miguel Quijano, a noted lawyer of the time.

The Marqués de las Torres de Rada had died in 1713, and all of his property had been adjudicated to the widow to pay his debts, to reimburse her for her dot, and as an allowance for two children. In 1721, Don Joseph Lorens and Don Francisco Lorens, the nephews of the Marqués, started suit against the widow, but the *Audiencia* decided in favor of the Marquesa. Later, the widow married the Marqués de Villa-Puente. Villa-Puente was a very rich man and noted for his benefactions, especially to the Jesuit missions in California. Later both he and the Marquesa died, and she left her property to these Jesuit missions.

In 1749 Don Joseph Lorens went before the Council of the Indies in Madrid and secured a decree in his favor by which the original inventories of the estate of Torres de Rada were declared null and void. As the missions were not cited to appear at the hearing before the Council, this plea of Quijano in their behalf was presented to the *Audiencia.* The question was largely concerning the value and disposition of jewels and articles of luxury that were left by Torres de Rada, and this evidence presents a very good picture of social conditions in Mexico of the period 1713-20. There is nothing about California in it.

137. TORRUBIA: Fr. José

I Moscoviti Nella California O Sia Dimostrazione Della Verita' Del Passò All' America Settentrionale Nuovamente scoperto dai Russi, e di quelle anticamente praticato dalli Popolatori, che vi trasmigrarono dall' Asia. Dissertazione Storico-Geografica Del Padre F. Giuseppe Torrubia Minore Osservante di S. Francesco, Cronologo di tutto l'Ordine, e Commissario Generale della Curia Oltramontana. [Ornament.]

In Roma MDCCLIX. Per Generoso Salomoni Con lic. de' Sup.

8°, title, 5 unnumbered leaves of preliminaries, and pages [13]-83.

Preliminaries: Dedication to Father Clemente of Palermo, dated August 25, 1759, licenses dated Rome, September 1 and August 31 respectively, an approbation of Antonio Baldani, and finally the license to print.

Copies: C, Cw, Cal. State library, H, JCB, TWS.

I MOSCOVITI NELLA CALIFORNIA

O SIA

DIMOSTRAZIONE DELLA VERITA'
DEL PASSO ALL' AMERICA
SETTENTRIONALE

Nuovamente scoperto dai Russi, e di quello anticamente praticato dalli Popolatori, che vi trasmigrarono dall'Asia.

DISSERTAZIONE
STORICO-GEOGRAFICA

DEL PADRE

F. GIUSEPPE TORRUBIA

Minore Osservante di S. Francesco,
Cronologo di tutto l' Ordine,
e Commissario Generale della
Curia Oltramontana.

IN ROMA MDCCLIX.

PER GENEROSO SALOMONI
Con lic. de' Sup.

This little work is chiefly directed to a discussion of the possible origin in Tartary of the Mexicans, and the possible manner in which they might have passed from Tartary to America. The discussion was precipitated by the discovery of Bering strait, and especially by the publication in 1750-54 of the geographical works of M. Buache and M. De l'Isle on the discoveries of the Russians and the passage from the North sea to the Pacific. Father Torrubia, who was the chronologist of the Franciscans, and, at the time of writing the above book, the commissary general of the order in Rome, had lived both in Mexico and the Philippines, and was well qualified to discuss the question, being well informed on all the Pacific voyages and discoveries. He begins by referring to the Dutch story of the passage from the Bacalaos to the South sea, which he says came into the hands of Philip III, who immediately ordered the Count of Monterey to send an expedition to verify the story. He then gives an account of the English navigations for the discovery of a northwest passage, taken from Ellis' chronology. Then follow an account of the so-called Chinese voyage to Fusang, and a discussion of the famous maps of Buache and De l'Isle issued in 1752 and 1753.

On page 44 begins an account of the Russian discoveries. Torrubia states that Bering strait was first discovered in 1640 by some Russians who passed through from the Arctic sea, and he intimates that the Germans had concealed this fact in order to give the credit to Bering, who, they said, first discovered the strait in 1728. The author states that the Russians came down as far as 55°, as shown on De l'Isle's map of 1752, and incidentally states that 41° north was considered the end of California. The end of the book is devoted to the apocryphal voyage of Fonte, seeming to follow Father Burriel's opinion in the matter.

I cannot imagine why Torrubia printed this book in Rome and in Italian, as he was a Spaniard and one object in printing it seems to have been a desire to call the attention of the Spanish authorities to the steady progress of the Russians on the northwest coast. The author was a prolific writer, chiefly on ecclesiastical matters and questions of jurisdiction. In 1756 he published in Rome his *Chrónica* of the Franciscan order, a standard work on the subject.

In 1760 this little pamphlet was printed in a *Nueva raccolta d'opuscoli scientifici,* an annual publication, this being volume VII issued in Venice in 1760. It occupies pages 471-536.

138. BARRIO Y JUNCO: Pedro de

Relacion De Los Meritos, Y Servicios De Don Pedro De Barrio, y Junco, Governador, y Capitan General que hà sido del Nuevo Reyno de Leon en la Nueva España.

Folio, 6 unnumbered pages, the last being a resumé of his services printed in a strip on one end, obviously for filing purposes. The *Relación* is dated at the end, Madrid, November 29, 1760.

Copies: AGI, 103-3-28, AGM.

With the copy in AGI is found another:

Expression Mas Individual de las particulares confianzas, y satisfacciones, que en los Emplèos, y encargos de el Real Servicio han merecido, por lo bien que los han practicado, con toda exactitud, lealtad, y desinterès, el Governador, y Capitàn General, que fuè de el Nuevo Reyno de Leon, comprehendido en la Nueva España, Don Pedro de Barrio y Junco: Su Padre el Theniente de Navio Don Phelipe de Barrio: y su Tio (Hermano del

Padre) el Coronèl Don Pedro de Barrio, Caballero del Orden de Santiago, cuyos meritos mas sucintamente se contienen en las Relaciones de ellos, que se les han dado por la Secretarìa de la Nueva España, en virtud de los Documentos, que en ella presentaron, y bolvieron à recoger, de los que se reconoce lo siguiente: Don Pedro De Barrio Y Junco.

Folio, 12 unnumbered pages, unsigned and undated.

From these it seems that Barrio was governor of Nuevo León from December 22, 1740, to November, 1746, and in 1747 was appointed governor of Texas by Revilla Gigedo. He took possession of his office, June 16, 1748, and served to July 10, 1751, at which time he delivered the office to Jacinto de Barrios y Jáuregui. His *residencia,* taken in 1752, absolved him of all charges.

On December 25, 1752, he again became governor of Nuevo León, and served five years. While there, he says, he founded four missions. In 1767-68 Barrio was governor of the Pueblo of El Paso.

Inserted in the latter document is a copy of the *sentencia* on the *autos* of *residencia* taken by Barrios on Don Pedro as governor in Texas.

139. GARCÍA: Fr. Bartholomé

Manual Para Administrar Los Santos Sacramentos De Penitencia, Eucharistia, Extrema-Uncion, Y Matrimonio: Dar Gracias Despues De Comulgar, Y Ayudar A Bien Morir A los Indios de las Naciones: Pajalates, Orejones, Pacaos, Pacóas, Tilijayas, Alasapas, Pausanes, y otras muchas diferentes, que se hallan en las Missiones del Rio de San Antonio, y Rio Grande, pertenecientes â el Colegio de la Santissima Cruz de la Ciudad de Queretaro,

PARA ADMINISTRAR
LOS SANTOS SACRAMENTOS
DE PENITENCIA,
EUCHARISTIA, EXTREMA-UNCION,
Y MATRIMONIO:
DAR GRACIAS DESPUES DE COMULGAR,
Y AYUDAR A BIEN MORIR

A los Indios de las Naciones: Pajalates, Orejones, Pacaos, Pacóas, Tilijayas, Alaſapas, Paulanes, y otras muchas diferentes, que ſe hallan en las Miſſiones del Rio de San Antonio, y Rio Grande, pertenecientes â el Colegio de la Santiſſima Cruz de la Ciudad de Queretaro, como ſon: Los Pacuâches, Meſcàles, Pampôpas, Tâcames, Chayopînes, Venados, Pamâques, y toda la Juventud de Pihuiques, Borrados, Sanipaos, y Manos de Perro.

COMPUESTO
POR EL P. Fr. BARTHOLOME GARCIA,
Predicador Apoſtolico, y actual Miſſionero de la Miſſion de N. S. P. S. Franciſco de dicho Colegio, y Rio de San Antonio, en la Provincia de Texas.

Impreſſo con las Licencias neceſſarias en la Imprenta de los Herederos de Doña Maria de Rivera, en la Calle de San Bernardo y eſquina de la Plazuela de el Volador Año de 1760.

como son: Los Pacuâches, Mescáles, Pampôpas, Tàcames, Chayopînes, Venados, Pamàques, y toda la Juventud de Pihuiques, Borrados, Sanipaos, y Manos de Perro. Compuesto Por El P. Fr. Bartholome Garcia, Predicador Apostolico, y actual Missionero de la Mission de N. S. P. S. Francisco de dicho Colegio, y Rio de San Antonio, en la Provincia de Texas.

Impresso con las Licencias necessarias en la Imprenta de los Herederos de Doña Maria de Rivera, en la Calle de San Bernardo y esquina de la Plazuela de el Volador. Año de 1760.

4°, title, 7 unnumbered leaves of preliminaries, and 88 numbered pages. [At the end:] Se acabò de imprimir el dia 15. de Octubre de 1760.

Preliminaries: 1 page of *aprobación* by Fr. Joseph Guadalupe Prado, 1 page of *parecer* of the same, 6 pages of *sentir* by the same, 1 page of licenses, that of the government being dated July 5, 1760, 1 page of order to Prado to pass on the work, 1 page of *nota,* 1 page of *consectario moral,* 2 pages of *advertencias prologales.*

Copies: A, BM, Har, H, J, JCB, LAP, LC, NYP, Texas State Library, TWS, Y.

From the preliminaries it appears that Father García had been a missionary for twelve years in Texas, and that the book had been submitted to Father Prado because he was the only one competent to pass on it. In his *aprobación* and *sentir* Father Prado states that he had spent twenty-two years in the missions of Coahuila and Texas, and notes the difficulties of the missionaries in making themselves understood by the natives. Acting through interpreters is the worst kind of practice because the interpreters do not know Spanish well, or else through ignorance or malice do not properly explain the mysteries. He states that this situation is much more serious in San Antonio because there are so many different languages there that it seems like Babylon. In order to get any results it would be necessary that the commonest language be chosen which the principal Indians would have to learn first in order to instruct the others.

This is the only work published on the languages of the Texas Indians during the Spanish régime.

140. GAMBOA: Francisco Xavier de

Comentarios A Las Ordenanzas De Minas, Dedicados Al Catholico Rey, Nuestro Señor, Don Carlos III. (Que Dios Guarde) Siempre Magnanimo, Siempre Feliz, Siempre Augusto, Por Don Francisco Xavier De Gamboa, Colegial de el Real, y mas antiguo de San Ildefonso de Mexico, Abogado de la Real Chancillerìa de aquella Ciudad, y de Presos de el Santo Oficio de la Inquisicion, su Consultor por la Suprema, y Diputado de el Consulado, y Comercio de la Nueva-España en la Corte de Madrid. Con Aprobacion, Y Privilegio Del Rey.

Madrid. En la Oficina de Joachin Ibarra, calle de las Urosas. Año MDCCLXI.

Folio, half title, title, 12 unnumbered leaves of preliminaries, 534 pages numbered except the first, and 3 plates of figures.

Preliminaries: 5 pages of dedication to the king, 2 of licenses, 2 of errata and *tasa,* 9 of indexes, and 6 of prologue.

Pages 490-510 contain a glossary of obscure words in use in the mining region, and an index of mining districts; pages 511 to the end contain an alphabetical index.

Copies: Har, J, JCB, LC, NYP, TWS, UT.

Translated into English by Richard Heathfield, and published in London in 1830 in 2 volumes, as *Commentaries on the Mining Ordinances of Spain.*

In 1743 one Domingo Reborato y Solar proposed the formation of a company, with a capital of two million pesos, to act as *aviadores.* An *aviador,* in the Spanish mining law, was a person who advanced money to work a mine, and in such capacity had certain well-defined rights. At this time many of the principal mines had got down to water level, and as the art of raising water was still in its infancy, many mines which had been very profitable had, on reaching water level, been compelled to suspend operations. The idea was to raise sufficient capital to undertake various serious operations of unwatering mines. Considerable literature exists on the subject of this bank, as it is sometimes called, and a number of valuable reports were made by the leading miners of the day, most of which remain still unpublished. These reports give a thorough insight into the condition of the mining industry of the time. Gamboa has inserted in his book extracts from several of these reports, most of which were unfavorable to the proposal.

Gamboa, the author of these commentaries, was perhaps the most eminent juris-consult who lived in Mexico during the viceregal period. He devoted himself especially to mining litigation, and consequently was well equipped to handle this subject. Mixed in with the learned commentaries on the ordinances will be found numerous observations regarding the history and current state of mining and metallurgy in Mexico. He cites nearly all the known books on the latter art current in that day, whether in Spanish or in other languages, and discusses at some length the development made in Mexico and Peru in the art of extraction of silver from ores. Mining was the principal business in Mexico for several

RELACION

DEL ATENTADO SACRILEGIO,

COMETIDO POR TRES INDIOS

1760 DE UN PUEBLO

DE LA PROVINCIA

DEL NUEVO MEXICO;

Y DE EL SEVERO CASTIGO,

QUE EXECUTÒ

LA DIVINA JUSTICIA

CCN EL FAUTOR PRINCIPAL

DE ELLOS.

Impressa, con las licencias necessarias, en Mexico en la Imprenta de la Bibliotheca Mexicana, en la Puente del Espiritu Santo. Año de 1763.

hundred years, and a very complete system had been worked out of mining and treating ores and marketing the product.

141. RELACIÓN

Relacion Del Atentado Sacrilegio, Cometido Por Tres Indios De Un Pueblo De La Provincia Del Nuevo Mexico; Y De El Severo Castigo, Que Executò La Divina Justicia Con El Fautor Principal De Ellos.

Impressa, con las licencias necessarias, en Mexico en la Imprenta de la Bibliotheca Mexicana, en la Puente del Espiritu Santo. Año de 1763.

4°, title leaf and 5 unnumbered pages, signed at the end, Pedro, Obispo de Durango.

Copies: BA, according to Medina, *La Imprenta en México*, no. 4819, WBS (No doubt the BA copy).

Don Pedro states that this is an extract taken from a *relación* which he is making up by order of his Majesty, giving a general account of his bishopric.

142. VILAPLANA: Fr. Hermenegildo de

Vida Portentosa Del Americano Septentrional Apostol El V. P. Fr. Antonio Margil De Jesus, Fundador, y Ex-Guardian de los Colegios de la Santa Cruz de Queretaro, de Christo Crucificado de Guatemala, y de nuestra Señora de Guadalupe de Zacatecas. Relacion Historica De Sus Nuevas, Y Antiguas Maravillas, Escrita Por El R. Padre Fray Hermenegildo de Vilaplana, Missionero Apostolico, Lector de Sagrada Theologia, Calificador del Santo Oficio, y Chronista del referido Colegio de la Santa Cruz. Dedicala Al Rey Nuestro Señor D. Carlos III. En Su Real, Y

Supremo Consejo De Las Indias, El M.R.P. Fr. Manuel De Naxera, Lector Jubilado, Procurador General de Indias, que fuè en la Corte de Madrid, Ex-Custodio de la Provincia de el Santo Evangelio, Padre de la de Santa Helena de la Florida, y Comissario General en esta Nueva España del Orden de N.P.S. Francisco.

Impressa En Mexico, Con Las Licencias Necessarias. En la Imprenta de la Bibliotheca Mexicana. Año de 1763.

4°, title, 16 unnumbered leaves of preliminaries, copper plate engraving of Father Antonio preaching to the Indians, 336 numbered pages.

Preliminaries: 5 pages of dedication by Naxera, 4 pages of *parecer* by Carrillo, 5 pages of *parecer* by Augustín Joseph de Quintela, 12 pages of *sentir* by Fr. Pablo Antonio Pérez, 1 page of license of the *Superior Gobierno* dated April 15, 1763, and license of the ordinary, 1 page of license of the order, 2 pages of prologue, 1 page of *protesta,* and 1 page of errata. The index occupies pages 331-336.

Copies: A, BM, J, JCB, NYP, S, TWS, UT, Y.

The account of Father Antonio's experiences in the north occurs in chapters XX and XXI, pages 149-163.

142a

Vida Portentosa Del Americano Septentrional . . . Madrid, Juan de San Martin, 1775.

4°, title, 6 unnumbered preliminary leaves, 335 pages, 1 plate.

143. BRAUN: P. Bartholomé

Carta Del P. Bartholome Braun Visitador De La Provincia Tarahumara A Los PP. Superiores De Esta Provincia De Nueva España Sobre La Apostolica Vida, Virtudes, Y Santa Muerte Del P. Francisco Hermano Glandorff. [Jesuit device.] Con Las Licencias Necessarias:

Impressa en el Real, y mas antiguo Colegio de San Ildefonso de Mexico, año de 1764.

4°, title, 33 pages numbered, and 1 unnumbered of *protesta.* Copy: J.

Father Francisco, the subject of this *Carta,* was one of the most noted Jesuit missionaries of the eighteenth century. He was born in Osnaburg, October 29, 1687, became a Jesuit on the 27th of May, 1708, and was assigned to the Mexican missions in 1717. Father Braun does not say just when he went to the Tarahumara as a missionary, but he must have gone about 1730, although Braun says in one place that he was a missionary more than forty years. He was located at Tomochi, which was said to have been one of the most difficult of all the Tarahumara missions. Like most books of this character laudatory of the dead, this contains many examples of Father Glandorff's marvelous experiences. He finally died at Tomochi, August 9, 1763, and Father Braun wrote this letter from the mission of Temosachi, May 30, 1764.

The Tarahumara Indians were rather susceptible to religious influence, and the Jesuits built up a great province in their territory. There was a very large number of missions, most of them very successful, and many of the churches which the Jesuits built are still standing at this day. There were many mines in the province, in which these Indians, although they were not particularly robust, worked. The country is very inaccessible, and these Indians did not suffer as much from the Apaches as the Indians in Sonora. For one reason or another, however, their number has greatly diminished, large numbers hav-

CARTA
DEL PADRE PROVINCIAL FRANCISCO ZEVALLOS
SOBRE LA APOSTOLICA VIDA, Y VIRTUDES
DEL P. FERNANDO KONSAG
INSIGNE MISSIONERO DE LA CALIFORNIA.

Impressa en el Real, y mas antiguo Colegio de San Ildefonso de Mexico, año de 1764.

ing been absorbed in the surrounding population and become good Mexicans; but there are still to be seen, occasionally around the larger towns, small bodies of them who are just about in as great a state of savagery as they were when the Jesuits first went there. It is only about forty years since the famous battle at Tomochic [as it is now spelled], in which large numbers of the Indians were killed in a fight with Don Porfirio's troops. They barricaded themselves in the church, finally, and were nearly all annihilated. The affair caused a tremendous scandal in Mexico as it grew out of an effort to take the land of the Indians away from them. They refused to be ousted peaceably and put up a fight. At first they had some success, but a large number of troops having been sent in, the natural result followed.

144. CATALOGUS

Catalogus Personarum, et officiorum Provinciæ Mexicanæ Societatis Jesu In Indiys 1764 [Jesuit device.]

Mexici. Typis Reg. & Ant. D. Ildefonsi Seminarij Collegij.

8°, title, unnumbered leaf with index of the colleges and convents, and 55 numbered pages.

Copies: JCB, and reprinted in full in Dr. Nicolás León's *Bibliografía Mexicana del Siglo xviii,* as no. 44 of vol. 3.

145. ZEVALLOS: P. Francisco

Carta Del Padre Provincial Francisco Zevallos Sobre La Apostolica Vida, Y Virtudes Del P. Fernando Konsag Insigne Missionero De La California. [Jesuit device.]

Impressa en el Real, y mas antiguo Colegio de San Ildefonso de Mexico, año de 1764.

DOCTRINA CHRISTIANA, Y PLATICAS DOCTRINALES,

TRADUCIDAS EN LENGUA OPATA

POR EL P. RECTOR MANUEL AGUIRRE de la Compañia de JESUS.

QUIEN LAS DEDICA

AL ILLMO. SEÑOR DOCTOR

PEDRO TAMARON

DEL CONSEJO DE S. M.

DIGNISSIMO OBISPO DE DURANGO.

CON LAS LICENCIAS NECESSARIAS:
Impressas en la Imprenta del Real, y mas antiguo Colegio de San Ildefonso de Mexico, año de 1765.

4°, title, leaf of *parecer,* leaf of *dictamen* and 2 licenses, all unnumbered, 31 numbered pages, and 1 unnumbered of *protesta.*
Copies: BM, H, P.

According to the account of Father Francisco Zevallos, Consag was a Hungarian, born in 1703 in Uvaradin, a city in Slavonia on the river Drave. He died September 10, 1759.

Coming to Mexico in 1730, he was destined for California and was first located at the mission of San Ignacio, in 1732. In 1746, on the 9th of June, he started on his exploration of the coast to the river Colorado, and in forty-six days he arrived at its mouth. His diary of this expedition, together with a map which he made, is to be found as appendix number 3 to the *Noticia de la California,* 1757. This expedition finally disposed of any doubt as to whether or not California was an island. In 1751, on the 22d of May, he started on another expedition by land; and in 1753, in June and July, he made another expedition by land to the north in company with Captain Fernando Rivera y Moncada. Zevallos gives a short account of all three expeditions, but the diary of the second expedition is to be found in the *Apostólicos Afanes,* pages 391-429. This book contains an excellent account of the founding of the northern missions in Lower California.

146. AGUIRRE: P. Manuel

Doctrina Christiana, Y Platicas Doctrinales, Traducidas En Lengua Opata Por El P. Rector Manuel Aguirre de la Compañia de Jesus. Quien Las Dedica Al Illmo. Señor Doctor Pedro Tamaron Del Consejo De S. M. Dignissimo Obispo De Durango. [Jesuit device.] Con Las Licencias Necessarias:

CONSTITUCIONES
DE LA CONGREGACION
DE NUESTRA SEÑORA
DE LA
LUZ,
Erigida en la Villa de Santa Fee Carital
de la Provincia de la Nueva Mexico,
y aprobada del Illmó. Señor D. Pedro
Tamaron Obiſpo de Durango.
A ſus expenſas las dà al publico
D. FRANCISCO ANTONIO
Marin del Valle, Governador, Capitan
general que fue de dicha Provincia, Hermano mayor de ſu Congregacion.
DEDICANSE
A la miſma Emperatriz Soberana.

IMPRESAS EN MEXICO,
con las licencias neceſſarias, por D.
Phelipe de Zuñiga, y Ontiveros, en la
calle de la Palma, año de 1766.

Impressas en la Imprenta del Real, y mas antiguo Colegio de San Ildefonso de Mexico, año de 1765.

4°, title, leaf of approval and license to print of Bishop Pedro Tamarón, dated Durango, October 26, 1761, leaf *Al que Leyere,* 162 numbered pages, and an unnumbered leaf of index, verso blank.

Copies: A, BM, J, JCB.

Bishop Tamarón in his approval states that he had submitted the work to Fathers Joseph Roldán and Juan Nentuig, also Opata missionaries, who both had advised him that it would prove very useful.

Father Aguirre was a missionary to the Opata Indians of Bacadeguachi, of Mochopa, and of Nacori in the province of Sonora.

146A. CONSTITUCIONES

Constituciones De La Congregacion De Nuestra Señora De La Luz, Erigida en la Villa de Santa Fee Capital de la Provincia de la Nueva Mexico, y aprobada del Ilmó. Señor D. Pedro Tamaron Obispo de Durango. A sus expensas las dà al publico D. Francisco Antonio Marin del Valle, Governador, Capitan general que fue de dicha Provincia, Hermano mayor de su Congregacion. Dedicanse A la misma Emperatriz Soberana.

Impresas En Mexico, con las licencias necessarias, por D. Phelipe de Zuñiga, y Ontiveros, en la calle de la Palma, año de 1766.

8°, title, with a cut of Nuestra Señora de la Luz on the verso, 5 pages of dedication to Soberana Señora, 4 pages to the Ilmō. Señor, and 45 pages of *Constituciones,* 7 pages of *aprobación* dated Santa Fe, June 3, 1760, signed by Pedro Obispo de Durango, 7 pages of the minutes of the meeting for the election of officers, 2 pages of *notoriedad,* 2 pages of *diligencias,* and 2 of license, or, besides the title leaf, a total of 74 pages, all unnumbered.

The formation of this *cofradía* took place in 1750 while Bishop Tamarón was in Santa Fe, but the *Constitución* seems not to have been formulated until 1760 and the printing was delayed six years more. The names signed to the *Constitución* and to the minutes of the election of officers are those of the outstanding citizens of New Mexico of the day, the first signature, in both cases, being that of the governor.

147. SOFERRÓN Y LARREA: Joseph del Campo

Relacion de los meritos, y servicios de Don Joseph del Campo Soferròn, y Larrea, Governador interino que ha sido de la Provincia de la Nueva Vizcaya, y actualmente Teniente de aquel Govierno.

Folio, 3 unnumbered pages, and 1 of *résumé,* apparently dated at the end, May 18, 1768.

Copy: Medina, *Biblioteca Hispano-Americana,* no. 4312, locates a copy in AGI, but I was unable to find it.

148. DÍAZ DE OROPESA: Joseph

Relacion De Los Meritos, Y Servicios De Don Joseph Diaz de Oropesa, Sargento mayor de las Compañias de Infanteria Española Miliciana del Nuevo Reyno de Leon.

4°, 4 unnumbered pages, dated Madrid, March 9, 1769.

Copy: AGI, 104-6-12.

Díaz de Oropesa, a native of Mexico and sergeant major of the militia in Nuevo León, says he had furnished food and supplies to the presidios of Rio Grande del Norte and San Antonio de Béjar, having dedicated himself to the pacification and settlement of the frontiers of the provinces of Monclova and Texas. His appointment was made by the Marqués de Croix.

149. COSTANSÓ: Miguel

Diario Historico De Los Viages De Mar, Y Tierra Hechos Al Norte De La California De Orden Del Excelentissimo Señor Marques De Croix, Virrey, Governador, y Capitan General de la Nueva España: Y Por Direccion Del Illustrissimo Señor D. Joseph De Galvez, Del Consejo, y Camara de S.M. en el Supremo de Indias, Intendente de Exercito, Visitador General de este Reyno. Executados por la Tropa destinada à dicho objeto al mando De Don Gaspar De Portola, Capitan de Dragones en el Regimiento de España, y Governador en dicha Peninsula Y por los Paquebots el S. Carlos y el S. Antonio al mando De Don Vicente Vila, Piloto del Numero de primeros de la Real Armada, Y De Don Juan Perez, de la Navegacion de Philipinas.

De Orden Del Excmo. Sr. Virrey, En la Imprenta del Superior Gobierno.

Folio, title, and 56 numbered pages, dated at the end, Mexico, 24th of October, 1770, and signed D. Miguel Costansó.

Copies: A, AGI, BM, H, J, JCB, LC, LAP, NYH, TWS.

On October 28, Viceroy Marqués de Croix addressed a letter to Julián de Arriaga of the Council, enclosing a copy of the work which was accompanied by a manuscript map made by Costansó which was published the following year in Madrid by Tomás López, engraved by Hipólito Ricarte, with the following title, "Carta reducida del Oceano Asiático ó mar del Súr que comprehende la costa Oriental y occidental de la Peninsula de la California, con el Golfo de su denominacion antiguamente conocido por la de Mar de Cortés y de las costas de la América Septentrional desde el Isthmo que úne dicha Peninsula con el continente hasta el Rio de los Reyes y desde el Rio Colo-

An Historical Journal
of the
Expeditions, *by* Sea *and* Land,
to the North of
CALIFORNIA;
in
1768, 1769, and 1770:

when
Spanish Establishments
Were first made at
San-Diego *and* Monte-Rey.

From a *Spanish MS.* Translated by *William Reveley*, Esq.

Published by *Dalrymple.*

1790.

LONDON,
Printed by GEORGE BIGG.
Sold by *P. Elmsly*, opposite Southampton Street, Strand; *J. Sewell*, Cornhill; *F. Wingrave*, (Successor to Mr. *Nourse)* opposite Catherine Street, Strand, and *J. Stockdale*, Piccadilly.

rado hasta el Cabo de Corrientes, Compuesta de orden del Virrey de Nueva España Marqués de Croix." At the end is the notation, Mexico, October 30, 1770, Miguel Costansó.

149a

An Historical Journal of the Expeditions, by Sea and Land, to the North of California; in 1768, 1769, and 1770: when Spanish Establishments Were first made at San-Diego and Monte-Rey. From a Spanish MS. Translated by William Reveley, Esq. Published by Dalrymple. 1790.

London, Printed by George Bigg. Sold by P. Elmsly, opposite Southampton Street, Strand; J. Sewell, Cornhill; F. Wingrave, (Successor to Mr. Nourse) opposite Catherine Street, Strand, and J. Stockdale, Piccadilly.

4°, title, leaf, and 76 pages numbered except the first, 4 maps on 2 sheets.

Maps: A large folded map—Chart of California by Miguel Costansó, 1770. Engraved by Tomás López, Madrid, 1771, entitled [the original title].

Plan of Port San Francisco in New-Albion, Lat. 37° 13 North, from a Spanish MS.

Plan of Port Bandera on the west-coast of Mexico, Lat. 20°40 N.

Chart of the west-coast of California from a Spanish MS. The two plans and the chart are engraved on a single sheet.

Copies exist with four more maps than those above described:

Plan of Port of S^{n}. Francisco on the West Coast of California . . . From a Spanish MS. Communicated by John Henry Cox Esq. [dated at the bottom] Jany 17th 1789. 11¼x12½ inches.

Plan of Monterey in California by Don Josef Tobar y Tamariz 7th December 1786.

Plan of the Road del Principe in the Channel of S^n Barbara by Don Josef Tobar y Tamariz 1786.

Plan of Port S^n Diego on the West Coast of California.

The last three plans were printed on one sheet 11¼x 8¼ inches, which contains the following note: N. B. These Plans were taken from Spanish MSS Communicated by John Henry Cox, Esq. Dated Jany 14th 1789.

Copies: BM, H. [8 maps], JCB, Mrs. Frederick Rindge [8 maps], TWS.

The translation of the account by Costansó ends on page 46. Pages 47-64 contain an extract from the *Navegación Especulativa y Práctica* of González Cabrera Bueno, printed in Manila in 1734. This consists of sailing directions along the shore from Cape Mendocino towards the port of Acapulco. Pages 65-74 contain *Journal of M. Sauvague le Muet, officer of the ship Comtesse de Pontchartrain, 1714.* Pages 75 and 76 contain a description of Port Bandera.

The leaf after the title is headed *Advertisement, November 1790,* and is signed at the end, *Dalrymple.* In this, Dalrymple states that he received in 1783 from Doctor Robertson, the manuscript in Spanish, which at his request had been translated by Mr. Reveley, and afterwards corrected by a Spanish friend. The manuscript was apparently not signed, but Dalrymple states that he knew the name of the author who wrote the report, which for certain reasons he does not give. He further states that he is inserting the map of California by Costansó, some views of the coast from a French manuscript, a plan of San Francisco, a chart of the west coast, and a view of Bandera on the same plate.

The Portolá expedition reached Monterey in May, 1770, took formal possession June 3d, and drew up the requisite *autos,* the originals of which still exist in the Mexican archives. On July 9, together with Costansó and Juan Pérez, Portolá left for San Blas, where he arrived August 1. Portolá immediately sent off to Mexico the documents relating to the taking of possession, and he at once followed the manuscripts, arriving in Mexico on August 10; and by August 16 the *Estracto de Noticias del Puerto de Monterey* was printed by the viceroy. At this date the journals of the expedition which had been sent overland from California had not yet arrived. Both the printed accounts of this expedition appeared from the press of the government in Mexico, almost certainly for private circulation, and judging from their extreme scarcity, in a very small edition. I think this was the case notwithstanding the statement in Paloú's *Noticias* that the *Estracto* was distributed to the public. At this time there was in effect a decree of the Spanish government that no one could publish anything concerning America without the knowledge and consent of the Council of the Indies. Obviously the government of Mexico published these accounts without this consent, and for this reason I do not think they were intended for public circulation.

Juan Pérez, Vicente Vila, Costansó, and Pedro Fages all received promotion as a reward for their share in the expedition.

In 1901 Mr. Charles F. Lummis, at that time editor of the *Land of Sunshine* in Los Angeles, obtained a copy of the original from Mr. Edward E. Ayer of Chicago, translated it, appending thereto a few unimportant notes, and published it in the June and July [1901] numbers. Mr. Lummis followed this with a translation of the *Estracto de Noticias* which was attached to Mr. Ayer's copy of the *Diario Histórico.*

In 1909, under the editorship of Mr. F. J. Teggart, the Academy of Pacific Coast History undertook the publication of the original text with translations of the various accounts of the Portolá expedition. In vol. I, no. 2, of its publications appeared the *Estracto de Noticias,* in no. 3 the diary of Portolá from a manuscript copy in the Bancroft library. The latter is of no interest whatever, being just as brief as the regulations would permit. In 1910 no. 4 appeared, with the *Diario Histórico* of Costansó and a translation made by Adolph Van Hemert-Engert, together with a facsimile of the title page and another of Costansó's map. The text was taken from a copy in the Los Angeles Public library. In 1911 in vol. II, no. 1, appeared the diary of Vicente Vila from a MS. copy in the Sutro collection, together with a translation. This is the log book of the *San Carlos,* or a copy of it, from January 9, 1769, to May 12, and again from August 1 to August 24, 1770. In no. 4 appeared the diary of Miguel Costansó together with a translation from a MS. copy in the Sutro collection collated with a copy of the original in the Archivo General de la Nación, Mexico, Section *Historia,* vol. 396. This covers the period from July 14, 1769, the day of leaving San Diego, to the day of the return there, January 4, 1770, and is the most valuable document known regarding this expedition.

Father Juan Crespi also kept a diary of the journey, which was published in 1927 by Herbert E. Bolton with various Crespi letters as, *Fray Juan Crespi, Missionary Explorer on the Pacific Coast, 1769-1774.*

Fages wrote an account of this expedition in 1775, which was embodied in a *Suplemento* to the two accounts which had been printed in 1770. Translated into French by Ternaux-Compans either in whole or in part from a manuscript in his possession, it was published in the *Nouvelles Annales des Voyages* in 1844, vol. 101, pages 145-182, and 311-347. A translation from the original Spanish was published by Herbert Ingram Priestley in the *Catholic Historical Review* in 1919. This has just been reprinted (1937) by the University of California Press in a separate volume under the title, *A Historical, Political, and Natural Description of California by Pedro Fages, Soldier of Spain.* All the writings of Fages which have survived are of the greatest interest, as he paid much attention to the natives encountered.

The founding of Monterey marks the definite settlement of Upper California, the main object of the Spanish government in planning and sending out the Portolá expedition. A full account of the origin, progress, and immediate results of this expedition will be found in C. E. Chapman's *Founding of Spanish California.*

149b

Bericht von Spanischen Expedetionem Zur See und zu land nach dem nordlichen Californien in dem jahren 1768. 1769. 1770.

This German edition of Costansó is found in volume I of Bruns' *Repositorium,* Tübingen, 1792, pages [1]-32, with a folding map: Carte von Californien von M. Costanso 1770.

150. ESTRACTO DE NOTICIAS

Estracto De Noticias del Puerto de Monterrey, de la Mission, y Presidio que se han establecido en èl con la denominacion de San Carlos, y del sucesso de las dos Expediciones de Mar, y Tierra que à este fin se despacharon en el año proximo anterior de 1769.

[Colophon:] Con Licencia y Orden, del Exmo. Señor Virrey. En la Imprenta del Superior Govierno.

Folio, 3 leaves with the verso of the last blank, dated at the end, Mexico, 16 de Agosto de 1770. It has a caption title occupying the upper half of the first page.

Copies: A, AGI, B, BNMS, H, J, P.

Estracto De Noticias del Puerto de Monterrey . . . [The same title as the preceding.]

4°, 8 unnumbered pages, with the caption title occupying the upper part of the first page.

Copies: B, H, J, WBS.

Both editions have the same text except for a few typographical differences.

Mr. Robert E. Cowan, in his *Bibliography of California,* 1914, states that the quarto edition is the second edition, but I have never been able to discover any contemporary statement as to which was printed first. They were probably both printed at the same time, the folio being for official circulation and the quarto for public circulation. We have Father Paloú's statement that it was issued for public circulation.

Paloú reprinted it in his life of Serra and also inserted it in his *Noticias de la Nueva California.*

It was first translated into English and published in the *Land of Sunshine* for July, 1901, and again in no. 2 of vol. 1 of the Publications of the Academy of Pacific Coast History.

Portolá and Costansó arrived in Mexico city on the 10th of August, 1770, bringing the first news of the occupation of Monterey; so it will be seen that the government lost very little time in having the account of the occupation of the port printed.

151. IRIARTE: Fr. Juan Pedro de

A Los M. RR. PP. MM. Prior, Rector, O Principal Presidente, y à todos los demás Religiosos de esta gravisima Comunidad, á cuya noticia llegasen las presentes Letras: Fr. Juan Pedro de Iriarte, Maestro en Sagrada Theologia, de la Provincia de Santiago de Mexico, Orden de Predicadores, y

Vicario General de esta Mision: Gracia, salud, y verdadero zelo por la conversion de las Almas.
[Madrid, 1770?]

Folio, 4 unnumbered pages, with the title occupying the first 6 lines on the first page.
Copies: AGI, 105-1-25, H.

This is a circular letter signed by Fr. Juan Pedro de Iriarte, [no day,] 1770. Part of it consists of a letter dated the 13th of June, by the general of the Dominican order, advising that the government had granted the right to the order to found a new mission on the frontier of California on the peninsula, and granting the right to Father Iriarte to take volunteers from Spain. Father Iriarte then emphasizes the importance of this mission and calls on the charitable feelings of his fellow members to come forward and volunteer. Iriarte was in Spain a long time engaged in this business, which was not brought to a conclusion for a number of years. The archives contain a number of petitions, *consultas,* etc., on the matter of the occupation by the Dominicans of the missions in Lower California.

152. LORENZANA: Francisco Antonio

Historia De Nueva-España, Escrita Por Su Esclarecido Conquistador Hernan Cortes, Aumentada Con Otros Documentos, Y Notas, Por El Ilustrissimo Señor Don Francisco Antonio Lorenzana, Arzobispo De Mexico. [Engraving.] Con Las Licencias Necesarias.

En México en la Imprenta del Superior Gobierno, del Br. D. Joseph Antonio de Hogal en la Calle de Tiburcio. Año de 1770.

Folio, title in red and black, engraving, 9 unnumbered leaves, xvi, 400 numbered pages, 9 unnumbered leaves of index, 2 maps, plate of the Great Temple of Mexico, plate of the Mexican calendar, and 31 leaves inserted between pages 175 and 177.

Preliminaries: 6 leaves of dedication to the bishops, etc., of the Mexican province, 2 leaves of prologue, and leaf with errata on the recto, verso blank.

Maps: Plano De La Nueva España en que se señalan los Viages que hizo el Capitan Hernan Cortes . . . Dispuesto por D[n] Jph Ant. de Alzate y Ramirez año de 1769;

[California] Domingo del Castillo Piloto me Fecit en Mexico . . . MDXLI.

The 31 leaves inserted consist of a printed title, *Cordillera De Los Pueblos, Que Antes De La Conquista Pagaban Tributo A El Emperador Muctezuma, Y En Que Especie, Y Cantidad,* and 31 copper plates illustrative of a Mexican codex. The first 13 of these are unnumbered, and the following numbered 15-32.

This consists of a reprint of the three previously published letters of Cortés, with notes and some preliminary remarks by Lorenzana. Pages 11-36 contain an account of the various viceroys of Mexico down to the Marqués de Croix, and pages 322-328 contain an account of the voyage of Cortés to the peninsula of California and notices of the subsequent expeditions down to 1769. To illustrate this account the map of Castillo was inserted, which Lorenzana states was copied from the original in the archives of the Marquesado, that is, of the Cortés family. Since that time the original has never appeared, so we are still at a loss to know whether Castillo or Lorenzana put the name "California" on the map.

153. ORTIZ PARRILLA: Diego

Relacion De Los Meritos, Y Servicios Del Coronel Don Diego Ortiz Parrilla, Governador interino que hà sido de las Provincias de Sinaloa, y Sonora, y de la de Coaguila en la Nueva España, de la Plaza de Panzacola, y Capitan del Presidio de Santa Rosa del Sacramento.

Folio, 8 unnumbered pages dated Madrid, May 3, 1770, on page 7. Page 8 contains a strip of résumé of services, for filing purposes.

Copy: AGI, 104-6-17.

Ortiz Parrilla had a distinguished career in the northern provinces of Mexico beginning in 1749, when he was appointed governor of Sonora and Sinaloa; and the archives contain many extensive *expedientes* of accounts of his campaigns against the Seris and Pimas Altos.

Ortiz was also charged with the removal of the presidio of San Xavier to San Sabá in 1756 and erecting the new one. In 1760 he was appointed commandant of the presidio of Santa Rosa de Sacramento. In 1761 he was sent to Florida on account of a revolt of the Talapuses and Apiscas, and in 1763 delivered the presidio of Pensacola to the British under the treaty terms. In January, 1764, he was asked to return to Santa Rosa to become *governador interino* of Coahuila, where he remained until 1766.

154. INSTRUCCIÓN

Instruccion Para Formar Una Linea ó Cordon De Quince Presidios Sobre las Fronteras de las Provincias Internas de este Reino de Nueva-España, Y Nuevo Reglamento Del número y calidad de Oficiales y Soldados que estos y los demas han de tener, Sueldos que gozarán desde el dia primero de Enero del año próxîmo de mil setecientos setenta y dos, y servicio que deben hacer sus Guarniciones. Año de [Arms of Spain] 1771.

De Orden De Su Excelencia.

En Mexico en la Imprenta del Br. D. Joseph Antonio de Hogal, Calle de Tiburcio.

Folio, title, and 80 numbered pages, signed at the end, El Marqués de Croix, Mexico, July 18, 1771.
Copies: AGI, B, J, JCB, MNM.

This consists of fifty-five orders or instructions preceded by four pages of explanation in which a short statement of the antecedent facts is given. At the end of this introduction, after observing that he had the consent of Gálvez and the *Junta de Guerra y Hacienda,* Croix orders the instruction to be put into effect from the beginning of the year 1772, to be observed until the king confirms or reforms it according to his wish. If it ever became effective is was only for the brief period between January 1, 1772, and the time when the new *reglamento* promulgated in Madrid, September 10, 1772, arrived in Mexico. This last embodied practically all the principal points covered by the *Instrucción.*

The immediate cause of the issuance of new rules for the frontier provinces was the report made to the viceroy and the Crown by the Marqués de Rubí as the result of his prolonged visit to the frontier in 1766 and 1767. Colonel Hugo O'Connor had a special commission to examine the province of Texas, and he also furnished detailed and extensive reports and recommendations for future action.

155. NOTICIA BREVE

Noticia Breve De La Expedicion Militar de Sonora y Cinaloa, su exîto feliz, y ventajoso estado en que por consecuencia de ella se han puesto ambas Provincias.

Folio, 12 numbered pages, dated at the end, Mexico, 17th of June, 1771. The title occupies the first four lines of page 1.
Copies: A, AGI, B, H, J, JCB, TWS.

This document contains the results of the famous expedition to Sonora of José de Gálvez, at least as he would like to have had them known. It was composed by someone in his interest, and is usually supposed to have been written by Gálvez himself, but I have never seen any precise statement as to the authorship.

There is a large amount of material extant regarding this expedition which was not written by Gálvez or anyone in his behalf, but on the contrary by enemies of the famous *visitador,* professed or otherwise. They present the facts in an entirely different way from this narrative, and, instead of leaving the province pacified, the truth seems to be that he accomplished very little. Dr. Herbert I. Priestley, of the University of California, has issued an exhaustive treatise on Gálvez' operations in the north of Mexico. My own impression, after reading both sides, is that Gálvez went a little crazy in Sonora, either on account of the heat or native liquor, and as a result indulged in some rather unwarranted proceedings. Aside from Portolá's expedition to California, which had some results, the country had very little to show for the enormous amount of money spent on the Gálvez enterprises.

156. PLAN DE UNA COMPAÑÍA

Plan De Una Compañia de Accionistas para fomentar con actividad el beneficio de las ricas Minas de Sonora y Cinaloa, y restablecer la Pesquería de Perlas en el Golfo de Californias.

4°, 8 unnumbered pages dated at the end, Mexico, April 15, 1771.

Copies: AGI, 104-6-14, BA.

This is a prospectus of a company that was to be formed in Mexico with shares at the moderate price of five hundred pesos each. The subscription was to remain

Nachrichten

von der

Amerikanischen Halbinsel

Californien:

mit einem

zweyfachen

Anhang falscher Nachrichten.

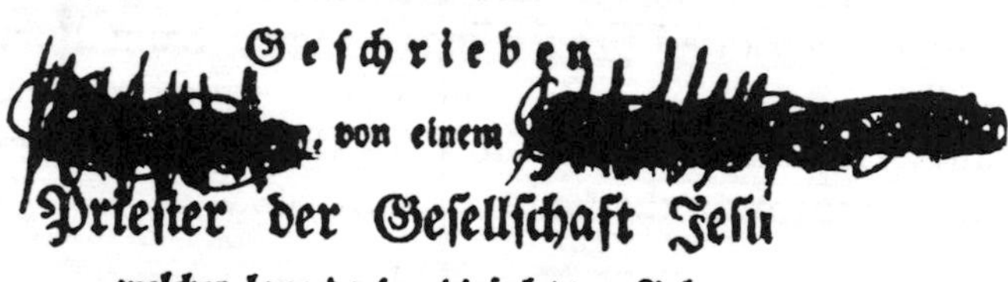
Geschrieben

von einem

Priester der Gesellschaft Jesu

welcher lang darinn diese letztere Jahr

gelebt hat.

Mit Erlaubnuß der Oberen.

Mannheim,

gedruckt in der Churfürstl. Hof- und Academie-

Buchdruckerey 1772.

open until eight hundred or a thousand shares had been subscribed, but the company was to begin to operate as soon as three hundred shares had been subscribed. The company proposed to work old mines which had been deserted, prospect for new ones, deal in goods, purchase gold dust, and finally, dive for pearls in the famous pearl beds which are found in California. The prospectus then proceeds to state that the pearl fishery has been almost abandoned for many years and is only carried on with canoes.

157. BAEGERT: Jacob

Nachrichten von der Amerikanischen Halbinsel Californien: mit einem zweyfachen Anhang falscher Nachrichten. Geschrieben von einem Priester der Gesellschaft Jesu, welcher lang darinn diese letztere Jahr gelebt hat. Mit Erlaubnuss der Oberen.

Mannheim, gedruckt in der Churfürstl. Hof- und Academie-Buchdruckerey 1772.

8°, title, 5 leaves of introduction and 2 of contents, unnumbered, 358 pages numbered except the first, 1 unnumbered leaf of errata, a map, and 2 plates.

Map: California per P. Ferdinandum Consak S. I. et alios. 175x220 mm.

Plates: Ein Californier and Eine Californierin.

Copies: B, C, Cw, JCB, NYP, Southwest Museum, TWS (1773).

The work also appears dated 1773, and according to Bancroft, with some corrections.

157a

An account of the aboriginal inhabitants of the Californian peninsula, as given by Jacob Baegert, a

German Jesuit missionary who lived there seventeen years during the second half of the last century. Translated and arranged for the Smithsonian institution by Charles Rau, of New York city.
Washington: 1866.

8°, 48 pages.

This is a large extract from the *Nachrichten,* which originally appeared on pages 352-369 and 378-399, respectively, of the reports of the Smithsonian Institution for 1863 and 1864, reprinted in separate form also in 1865 and 1875. It largely relates to the Indians.

The author of this work was a German Jesuit named Jacob Baegert. He was born December 22, 1717, entered the order September 27, 1736, and went to California in 1751. At the time of the expulsion he was located at the mission of San Luis Gonzaga. According to Bancroft, *North Mexican States,* I, page 478, he died at Neuberg, Bavaria, in 1772.

Towards the end of the Jesuit régime in California the missionaries there, especially the Germans, were very dissatisfied, and Baegert in his book reflects this attitude of mind.

There are two other accounts of the last days of the Jesuits in California, both printed in Murr's *Nachrichten: Reisebeschreibung aus Californien durch das Gebiet von Mexico nach Europa,,* 1767, by Franz Benno Ducrue, and *Nachrichten von Californien,* by Wenzel Link.

158. CHAPPE D'AUTEROCHE: Jean

Voyage En Californie Pour L'Observation Du Passage De Venus Sur Le Disque Du Soleil, Le 3 Juin 1769; Contenant les observations de ce phénomene, & la description historique de la route de l'Auteur à travers la Mexique. Par feu M. Chappe d'

Auteroche, de l'Académie Royale des Sciences. Rédigé & publié par M. de Cassini fils, de la même Academie, Directeur en survivance de l'Observatoire Royal de Paris, Etc.

A Paris, Chez Charles-Antoine Jombert, Libraire du Roi pour l'Artillerie & le Génie, rue Dauphine, à l'Image Notre-Dame. M.DCC.LXXII. Avec Approbation, Et Privilege Du Roi.

4°, half-title, title, 170 pages, 1 leaf with the privilege, plan of the city of Mexico, folding table at pages 50-51, and 3 plates. The plan of the city of Mexico was engraved probably from one made by José Antonio Alzate.

The journal of Monsieur Chappe d'Auteroche concludes on page 39, shortly after his arrival at the mission of San Joseph. It seems that a few days after he arrived there he died of some contagious malady which at that time was ravaging the country. As a result of this unfortunate ending of the enterprise his companions contented themselves with simply taking the observations of the transit of Venus without indulging in anything more than very cursory remarks on California, none of any value.

158a

A Voyage to California, To Observe The Transit Of Venus. By Mons. Chappe D'Auteroche. With An Historical Description Of The Author's Route Through Mexico, And The Natural History Of That Province, Also, A Voyage To Newfoundland And Sallee, To Make Experiments On Mr. Le Roy's Time Keepers. By Monsieur De Cassini.

London: Printed For Edward And Charles Dilly, In The Poultry. MDCCLXXVIII.

8°, half title, title, leaf of advertisements, leaf of contents, 215 pages (wrongly marked 315), plan of the city of Mexico reëngraved on a smaller scale.

REGLAMENTO,
E INSTRUCCION
PARA LOS PRESIDIOS
QUE SE HAN DE FORMAR
EN LA LINEA DE FRONTERA
de la Nueva España.

RESUELTO POR EL REY N. S.
en Cedula de 10. de Septiembre
de 1772.

DE ORDEN DE SU MAGESTAD.

MADRID: Por Juan de San Martin , Impresor de la Secretarìa del Despacho Universal de Indias.
Año de 1772.

All that is translated from the French edition will be found in the first 105 pages, the remainder being the voyage to Newfoundland . . .

159. REGLAMENTO

Reglamento, E Instruccion Para Los Presidios Que Se Han De Formar En La Linea De Frontera de la Nueva España. Resuelto Por El Rey N. S. en Cedula de 10. de Septiembre de 1772. [Printer's device.] De Orden De Su Magestad.

Madrid: Por Juan de San Martin, Impresor de la Secretarìa del Despacho Universal de Indias. Año de 1772.

4°, leaf with the arms of Spain, title, and 122 pages numbered except the first. At the end, San Ildefonso September 10, 1772—I the King—Don Julian de Arriaga.

Copies: A, AGI, B, J, UT.

159a

Reglamento, E Instruccion Para Los Presidios Que Se Han De Formar En La Linea De Frontera de la Nueva España. Resuelto Por El Rey N. S. en Cedula de 10. de Septiembre de 1772. [Arms of Spain.] De orden de el Excelentissimo Sr. Virrey de esto Reyno.

Reimpresso en Mexico: En la Imprenta del Br. D. Joseph Antonio de Hogal, Calle de Tiburcio: año de 1773.

4°, title, 132 pages.

Copies: B, C, LC.

159b

Reglamento E Instruccion Para Los Presidios Que Se Han De Formar En La Linea De Frontera de la Nueva España. Resuelto Por El Rey N. S. en

REGLAMENTO

E INSTRUCCION

PARA LOS PRESIDIOS

QUE SE HAN DE FORMAR

EN LA LINEA DE FRONTERA

DE LA NUEVA ESPAÑA.

RESUELTO POR EL REY NUESTRO SEÑOR

en Cedula de 10 de Septiembre de

1772.

Cedula de 10. de Septiembre de 1772. [Arms of Spain.] De orden del Exmô Sr. Virrey de esto Reyno.

Reimpresso en Mexico, por D. Felipe de Zuñiga y Ontiveros, año de 1790.

4°, title, 91 pages.
Copies: AGI, WBS.

159c

Reglamento E Instruccion Para Los Presidios Que Se Han De Formar En La Linea De Frontera De La Nueva España. Resuelto Por El Rey Nuestro Señor en Cedula de 10 de Septiembre de 1772.

4°, title, and 46 numbered pages.
Copy: J.

This edition contains no imprint but has all the appearance of having been printed in one of the frontier provinces before 1825, very likely at Saltillo or Monterey.

159d

Reglamento E Instruccion Para Los Presidios Que Se Han De Formar En La Linea De Frontera De La Nueva España. Resuelto Por El Rey Nuestro Señor en cédula de 10 de Septiembre de 1772.

Monterrey de Nuevo Leon, Imprenta del Gobierno à cargo del C. Lorenzo A. de Melo, Año de 1827.

4°, title, and 54 pages.
Copy: Y.

There is a notice in the catalogue of the Andrade sale of an edition in 30 pages folio, Mexico, 1834, and I have seen a notice of another edition of Madrid, 1822, in 4°.

•

This *Reglamento* grew out of the tour of inspection of the Marqués de Rubí and contains the substance of the

Instrucción which was prepared in Mexico and printed in 1771. It was in effect for a long time, as can be seen from the number of editions printed. The line of presidios marked out by Rubí formed a cordon of fifteen. It extended from Altar in Sonora to La Bahía in Texas and was maintained with a few exceptions until the Revolution, and in fact even later. The republican government in Mexico made a few changes in location, but generally speaking the system lasted until nearly 1850.

160. OCA Y ALEMÁN: Manuel Antonio de

Relacion De Los Meritos, Y Servicios Del Teniente Coronel De Milicias D. Manuel Antonio de Oca y Alemán.

Folio, 3 unnumbered pages certified to at the end, Madrid, November 5, 1773.

Copy: AGI, 104-6-17.

He was commandant of the presidio of San Sabá, but does not state at what period. Later he refers to being, in 1770, at San Fernando de Austria, to which place the presidio of San Sabá had been moved.

161. UGALDE: Juan de

Relacion De Servicios, Y Meritos Del Coronel D. Juan De Ugalde, Gonzalez, Castillo, y Tazo.

Folio, 4 unnumbered pages dated at the end, Madrid, December 9, 1774.

Copy: AGI, 103-5-21.

From this it appears that Ugalde was a native of Cádiz, and forty-five years of age in 1766; since 1767 he had served in Peru. Ugalde was evidently an applicant for some post in New Spain. Later he had a distinguished career in the frontier provinces.

162. SUMMARY OBSERVATIONS

Summary Observations And Facts Collected From Late And Authentic Accounts Of Russian And Other Navigators, To Show The Practicability And Good Prospect Of Success In Enterprises To Discover A Northern Passage For Vessels By Sea, Between The Atlantic And Pacific Oceans, Or Nearly To Approach The North Pole; For which the offers of Reward are renewed by a late Act of Parliament.

London: Sold by John Nourse, Bookseller to the King, and to the Board of Longitude. M.DCC.LXXVI.

4°, title, and 29 pages.
Copy: H.

Pages 28-29 contain a translation from the Spanish of a short account of the voyage of Hezeta and Bodega in 1775 to the northwest coast. They were seeking to verify rumors of Russian and English activities in the North Pacific area.

163. BREVE APOSTÓLICO

Breve Apostólico De Pio Sexto, Y Estatutos Generales Para La Ereccion Y Gobierno De Las Custodias De Missioneros Franciscos Observantes De Propaganda Fide En Las Provincias Internas De Nueva España. [Printer's device.]

Madrid MDCCLXXXI. Por D. Joachîn Ibarra, Impresor de Cámara de S. M. Con superior permiso.

4°, title, 42 pages of *Breve,* and 210 pages of *Bullas Apostólicana,* no. 4983. I have not, however, seen any copy with the 210
Copies: Collation from Medina, *Biblioteca Hispano-Americana,* no 4983. I have not, however, seen any copy with the 210 pages of *Bullas.* My own copy contained 122 pages of *Bullas*

only, and an index to the same, pages 121-133. Mr. W. B. Stephens has a copy without the *Bullas*. The University of Texas has a copy which is complete. It contains 42 pages of *Breve* and 210 of *Bullas*.

The *Breve of* Pio Sexto, dated Rome, November 17, 1779, orders the erection of *custodias* in the provinces of California, Sonora, Sinaloa, Nueva Viscaya, and New Mexico. The *Breve* begins by setting forth the disturbances which had occurred in these provinces after the expulsion of the Jesuits, apparently arising from some conflict between the superior authorities and the Franciscans. The pope conceded to the king the right to establish these *custodias,* and the king by *cédula* erected four, namely San Carlos in Sonora, San Gabriel in California, San Antonio in Nueva Viscaya, and Concepción in New Mexico.

Under the authority of the pope, Fr. Manuel de la Vega formed the *Estatutos* to govern the *custodias,* and these are added to the *Breve* of the pope. Under these *Estatutos* the missionaries in Sonora and California carried on their work until the secularization. According to them the college of San Fernando and the province of Michoacán were to furnish the missionaries for the *custodia* of San Gabriel, the province of Santo Evangelio for that of Concepción, the province of Santiago de Jalisco and the college of Santa Cruz for that of San Carlos, and the province of Zacatecas and the college of the Señora de Guadalupe for that of San Antonio.

The *Bullas Apostólicas* relate to the missionary colleges which were erected in Mexico, and chiefly contain rules for their regulation and government.

164. MOURELLE: Francisco Antonio

Journal Of A Voyage In 1775. To explore the coast of America, Northward of California, By the second Pilot of the Fleet, Don Francisco Antonio Maurelle, in the King's Schooner, called the Sonora, and commanded by Don Juan Francisco de la Bodega.

[London, 1780 or 1781.]

4°, title, iii-ix, 3-67 pages, map without title but showing the Pacific coast from about 15° to 60° of north latitude. Page 67 contains on the recto a note of addenda to page 18.

Copies: B, J, LC.

The pages printed with Roman numerals contain an introduction, evidently by the translator. In a footnote he refers to a projected expedition to be sent by the Empress of Russia from Kamchatka to the northwest coast in 1781 in the proper season. From this it seems likely that the introduction, at least, was not printed until that year, or possibly the one previous. In spite of this fact, Mourelle, in a relation of his services printed June 1, 1814, states that Captain Cook on his last voyage of discovery had with him a copy of his journal, printed, translated in London by the Honorable Barrington. It is possible, of course, that Cook did have with him a translation of the journal printed by the Admiralty, but it could hardly have been one of these copies with the introduction of the translator.

In 1781 it was included by Daines Barrington in his *Miscellanies,* with the same title, and paged 471 star to 477 star and 471 to 534, with the same chart. It is, page for page, the same as the other but with different pagination and also different signatures, and with the addenda on page 552.

The original from which this translation was made does not seem to be known. There are various accounts of the expedition in the archives, and it is possible that this translation may have been made from a diary of Mourelle to be found in vol. 324 of the section of *Historia* in the Archivo

General de la Nación, Mexico, but if so, many changes were made, the translation being in every respect far inferior to the original.

165. PAGÈS: Pierre Marie François

Voyages Autour Du Monde, Et Vers Les Deux Poles, par Terre Et Par Mer, Pendant les Années 1767, 1768, 1769, 1770, 1771, 1773, 1774 & 1776. Par M. de Pagès . . . Tome Premier.

A Paris: Chez Moutard. M.DCC.LXXXII.

8°, 432 pages; 272 pages, 7 maps, and 3 plates.
One map shows New Spain and Louisiana.

165a

Travels Round the World, In The Years 1767, 1768, 1769, 1770, 1771. By Monsieur de Pagés . . . Translated From The French. Volume The First.

London: J. Murray. MDCCXCI.

8°, frontispiece, xiv, 289 pages; iv, 257 pages, page 261 misnumbered for 257.

165b

Travels Round the World, . . . [The same.] The Second Edition Enlarged.

London: J. Murray. MDCCXCII.

8°, xx, 300 pages and folding table; xii, 268 pages; xxii, [2], 303 pages.
Some of these volumes sometimes appear with MDCCXCIII on the title page.

Pagès is supposed to have made a journey through Texas on horseback in 1767, passing from Natchitoches to the Rio Grande. The book contains numerous observations on Texas and the missions, but I have never been able to persuade myself that the author ever saw Texas. The work has all the appearance of being one made up in

Paris, simulating a real journey, a common enough trick of the times.

166. REGLAMENTO

Reglamento Para El Gobierno De La Provincia De Californias. Aprobado por S. M. en Real Orden de 24. de Octubre de 1781. [Arms of Spain.]

En Mexico. Por D. Felipe de Zuniga y Ontiveros, calle del Espiritu Santo, año de 1784.

Folio, title, 37 numbered pages and 1 unnumbered. The *Reglamento* ends on page 37, and is dated and signed, San Carlos de Monterey, June 1, 1779, Felipe de Neve. The unnumbered page contains the order of Gálvez to the viceroy, dated San Lorenzo, October 24, 1781, to put the same into effect, and the order of the viceroy, dated Mexico, March 26, 1782, to print the corresponding examples to be directed to the necessary public officials.

Copies: A, AGI, DLG, H, NYP.

John Everett Johnson prepared an English translation of this *Reglamento,* in two volumes, one of which contains the Spanish text. The Grabhorn Press published the work in 1929 and entitled it, *Regulations for Governing the Province of the Californias; Approved by His Majesty by Royal Order, dated October 24, 1781.*

166a

Reglamento [the same title]. California Historical Society's publication. Re-impresso en la imprenta del Colegio de Santa Clara, 1874.

8°, 68 pages.

It is generally stated that all the copies of this reprint except six were destroyed by fire; at any rate, it is almost as rare as the original.

This *Reglamento* was prepared in consequence of a *cédula* of March 21, 1775, and, as will be seen by the date, was prepared in 1779. At this time there were eight missions in California, and three more had been ordered erected, as well as a new presidio in the center of the Santa Barbara Channel coast. Article 14 treats of settlers, their rights, privileges, and duties, particularly important at that time in view of the fact that San José had just been founded and it had been decided to found another town with families from Sonora and Sinaloa.

These regulations governed the conduct of affairs in the Californias until Mexico became independent.

167. INSTRUCCIÓN

Instruccion Formada en virtud de Real Orden de S. M., que se dirige al Señor Comandante General de Provincias internas Don Jacobo Ugarte y Loyola para gobierno y puntual observancia de este Superior Gefe y de sus inmediatos Subalternos.

Folio, 56 pages, with a caption title at the head of page 1. At the end it is signed by the Conde de Gálvez and dated Mexico, August 26, 1786. Page 55 is incorrectly numbered 52.

Copies: AGM, DLG (first page defective), H.

167a

Instruccion Formada [the same title as the preceding].

Folio, 60 pages.

Copies: AGI, J, JCB, Texas State library, TWS, WBS.

Each of the above contains 216 numbered paragraphs, and their contents are identical. They are both set up with the same type, and must have been printed about the same time.

I have no means of determining which was printed first, nor have I ever been able to discover why the document was reprinted.

The document deals with the Indians and the offensive operations of the continuous Apache wars.

Although Ugarte was the *comandante general* he had two subordinates, and the frontier provinces were divided between them, Ugarte being in charge of Sonora and California, the inspector, Don Joseph Rengel, of Neuva Vizcaya and New Mexico, and Colonel Don Juan Ugalde, of Texas and Coahuila. Trading with the Indians was prohibited except in the presence of the *comandante.* In paragraph no. 112 Gálvez states that the punishment of the Yumas for their crime would have to wait until the Apaches were conquered. Paragraphs 162-170 treat of New Mexico, and 171-191 of Texas and Coahuila.

167A. EL REY

El Rey. Por quanto por Don Fray Antonio de los Reyes, Obispo de Sonora, y Don Felipe de Neve, Comandante General que fué de las Provincias Internas de Nueva España, se me ha representado con fechas de veinte y seis de Enero, y tres de Abril de mil setecientos ochenta y quatro, y correspondientes documentos, lo ocurrido acerca de la ereccion de la Custodia de San Gabriel, y arreglo de las Misiones de Californias . . . [At end]: Fecha en el Pardo á Vte y vno de Marzo de mil setecientos ochenta y siete.

Apparently this document is the original imprint of [illegible]80, which was printed in Mexico.

Folio, 2 unnumbered leaves.
Copy: JCB.

168. PALOÚ: Fr: Francisco

Relacion Historica De La Vida Y Apostolicas Tareas Del Venerable Padre Fray Junipero Serra, Y de las Misiones que fundó en la California Sep-

RELACION HISTORICA
DE LA VIDA
Y APOSTOLICAS TAREAS
DEL VENERABLE PADRE
FRAY JUNIPERO SERRA,

Y de las Misiones que fundó en la California Septentrional, y nuevos establecimientos de Monterey.

ESCRITA

Por el R. P. L. Fr. FRANCISCO PALOU, Guardian actual del Colegio Apostólico de S. Fernando de México, y Discipulo del Venerable Fundador:

DIRIGIDA

A SU SANTA PROVINCIA

DE LA REGULAR OBSERVANCIA

DE NRÒ. S. P. S. FRANCISCO

DE LA ISLA DE MALLORCA.

A EXPENSAS

DE DON MIGUEL GONZALEZ CALDERON

SINDICO DE DICHO APOSTOLICO COLEGIO.

Impresa en México, en la Imprenta de Don Felipe de Zúñiga y Ontiveros, calle del Espíritu Santo, año de 1787.

tentrional, y nuevos establecimientos de Monterey. Escrita Por el R. P. L. Fr. Francisco Palou, Guardian actual del Colegio Apostólico de S. Fernando de México, y Discípulo del Venerable Fundador: Dirigida A Su Santa Provincia De La Regular Observancia De Nrô. S.P.S. Francisco De La Isla De Mallorca. A Expensas De Varios Bienhechores.

Impresa en México, en la Imprenta de Don Felipe de Zúñiga y Ontiveros, calle del Espíritu Santo, año de 1787.

4°, title, 13 unnumbered preliminary leaves, portrait of Serra, 344 numbered pages, and a map.

Preliminaries: 5 leaves of dedication, 1 page of *protesta,* 6 pages of *pareceres,* 1 page of licenses, 6 pages of index of chapters, and 2 pages of prologue. Pages 342-344 contain the errata. The license of the government is dated December 7, 1786.

Map: Californias: Antigua Y Nueva Notas. En èsta Carta no se escrib^{n}. los nombr^{s}. de tód^{s}. las Islas, P,^{tos} Rios, y demàs, p^{r}. ser hecha p^{a}. solo demostrar lo q^{e}. andubo, y Mision^{s}. q^{e}. fundò en la Nvā Calif^{a}. el V.P. Fr. Junipero Serra, Presid^{te}. de èllas. La long. ès arreglada al meridiano de S. Blas. Diego Troncoso Sc. Mex^{co}. a^{0}. 1787.

I have some reason to think that this map was published before the book and that the first edition was issued without the words "Mar Pacifico," as Mr. Robert E. Cowan has such a copy and only one other appears to be known.

Many copies have at the end of the title, in place of the last sentence, the following: A Expensas De Don Miguel Gonzalez Calderon Sindico De Dicho Apostolico Colegio.

Copies: A, B, C, Cw, H, Har, J, JCB, LC, LAP, P, S, Southwest Museum, TWS, UT.

It was reprinted in Mexico, 1852, as the second part, pages 125-252, of Clavijero's *Historia de la Antigua ó Baja California*.

This work of Father Paloú is perhaps the best known of all works relating to California, or perhaps it would be better said, the most noted. As it was written in Spanish and not translated, most English-speaking people who do not understand Spanish know it only by reputation. It evidently had a considerable circulation, as many copies of it are extant. Notwithstanding its immense importance for the early history of Upper California it was never translated in full until 1913, when this was done by C. Scott Williams, and published in Pasadena, California, with an introduction and notes by George Wharton James, with a reproduction of the portrait of Serra and the map, together with a photograph of Serra's monument in Golden Gate Park, San Francisco. Previously, in 1890, Father Adam published a small book in English with translations of a few of the chapters, but this translation is even scarcer than the original.

Father Paloú inserted at the end of his book a reprint of *Tanto que se Sacó de una Carta* of Father Benavides. Both Paloú and Serra were from Mallorca, devoted friends and companions. An interesting life of Serra was published by Francisco Torrens y Nicolau in Mallorca in 1913, which contains some letters of Serra directed to friends in Mallorca which had not previously been published.

168a

Noticias De La Nueva California, Escritas Por El Rev. Padre Fr. Francisco Paloú.

San Francisco: Imprenta De Edouardo Bosqui y Cia. 1874.

8°, 4 vols. Vol. 1: xx, 270 pages, view of the mission of San Diego in 1873, view of the olive orchard there, and 2 views of

San Diego; vol. II: 301 pages, view of San Buenaventura, and 4 views of San Diego; vol. III: 315 pages, view of San Luis Rey in 1842, ground plan of San Luis Rey, view of Santa Clara, 1849, and 4 small views of the modern buildings there, view of the corridor at Santa Barbara; vol. IV: 253 pages, view of the custom house at San Francisco, 1846, view of the mission of Santa Barbara, and 2 views of the ruins of San Carlos.

This was issued under the auspices of the California Historical Society at the expense of Joseph A. Donohoe, and only one hundred copies were printed.

The work was reprinted, as far as the account of Nueva California is concerned, from the *Documentos para la historia de Mexico,* Mexico, 1857, fourth series, vols. 5-7.

In this work Paloú brought the history of California down to 1784, and although it might be supposed to be confined to Nueva California it also includes notices of Antigua California. It was printed from a copy in the Archivo General in Mexico in a *Colección de Memorias de Nueva España,* vols. 22 and 23, made in 1792 from the original which then existed in the College of San Fernando in Mexico but has now disappeared.

A new four-volume edition of Paloú's *Noticias,* edited by Herbert E. Bolton, was published by the University of California Press in 1926. This translation is based on the Fray Francisco García Figueroa copy of the lost original. A number of Paloú letters appeared in volume four.

The work was compiled by Father Paloú while in California, and largely while at the Dolores mission at San Francisco from information derived from individuals connected with the various expeditions to and in California, and from original narratives. It has the appearance of having been intended for publication, but probably the idea was abandoned and instead Paloú wrote his life of Serra. This latter contains substantially all that is to be found in the *Noticias,* although, of course, written in an entirely different style and with less detail.

In the reprint, in place of the introduction by Paloú, appears an historical introduction by John T. Doyle at whose instance the reprint was made.

168b

El Rey. Por quanto por Don Fray Antonio de los Reyes, Obispo de Sonora, y Don Felipe de Neve, Comandante General que fué de las Provincias Internas de Nueva España se me ha representado con fechas de veinte y seis de Enero, y tres de Abril de mil setecientos ochenta y quatro, y correspondientes documentos, lo ocurrido acerca de la erección de la Custodia de San Gabriel, y arreglo de las Misiones de Californias, . . .

4°, 3 unnumbered pages of text, n.p., n.d., but undoubtedly printed in Mexico.

This is a royal *cédula,* with the date added in handwriting as of March 21, 1787. It commands the use of some Franciscans from the province of Michoacán, and regular reports, biennially or triennially, by the political governors. It refers to all missions, not merely to those of California.

This information was supplied by Roland D. Hussey, who saw the document in the Archives of the Indies.

169. SANTA MARÍA: Fr. Vicente

Relacion Historica de la Colonia del Nuevo Santander y Costa del Seno Mexicano. Escrita por el P. Fr. Vicente Santa Maria Presbitero de la orden de San Francisco, . . . A expensas de los Sres. Conde de Sierra Gorda y sus hermanos.

[Mexico, 1787?]

This entire piece is reprinted in Boletín no. 8, pages 389-515, of the Sociedad Bibliografía Mexicana, from a *folletín* of the *Periódico Oficial* of the state of Tamaulipas, published in Ciudad Victoria.

According to the account given by Doctor León, who reprinted this document, the pamphlet printed in Ciudad Victoria was the only one that has been found, and this itself had been reprinted from a copy which has now disappeared, and which had probably been printed in Mexico in 1787.

170. ESTADO GENERAL

Estado general de las Missiones que tiene á su cargo la Religión Seráfica en las dos Américas, é Islas Filipinas, según consta de los documentos más modernos y seguros que se han remitido á este Oficio de la Comisaria General de Indias.

Madrid: En la oficina de Benito Cano, año de MDCCLXXXVIII.

Folio, title, 28 numbered pages.
Copies: AGI, 154-7-16, M.

This very rare pamphlet was republished in 1915 as appendix no. 2 to Maas' *Documentos*. It contains a list of all the Franciscan missions in the frontier provinces and in California, showing to which particular college or province they belonged.

171. LARRAÑAGA: Bruno Francisco

Prospecto de una Eneida Apostólico ô Epopeya, que celebra la predicacion del V. Apostol del Occidente Fr. Antonio Margil de Jesus: intitulada Margileida. Escrita con puros versos de P. Virgilio Maron, y traducida a verso castellano: la que se propone al publico de esta America Septentrional por subscripcion: Para que colectados

STORIA DELLA CALIFORNIA

OPERA POSTUMA

DEL NOB. SIG. ABATE

D. FRANCESCO SAVERIO CLAVIGERO.

TOMO PRIMO.

IN VENEZIA,

MDCCLXXXIX.

APPRESSO MODESTO FENZO.

Con Licenza de' Superiori, e Privilegio.

anticipadamente los gastos necesarios, se procede inmediatamente â su impression. Su autor Don Bruno Francisco Larrañaga.

Impressa en Mexico en la Imprenta nueva Madrileña de los Herederos del Lic. D. Joseph de Jauregui, Calle de S. Bernardo. Año de 1788.

4°, title, 1 unnumbered leaf, and 28 pages.

Preliminaries: The *protesta* on the verso of the title, leaf with opinion and the license of the government dated May 23. At the end of the text are the errata.

Copies: B, BM, M, UT.

According to this prospectus the work was going to appear in three volumes at the modest price of twelve pesos, but evidently subscribers were lacking as the work never appeared.

172. CLAVIJERO: P. Francisco Javier

Storia Della California Opera Postuma Del Nob. Sig. Abate D. Francesco Saverio Clavigero. Tomo Primo. [Printer's device.]

In Venezia, MDCCLXXXIX. Appresso Modesto Fenzo. Con Licenza de' Superiori, e Privilegio.

4°, 276 pages and an unnumbered leaf of errata; 212 pages and an unnumbered leaf of errata, map.

Preliminaries: Pages 3-13 of vol. I contain an account of Clavijero's writings, and pages 14-27 the preface to the work. Vol. II, pages 206-11, constitute the index, and page 212 is headed *Noi Riformatori*.

Map: Carta Della California suo Golfo e Contracoste Della Nuova Spagna, 273x368 mm. It was drawn by Don Raimondo Tarros, 1788, and engraved by J. Zambelli. In the introduction it is stated that the basis of the map was the one of Father Consag published in 1757 in the *Noticia de California*.

Copies: B, C, Cw, H, JCB, NYP, Southwest Museum, TWS, UT, W.

172a

Historia de la Antigua ó Baja California, Obra Postuma Del Padre Francisco Javier Clavijero, De La Compañia De Jesus. Traducida Del Italiano Por el presbitero don Nicolas Garcia de San Vicente. [Printer's device.]

Méjico. Imprenta De Juan R. Navarro, Editor. 1852.

8°, title, 2 leaves by the editor, 1 page by the translator, v pages of preface, 252 pages, and 6 unnumbered pages of index.

The book was issued as vol. II of the *Biblioteca Nacional y Extranjera,* and a leaf with this title is prefixed to the work. A few notes are added, among them the license conceded by the viceroy, February 6, 1697, to Fathers Salvatierra and Kino for their expedition to California. The editor states that he did not reproduce the map because it does not merit confidence, and in place thereof inserts a modern one, which he says presents greater possibilities of being exact. Pages 120-123 contain an appendix written by the translator, in which he refers briefly to the history subsequent to the expulsion of the Jesuits in 1767, and which contains a short account of the colonization of Upper California. Pages 125-252 contain a second edition of Paloú's life of Serra. I have never seen a copy with the map.

In the San Diego *Herald* of April 17, 1858, there began to appear a translation into English of this book, and the publication was continued until September 10, 1859, the translation getting as far as book II, chapter 30. According to correspondence left by Mr. E. W. Morse of San Diego it appears that Dr. John F. Hammond, an army doctor, was the translator. The suspension of the *Herald* in 1860 apparently ended the work.

About 1862 or 1863 some very short extracts were published in the *Historical Outline of Lower California.* Most of the facts regarding the Lower California missions in this pamphlet seem to have been derived from Clavijero, together with such information as the translator, M.E.R., was able to obtain in 1862. This pamphlet was published in San Francisco by Henry Payot in 79 pages, octavo.

173. LARRAÑAGA: Bruno Francisco

Apologia Por La Margileida Y Su Prospecto Y Satisfaccion de las notas de la Gazeta de Literatura Num. 1 de la Segunda subscripcion.

[Colophon:] Imprenta de los Herederos del Lic. D. Joseph de Jauregui año de 1789.

4°, 16 pages, with caption title only.

Copies: Georgetown University; to this is appended pages numbered 3-8 of poetry on Father Margil; UT.

This *Apología* was brought about by an attack in the *Gazeta,* probably the one which was written under the signature of J. L. M., that is, José Longinos Martínez.

174. ARRICIVITA: Fr. Juan Domingo

Crónica Seráfica Y Apostólica Del Colegio De Propaganda Fide De La Santa Cruz De Querétaro En La Nueva España, Dedicada Al Santísimo Patriarca El Señor San Joseph. Escrita Por el P. Fr. Juan Domingo Arricivita, Predicador Apostólico, ex-Prefecto, y Comisario habitual de las Misiones, Escritor Titular del Seminario, y su mas afecto Hijo. [Vignette.] Segunda Parte.

En México: Por Don Felipe de Zúñiga y Ontiveros, año de 1792.

Folio, title, 9 unnumbered leaves of preliminaries, 605 numbered pages of text, 1 of errata, and 7 of index unnumbered. Errors in pagination: 93 for 83, 94 for 84, 233 for 223, 213 for 313, 215 for 315, 884 for 484, and 334 for 534. Pages 247-250 are duplicated in some copies.

Preliminaries: 6 pages of dedication to San Joseph, 1 page of *parecer* of Miguel de Guevara, 1 page of license of the government, May 4, 1792, 1 page of *parecer* of Juan Antonio Chaves and the license of the ordinary, 1 page of approbation of Manuel Avella, 1 page of license of the commissary general, 4 pages of prologue, and 1 page of *protesta.*

Copies: A, B, GPH, Har, H, J, JCB, LAP, NYP, Southwest Museum, TWS, UT, Y.

From the *protesta* of the author and the space allotted to the life of Father Antonio Margil de Jesús it seems possible that the immediate cause of the publication of this work was the active proceedings taken in that particular year, 1792, in the *Causa* of his beatification.

The entire first book is devoted to the life of Father Antonio Margil de Jesús, while book II contains the lives of other illustrious members of the College, many of whom had been active in Texas. A long account is given of Fr. Francisco Hidalgo.

Pages 321-386 contain an account of the missions of Texas down to the time of the visit of the Marqués de Rubí, and pages 394-444 the history of the missions of Sonora beginning with the entry of the Franciscan fathers into that province in 1768.

Book IV contains the account of Father Francisco Garcés, with his various journeys and final murder on the Colorado river. For a long time this book was the principal, in fact only source for the history of the travels of Father Garcés and his two expeditions to California. Today, however, we have the diaries of these expeditions, which have to a large extent superseded this work; nevertheless the author has extracted from these diaries most of what is of any great importance.

174a

Sermon Que Èn Las Solemnes Honras Celebradas En Obsequio De Los VV. PP. Predicadores Apostólicos Fr. Francisco Tomas Hermenegildo Garcés: Fr. Juan Marcelo Diaz: Fr. José Matias Moreno: Fr. Juan Antonio Barreneche: Misioneros Del Colegio de Propaganda fide de la Santa Cruz de Queretaro, Fundadores de las Conversiones de la Purísima Concepcion, y de S. Pedro y S. Pablo del Rio Colorado entre los Gentiles Yumas, y muertos en ellas gloriosamente á manos de los mismos Bárbaros en los dias 17 y 19 de Julio de 1781 Dixo En La Iglesia De Dicho Colegio El 19 De Julio de 1794 En Que Se Sepultaron Sus Cenizas Fr. Diego Miguel Bringas De Manzaneda y Encinas, Misionero Apostólico, é Hijo del mismo Seminario, que reverente lo consagra á las Doctísimas, Religiosísimas y Santas Provincias de Franciscanos Observantes de la antigua y nueva España, á nombre del expresado Colegio de Misioneros de la Santa Cruz de Queretaro.

Madrid, Año 1819. En La Imprenta De D. Fermin Villalpando, Impresor De Camara De S. M.

4°, title, and pages numbered [3]-94.
Copies: J, UT.

For many purposes this sermon may be considered as a continuation of the work of Fr. Juan Domingo Arricivita, as the first part, to page 48, consists of historical notes about various Franciscan missionaries who labored in Sonora and Arizona at different times. There are also attached as footnotes to the sermon many valuable historical and geographical notes, together with much information, especially on Father Garcés.

In the first part will be found accounts of the following missionaries to the northern Indians from the College of Querétaro: Father Juan Chrisóstomo Gil de Bernabé who went to Sonora in 1767, became president of the missions, and founded one among the Seris, November 17, 1772, where he was killed by them on the 7th of March, 1773; Fr. Juan Alias, missionary to the Seris, who died in Querétaro July 31, 1799; Fr. Antonio Losilla; Fr. José del Rio, missionary for fifty-two years, chiefly in Texas and Sonora; Fr. Cayetano Aponte y Lis, who served ten years in Texas; Fr. Estevan de Salazar, missionary in Texas and Sonora; Fr. Sebastián Flores, the first *custodio* of San Carlos de Sonora; Fr. Marcos Guerena, missionary to Texas; Fr. Juan de Saróbe, who went to Sonora in 1768; Fr. Antonio Margil de Jesús; Fr. Felipe Guillén, who, after being two years in Texas, spent six years in Sonora, where he was killed by the Indians, April 27, 1778; and Fr. Francisco Roch, who spent twelve years in Sonora.

The author also refers to Fr. Francisco Casañas de Jesús María, who was killed by the Apaches (Jemez) in New Mexico in 1696 at the age of forty; Fr. José Guadalupe Ramírez de Pradò, missionary in Texas for twenty-seven years; Fr. Juan Salvador de Amaya, twenty-four years a missionary in Texas; and Fr. Diego Ursùa, missionary in Texas after 1758.

Long accounts are given of Fr. Pedro Font and Fr. Francisco Antonio Barbastro. Father Font became a missionary in 1763, and went to Sonora in 1773, where he died September 16, 1781, at the age of forty-three. Father Barbastro was the most noted of all the Franciscan missionaries of this epoch. He was almost always president of the conversions, and at one time was *custodio* of San Carlos. Father Barbastro was located at the pueblo Aconchi, where he died June 22, 1800, at the age of sixty-six. He left various writings, among others, notes for a history of Sonora. Father Bringas says that he visited him at Aconchi in 1795 and that he talked Opata as well as the Indians.

The account of the massacre of the four missionaries on the Colorado river in 1781 was apparently taken from the notes of Father Barbastro and from an account written by Don Pedro Fages.

Father Bringas, the author of this work, was a native of Alamos in Sonora, and was the most noted preacher in Mexico during the period from 1800 to the time of his leaving Mexico, probably in 1821. He was a very violent *realista* and published a number of pamphlets during the early days of the revolution, full of violent attacks on the revolutionists. In 1814 he was guardian of the College in Querétaro.

Although the Sermon was delivered in the College in 1794, I do not think that it was printed at that time or later in Mexico.

Dr. Elliott Coues published in 1900 in New York, *On the Trail of a Spanish Pioneer, the Diary and Itinerary of Francisco Garcés,* containing an appreciative account of that indefatigable explorer. In the introduction Dr. Coues refers to the loss of the original holograph of Father Garcés. What purported to be this original, together with an original map, was offered a few years ago by a well-known bookseller in Spain, but I understand that when it was sent to a collector in this country on approval it was pronounced only a copy.

Diario que formó el capitan D. José de Zúñiga en la espedicion destinada al reconocimiento, apertura y perfeccion del camino del Nuevo Mexico, para abrir el comercio con la provincia de Sonora: principiado en 9 de Abril de 1795.

Aurora. Periodico Cientifico Y Militar. Num. 1. Tomo 1. Mexico . . . 1835, pages 269-278.

This account was printed from the original diary of Captain Zúñiga with some notes of unknown origin but probably furnished by the editor of the periodical. The diary begins April 9, 1795, preceded by a list of the forces and officers who accompanied the expedition, and continues to their return on May 29 to the presidio of Tucson from which they had departed. They arrived at Zuñi on the 1st of May, where they found a Franciscan father. They remained there until the 7th, having sent a courier to Santa Fe to advise the governor of their arrival, but as no answer was received by that day, Zúñiga concluded to return. At the end is a *derrotero* from Zuñi to Tucson showing the distance marched to have been 108 leagues. In the notes at the end he states that he had with him the diary of Teniente Colonel Manuel Echeagaray of a reconnaissance which he had made in the year 1788 to the Sierra of San Francisco. Zúñiga had an Apache Indian as guide, and without him, he says, he would have had great trouble in finding the Spanish settlement. He mentions a previous expedition of Don José Saenz Rico, and another of Don Pedro de Mata, but it seems they did not go beyond what they called the San Francisco mountains.

Zúñiga's diary was translated into English by G. P. Hammond from the manuscript copy in the archives of the Indies and published in volume VI of the *New Mexico Historical Review,* January, 1931.

175. REAL ORDEN

Excmo. Señor En Papel de 21 del corriente me dice el Señor Conde del Campo de Alange lo que sigue . . .

San Lorenzo Nov. 23, 1792—Son copias. Mexico 12 Feb. 1793—Bonilla.

Folio, 4 pages.
Copy: LC.

This relates to a new constitution for the *comandancia general.*

176. PFEFFERKORN: Ignaz

Beschreibung der Landschaft Sonora samt andern merkwürdigen Nachrichten von den inneren Theilen Neu-Spaniens und Reise aus Amerika bis in Deutschland, nebst einer Landcharte von Sonora. Von Ignaz Pfefferkorn, eilfjährigen Missionar daselbst. Erster Band. [Woodcut.] Mit allergnädigster kaiserlicher Freiheit.

Auf Kosten des Verfassers gedrukt zu Köln am Rhein in der Langenschen Buchhandlung 1794.

8°, title, 7 unnumbered preliminary leaves, pages numbered 1-455, and 9 pages of register beginning on the verso of 455, map; title, pages numbered 1-447, register 13 pages beginning on the verso of 447. Sigs.: A-Ff; A-Ee, of eight leaves each, and Ff, of six each [besides the title].

Preliminaries: 4 pages of dedication, and 10 pages of *vorrede.*

Map: Folded map without the title showing Provincia de Sonora and Provincia de Ostimuri, also part of the peninsula of Lower California.

A third volume, dealing with Pfefferkorn's return to Germany, was apparently never issued.

Copies: LC, NYP.

Pfefferkorn came to America in 1755 in company with Joseph Och, Michael Gerstner, and Bernard Middendorf. They were at once sent out as missionaries among the Indians to replace those who had died or moved

Beschreibung
der
Landschaft

Sonora

samt
andern merkwürdigen Nachrichten
von den inneren Theilen

Neu-Spaniens
und
Reise aus Amerika
bis in
Deutschland,
nebst einer Landcharte von Sonora.

Von Ignaz Pfefferkorn,
eilfjährigen Missionar daselbst.

Erster Band.

Auf Kosten des Verfassers
gedrukt zu Köln am Rhein in der Langenschen
Buchhandlung 1794.

away. Father Middendorf went to the mission of Movas, Gerstner to Saric, and Och to Santa María Baseràca. Pfefferkorn was to reëstablish the mission of Sonóitac, but this plan was given up in favor of Ati, owing to the hostility of the Pápagos. He took up his post at Ati, among the Pimas, in 1756 and remained among them nearly seven years. Then, in ill health and in need of a change of environment, he was sent to Cucurpe, among the Eudebes, where he labored for four years, or until the expulsion of the Jesuits in 1767.

Pfefferkorn's account of Sonora consists largely of a detailed description of the province, including, in an introductory sketch, a discussion of its neighboring inhabitants and the efforts of the earlier missionaries, Kino, Sedelmeyer, and others, to convert the aboriginees. The author divides his work into a number of topics, volume I dealing with the following: the location and boundaries of Sonora; extent of Christianity in the province and attempts to found new missions; nature of the land, its fertility and climate; the vegetation of the region; mineral resources; discourse on the animal life of the area; appendices on the wild Apaches and Seris. Volume II (1795) treats mainly of the inhabitants, under the following divisions: physical appearance of the natives; their disposition and character; customs; ceremonies; dress, dwellings, and tools; scarcity of provisions; occupations of the men and women; mode of warfare; diseases, cures, and burial rites; religious practices of the unconverted; languages; behavior of the converted tribes, Opatas and Eudebes; establishment of the missions in Sonora; decline of the Indian population in America; local administration of the missions; the Spaniards in Sonora.

After the return to Germany of the expelled German missionaries, another wrote an account of his experiences,

NOTICIAS

DE LA PROVINCIA DE CALIFORNIAS

EN TRES CARTAS

DE UN SACERDOTE RELIGIOSO

HIJO DEL REAL CONVENTO

DE PREDICADORES DE VALENCIA

A UN AMIGO SUYO.

CARTA I.

EN VALENCIA
POR LOS HERMANOS DE ORGA.
M.DCC.XCIV.
CON LAS LICENCIAS NECESARIAS.

which was published in Murr's *Nachrichten*, Halle, 1809-11. I refer to the *Reise* of Father Och.

The best account extant of the Sonora missions just before the expulsion was written by Father Miguel Gerstner, a German missionary located at Saric, but for some reason it was never published, although evidently written for that purpose.

177. SALES: Fr. Luis

Noticias De La Provincia De Californias En Tres Cartas De Un Sacerdote Religioso Hijo Del Real Convento De Predicadores De Valencia A Un Amigo Suyo. Carta I.

En Valencia Por Los Hermanos De Orga. M.DCC.XCIV. Con Las Licencias Necesarias.

12°, title, leaf *Al que leyere,* text pages 5-104; new title the same as the first except Carta II, *Al que leyere* pages [3]-14, text pages 15-96; new title the same as the first except Carta III, *Al que leyere* pages [3]-6, text pages 7-104, and 2 folding tables between pages 98 and 99.

Tables: Estado general de las Misiones de la Provincia de California en el año 1787. Estado que manifiesta los Bienes que posee cada uno de las Misiones de esta Provincia en el año 1788.

Copies: A, B, BNP, Cw, C, H, J, JCB, LC, NYP.

I have seen it somewhere stated that the government was very much displeased at the publication of this book, which it seems had not been previously duly authorized, notwithstanding the fact that it contains on the title page "Con Las Licencias Necesarias." The letters are signed F. L. S., initials which have been identified as those of Fr. Luis Sales, a Dominican from Valencia.

Sales was located in Lower California and founded San Miguel, the most northerly and the last to be founded of the Lower California missions. His book is largely devoted to an account of the occurrences after the expulsion of the Jesuits, and contains accounts of the country, the animals, the Indians, and the trials of the missionaries. He states that the Venegas account is in error in certain respects because Venegas believed the Indians, and in any case did not know their ridiculous language. He thought that the Indians originated in Asia, and quotes Captain James Colnett as to the similarity of language of the northern Indians to that of the inhabitants in Asia. There are some remarks on the fur trade and the attempt of the Spanish government to initiate a trade with China on its own account. There are a few remarks on Upper California, which the author never saw, but he refers to a contemplated expedition from Monterey or the Rio San Francisco in 1785, eastward to New Mexico, which he offered to join, but which failed from lack of funds.

One of the chief elements of value in the *cartas* consists in a rather detailed account of the division of the province and the assignment of the lower part of it to the Dominicans. Sales inserts some copies of the original documents, a *cédula* to the viceroy, November 4, 1768, Father Iriarte's letter of July 10, 1770, and the Bishop of Sonora's letter from Alamos, December 13, 1783, to the *Comandante General.*

Pages 57-86 of Carta II contain—*Informe Que yo D. Josef Tobar y Tamáriz, primer Piloto de la Real Armada, doy al Excelentisimo Señor Virey de Nueva España, en obedecimiento de superior órden comunicada con fecha de 29 de Agosto de 1789.* This is an account of the Nootka expedition under Martínez, the capture of Colnett, and the occurrences while there, together with an account of the country and the Indians. Sales adds some remarks on the affair, and incidentally observes that he knew John Kendrick had coined money in his own name because he himself had four of these coins, which in one part had a sea with two ships on it and the name Washington, while on the other part were some letters which signified the expedition which he was undertaking to our continent. While Martínez did not molest Kendrick or Gray, Sales says that after the viceroy heard of the occurrences he sent an order to all the missions in California to seize Kendrick's ships in case they should appear at any of the ports.

The largest part of this *Informe* was reprinted in *El Viajero Universal,* tomo XXVI, Madrid, 1799, pages 157-168, from which extensive quotations were made by Bancroft in his *History of the Northwest Coast,* chapter VII of volume I, where will be found on page 186 a facsimile of the famous Columbian medal to which Sales refers.

The description of California contained in this book is copied largely into the same volume of the *Viajero Universal* in which the Tobar *Informe* appears. In fact that volume is made up almost entirely, so far as the account of California is concerned, from this book and that of Venegas, and contains no new material.

ERRATA

On page 234, line 10, and page 256, line 9, the words "Barcia Pinelo" should read "León Pinelo." Antonio León Pinelo's famous bibliography, *Epítome de la biblioteca, oriental i occidental, náutica i geográfica,* Madrid, 1629, was reissued by Andrés González Barcia as *Epítome de la bibliotheca, oriental y occidental, náutica y geográfica de Don Antonio de León Pinelo . . . añadido, y enmendado nuevamente, en que se contienen los escritores de las Indias orientales y occidentales,* Madrid, 1737-38, in 3 volumes.

BIBLIOGRAPHY

Alcazar, P. Bartolomé de. *Chrono-historia de la Compañia de Jesús en la Provincia de Toledo y elogios de sus varones illustres.* Madrid, 1710. 2 vols.

Contains in vol. II, p. 488, *Carta al Rector de Sinaloa de la Reduccion de los Indios del Rio Mayo por Diego Martinez de Hurdayde.*

Alcedo, Antonio de. *Biblioteca Americana. Catálogo de los autores que han escrito de la América en diferentes idiomas y noticias de su vida y patria, años en que vivieron y obras que escribieron. Compuesta año de 1807.*

This is a manuscript in the Harvard College library, formerly belonging to Jared Sparks, which has never been printed. There is another with the same title in the John Carter Brown library, no doubt another copy.

——*Diccionario geografico-histórico de las Indias occidentales ó América* ... Madrid, 1786-89. 5 vols. 4°.

This was translated into English, with additions, as: *The Geographical and Historical Dictionary of America and the West Indies.* By G. A. Thompson: London, 1812-15. 5 vols. and a large atlas of 19 maps by Arrowsmith. In the preface Thompson says that the original was suppressed by the Spanish government, but I doubt it. In the preface to part III Thompson has added a list of the chief books consulted by him in making the additions to the original. Part IV contains a table of the geographical observations. At present the work is of but little value except as used in conjunction with investigations of the period from 1775 to 1815. The atlas is now very scarce, as almost all copies have been broken up by dealers and the maps sold separately.

Alliot, Hector. *Bibliography of Arizona; being the record of literature collected by Joseph Amasa Munk, M.D., and donated by him to the Southwest Museum of Los Angeles, California.* Los Angeles, 1914.

This is the third edition, the first and second having been issued by Dr. Munk himself in 1900 and 1908. In 1908 Dr. Munk donated this very interesting collection to the Southwest Museum. The collection contains very few early works but had at least one rarity, the French edition of Benavides, Brussels, 1631, which Dr. Munk sold to Edward E. Ayer.

Andrade, José María. *Catalogue de la riche bibliothèque de . . . livres manuscrits et imprimés. Litterature Française et Espagnole . . .* Leipzig, 1869.

This was the first important collection of Mexican books to be sold at auction. The collection was made by Andrade, a bookseller in Mexico City, who sold it to the Emperor Maximilian. Many of the books passed into the possession of H. H. Bancroft and formed the nucleus of his famous collection.

Andrade, Vicente de P. *Ensayo bibliográfico Mexicano del siglo XVII.* Mexico, 1899.

This is a very scholarly work, now to a large extent superseded by Medina's bibliography of Mexico. It contains many facsimiles of the title pages of rare books, and many of the introductions containing valuable notices are reprinted. Andrade was the nephew of José María Andrade, and also a discriminating collector of rare books. Many of his valuable books passed into the hands of Federico Gómez de Orozco and subsequently into those of W. B. Stephens.

Antonio, Nicolás. *Bibliotheca hispana nova sive hispanorum scriptorum qui ab anno MD. ad MDCLXXXIV, floruere notitia. . . .* Matriti, Ibarra, MDCCLXXXII-VIII. 2 vols., folio.

This is the second edition, the first having appeared in Rome in 1672. This work contains information of much value, although the Spanish titles having been translated into Latin, great confusion arises in the identification of many works.

Atkinson, Geoffroy. *La littérature géographique française de la renaissance répertoire bibliographique.* Paris, 1927.

Backer, Augustin et Aloys de. *Bibliothèque des écrivains de la Compagnie de Jésus, ou notices bibliographiques: 1° de tous les ouvrages publiés par les membres de Jésus, depuis la fondation de l'ordre jusqu'á nos jours; 2° des apologies, des controverses religieuses, des critiques litteraires et scientifiques suscitees à leur sujet, par . . . de la meme Compagnie.* Liege, Grandmont-Donders, 1853-61. 7 vols. 4°.

A second edition was issued in Brussels, 1869-76, in 3 vols. This work is indispensable for a study of the bibliography of the subject.

Bancroft, Hubert Howe. *History of the North Mexican States and Texas.* San Francisco, 1884-89. 2 vols.

——*History of Arizona and New Mexico, 1530-1888.* San Francisco, 1889.

——*History of California.* San Francisco, 1884-90. 7 vols.

Bandelier, Adolph F. *Contributions to the history of the southwestern portion of the United States.* Cambridge, 1890. *Papers of the Archaeological Institute of America.* American Series, v.

——*Documentary history of the Rio Grande pueblos of New Mexico.* I. Bibliographic introduction. Archæological Institute of America, *Papers of the School of American Archaeology,* no. 13. Lancaster, Pa., 1910-11.

——*Final Report of investigations among the Indians of the Southwestern United States, carried on mainly in the years from 1880 to 1885.* Cambridge, Mass. Part I, 1890; Part II, 1892. *Papers of the Archaeological Institute of America.* American Series, III-IV.

——*The Gilded Man (El Dorado) and other pictures of the Spanish occupancy of America.* New York, 1893.

——*Historical introduction to studies among the sedentary Indians of New Mexico.* Boston, 1881. *Papers of the Archaeological Institute of America.* American Series, I.

——*Reports by A. F. Bandelier on his investigations in New Mexico during the years 1883-84.* Fifth *Annual Report* of the Executive Committee of the Archaeological Institute of America. Cambridge, 1884.

——*Report of an archaeological tour in Mexico in 1881.* Boston, 1884. *Papers of the Archaeological Institute of America.* American Series, II.

Barcia. See González Barcia.

Barrington, Daines. *Miscellanies.* London, 1781.

Contains Mourelle's Journal.

Beaumont, P. Pablo de la Purissima Concepcion. *Cronica de la provincia de los santos apostoles, S. Pedro y S. Pablo de Michoacan de la regular observancia de N. P. S. Francisco.* Mexico, 1873-74. 5 vols.

This work of Father Beaumont was written about 1780. Beaumont says that he had the papers of Pedro de Tovar, one of the principal figures in the Coronado expedition. For the early part he largely copied Father Tello. There are several manuscripts of this work in existence, one of which with maps and colored drawings is in the New York Public library. The manuscript fell into the hands of Bustamante, who published twenty-four chapters of the *Aparato* as *Historia del Descubrimiento de la America Septentrional por Christobal Colon, escrito por Fr. Manuel de la Vega.* In 1855 publication of it was begun in Morelia in the *folletín* of a newspaper and the *Aparato* and 184 pages of the *Crónica* were printed. At that time several manuscript copies of the book were in circulation, in Mexico, one of which belonged to José F. Ramírez and which was later sold at the Ramírez sale in 1880. Alfredo Chavero bought it and brought it back to Mexico, and it was from this copy that the book was finally printed in 1873, but without the map of Michoacán which was attached to the manuscript. The *Crónica* only covers events up to 1566. The author quotes extensively from all the well-known authorities. His account of Marcos de Niza, pages 143 *et seq.*, of vol. IV, is much confused.

Beristain y Souza, José Mariano. *Biblioteca Hispano-Americana Septentrional.* Mexico, 1816. Vol. II, 1819. Vol. III, 1821. Large 4°.

Stevens, in the *Historical Nuggets,* instead of putting a price on this work has marked it priceless. The facts are that vol. I is not an especially rare book, but Beristain having died, the other two volumes were brought out by his nephew, and probably on account of the troubled state of affairs in Mexico at the time, very few copies were sold; as a result these last two volumes are excessively rare, and only a few complete copies are known to exist. Lacking collations, this work today is valuable only for the immense amount of information it contains of manuscripts which then existed in the monastic libraries of Mexico.

——*Biblioteca Hispano Americana Setentrional.* Segunda edicion. Amecameca, 1883-1897. 3 vols. Tomo IV, Comprende los anónimos que dejó escritos el autor, las adiciones del Dr. Osores y otras añadidas posteriormente por las personas que se expresan. J. T. Medina publícalo ahora con una introducción bio-bibliográfica. Santiago de Chile, 1897. 8°, liii, 198 pp. and 1 p. of index.

——[The same]—adiciones y correcciones, etc. [of Ramírez] . . . *publícanlas Lic. Victoriano Agüeros y El Dr. N. Leon.* Mexico, 1898. 659 pp. and photo of José Fernández Ramírez.

This is the only available edition of Beristain. The supplementary volumes contain considerable valuable information.

Biblioteca de Autores Españoles desde la formación del lenguaje hasta nuestros dias. Historiadores primitivos de Indias. Colección dirigida é ilustrada por Don Enrique de Vedia. Tomo Primero. Madrid. 1852. 2 vols. 8°. Vol. I, 599 pp. Vol. II, 574 pp. Second edition, 1877.

Bibliotheca Mejicana. Catalogue of an extraordinary collection of books and manuscripts, almost wholly relating to the history and literature of North and South America, particularly Mexico. Sold by Puttick and Simpson, June 1, 1869, and seven following days.

This is the famous collection of Father Fischer down to no. 2038. The rest of the collection, also a rare and notable one, belonged to Dr. Berendt of Vera Cruz, and contained a number of very rare early American and English books.

Bolton, Herbert E. *Guide to materials for the history of the United States in the principal archives of Mexico.* Washington, D. C., 1913.

——*Spanish Exploration in the Southwest, 1542-1706.* New York, 1916.

——*Kino's historical memoir of Pimería Alta.* Cleveland, 1919. 2 vols.

The basis of this book is a translation of Kino's *Favores Celestiales,* the manuscript of which Dr. Bolton found in the Archives of Mexico. The substance of it had already been printed in the *Apostólicos Afanes,* published in Barcelona in 1754.

——*Historical memoirs of New California, by Fray Francisco Palóu, O. F. M.* Berkeley, 1926. 4 vols.

——*Anza's California expeditions.* Berkeley, 1930. 5 vols.

——*Rim of Christendom: a biography of Eusebio Kino, Pacific coast pioneer.* New York, 1936.

Bondoy, Fr. Francisco. *Chronica seraphica de la santa provincia de Mallorca de la regular observancia de N. S. P. S. Francisco . . .* Año de 1814.

See Civezza, *Saggio,* no. 84, for a long account of his manuscript, which contains a life of Serra.

Carayon, P. Auguste. *Bibliographie historique de la Compagnie de Jésus ou catalogue des ouvrages relatifs à l'histoire des Jésuites depuis leur origine jusqu'a nos jours.* Paris, 1864.

This contains, in the appendix, a list of the letters in Stöcklein.

Carrasco y Guisasola. *Documentos referentes al reconocimiento de las costas de las Californias, desde el cabo de San Lucas al de Mendocino recopiladas en el archivo de Indias.* Madrid, 1882.

Cartas de Indias. Publícalas por primera vez el ministerio de Fomento. Madrid, 1877.

This volume contains XVI, 877 pages of letter press, 67 leaves of facsimile reproductions from unpublished documents, 22 leaves of facsimile autographs, and 4 maps reproduced in facsimile from unique originals.

Cartas Edifiantes, y Curiosas, escritas de las missiones estrangeras, por algunos missioneros de la Compañia de Jesús: Traducidas del idioma francés por el Padre Diego Davin, de la Compañia de Jesus. Madrid, 1753-57. 16 vols. 4°.

The California material is contained in vol. III.

Cavo, P. Andrés. *Los tres siglos de Mexico durante el gobierno español hasta la entrada del ejército trigarante. . . .* Publícala con notas y supplemento el Lic. Carlos María de Bustamante. Mexico, 1836-38. 2 vols. and 2 of supplement.

Cavo, one of the expelled Jesuits, wrote only the part to 1766, Bustamante in his characteristic manner making two volumes with which Cavo had nothing to do. Cavo himself, who was born in 1739 and became a Jesuit in 1758, had very little first-hand knowledge of the subject, and wrote largely from previously published sources, concluding the work about 1790.

Chapman, Charles E. *Catalogue of materials in the Archivo General de Indias for the history of the Pacific coast and the American southwest.* Berkeley, 1919.

The documents for the earlier period occupy a very small space in the book, but from 1750 on the calendar is very voluminous. About 25,000 separate documents are listed, in chronological order, and they are described as to technical characteristics and contents. Approximately two-thirds of the material in the catalogue deals with the Californias.

——*The Founding of Spanish California, 1687-1783.* New York, 1916.

At the end are appended some bibliographical notes concerning printed sources and manuscript material.

——*A History of California, the Spanish period.* New York, 1921.

This work consists for the most part of Professor Chapman's lectures at the University of California, and is written in what might be called popular style. The basis for the book seems to be Professor Chapman's previous book, *The Founding of Spanish California,* and Bancroft's *History of California* for the later epoch.

Chronica Seraphica de la provincia de Castilla.

This is a manuscript in 3 vols. folio, now in the *Colegio Franciscana de Pastrana.* Civezza, no. 139, says it contains an account of the College of Santa Cruz de Querétaro, and much information on Florida and Mexico, and includes many biographies.

There is also in the same library another one-volume manuscript with the same title, but earlier than this.

Civezza. *See* Marcellino da Civezza.

Clemente P. Claudio (Juan Eusebio Nieremberg). *Tablas chronologicas, en que se contienen los sucesos eclesiásticos y seculares de España, Africa, Indias Orientales y Occidentales desde su principio hasta el año 1642.* Madrid, 1643, 12°

——[The same] . . . *illustradas é añadidas desde el año 1642 hasta el presente de 1689, por el Lic. Vicente Joseph Miguel* . . . Valencia, 1689. 4°, title, 7 preliminary leaves and 275 pages.

This work was much used and quoted by later Spanish authors, although now little known.

Cole, George Watson. *Catalogue of books relating to the discovery and early history of North and South America.* New York, 1907. 5 vols.

This is usually known as the Church catalogue, describing a very notable collection of books which passed into the hands of Henry E. Huntington. The catalogue records books dated as late as 1884.

Colección de documentos inéditos para la historia de España. Madrid, 1842-1895. 112 volumes, 4°.

This collection was begun by Martín Fernández Navarrete and Miguel Salvá, and was continued by various Spanish historians, including José Sancho Rayón and Francisco de Zabálburu. Vols. I, II, IV, XVI, XXII and CIV, contain documents relating to Cortés; vols. VIII and XIII documents relative to Andrés Marcos Burriel; vol. XV *Exámen historico critico de los viajes y descubrimientos apócrifos del capitán Lorenzo Ferrer Maldonado,* etc. by Martín Fernández Navarrete; vol. LIII contains another version of Motolinía's *Ritos Antiguos,* etc.; and vols. LXII-LXVI contain *Historia de las Indias* by Las Casas.

Colección de documentos inéditos relativos al descubrimiento conquista y colonizacion de las posesiones Españolas, en América y Oceanía. Madrid, 1864-1884. 42 vols., 8°.

This collection was published under the direction of Señores J. F. Pacheco, F. de Cárdenas, and L. Torres de Mendoza, and is usually known as the Pacheco-Cárdenas collection. Second series, 1900. 13 vols.

Colección de documentos para la historia de México. Mexico, 1858 and 1866. 2 vols. 4°.

This collection was printed by Joaquín García Icazbalceta, largely from documents in his possession. The notes which Señor García Icazbalceta has prefixed to the documents are not the least interesting part of the collection.

Cortés, Hernán. *Escritos sueltos de Hernán Cortés. Colección formada para servir de complemento a "las cartas de relaciones."* Mexico, 1871.

Coues, Elliott. *On the trail of a Spanish pioneer, the diary and itinerary of Francisco Garcés in his travels through Sonora, Arizona, and California, 1775-1776.* New York, 1900. 2 vols.

Dr. Coues edited Garcés' diary from two copies in manuscript, one of which is in the Bureau of American Ethnology in Washington, and from a printed copy in vol. 1, pages 225-374 of the second series of the *Documentos para la historia de Mexico.* The original diary of Garcés appears to be unknown. Recently a well-known Madrid bookseller offered what he asserted to be the original with a map, but I understand that on examination it proved to be a copy.

Court, J. *Catalogue de la précieuse bibliothèque de Feu M. le Docteur J. Court,* Paris, 1884.

This collection embraced many extremely rare and interesting early American works, and was arranged by Charles Leclerc, who has added collations to some of the rarest pieces.

Cowan, Robert E. *A bibliography of the history of California and the Pacific west, 1510-1906.* San Francisco, 1914.

This was the first bibliography of California which had been printed in book form, the only previous effort being that of Alexander S. Taylor, published in the Sacramento Daily Union, June 25, 1863, and supplements. This work of Mr. Cowan does not pretend to be a complete bibliography but only a selection of the more important works. Nevertheless for certain periods very little has been omitted.

——*A Bibliography of the History of California, 1510-1930.* By Robert Ernest Cowan and Robert Granniss Cowan. San Francisco, 1933. 3 vols.

The number of titles, in the original work, was about eight hundred and fifty. In this edition there are nearly five thousand.

Cuevas, P. Mariano, S. J. *Cartas y otros documentos de Hernán Cortés novisimamente descubiertos en el Archivo General de Indias.* Sevilla, 1915.

Included among these documents are several relating to Cortés' expeditions to California, a few of which had been previously printed.

——*Documentos inéditos del siglo XVI para la historia de Mexico.* Mexico . . . 1914.

This collection is made up chiefly from originals in the archives in Seville.

Davila y Arrillaga, José Mariano. *Continuación de la historia de la compañia de Jesús en Nueva España, del P. Francisco Javier Alegre.* Puebla, 1888-89. 2 vols.

Daza, Fr. Antonio. *Qvarta parte de la Chronica general de Ntro. Padre San Francisco y de su Apostolica Orden compuesta por Fray Antonio Daça . . . Año de 1611.* Impresa en San Francisco de Valladolid por Juan Godines de Millis y Diego de Cordova. Folio, engraved title, 13 leaves of preliminaries, 220, 375, 344, 304 pp., 9 leaves of index and one of colophon.

Díaz del Castillo, Bernal. *Historia verdadera de la conquista de la Nueva-España.* Madrid, 1632. Another edition without date with an extra chapter.

Diccionario universal de historia y de geografía. Mexico, 1853-56.

This work consists of ten volumes, the first seven being copied from the original printed in Spain, with many additions and changes, while the last three volumes, edited by Manuel Orozco y Berra, form a special appendix on Mexican subjects, the articles being contributed by the best known writers of the day, including Lucas Alamán, José María Andrade, Icazbalceta, and others. A number of original documents were published in this edition.

Documentos para la historia de Mexico. Mexico, 1853-57.

Series I consists of 7 vols., Series II of 5 vols., Series III of 4 parts in one large folio vol., and Series IV of 7 vols. Series III and IV contain the documents referring to Texas, New Mexico, Sonora, and California. The single volume of the third series is extremely rare, and is usually found imperfect. There is a perfect copy of it in the García collection at the University of Texas and another in the library of the University of Mexico. It is supposed to be complete in 932 pages. The fifth volume of the Second Series was never terminated.

Dorantes de Carranza, Baltasar. *Sumaria relacion de las cosas de la Nueva España* . . . La publica por primera vez el Museo Nacional de Mexico. Mexico, 1902.

Baltasar was the son of Andrés Dorantes, one of the three companions of Cabeza de Vaca. The book contains nothing of any value on the wanderings of the party.

Eguiara y Eguren, Juan Joseph de. *Bibliotheca Mexicana, sive eruditorum historia virorum qui in America Boreali nati, vel alibi geniti, in ipsam domicilio aut studijs asciti, quavis linguâ scripto aliquid tradiderunt.* Tomus Primus, exhibens Litteras ABC. Mexici: . . . in Aedibus Authoris, 1755. Folio, half-title, title, 78 preliminary leaves, 543 pages of text.

Engelhardt, Fr. Zephyrin. *The Franciscans in Arizona.* Harbor Springs, Michigan, 1899.

Father Engelhardt wrote this book largely from Arricivita's book published in 1792 and Bancroft's book for the subsequent period. The fact is that there are not many documents existing of the time after 1791.

——*The missions and missionaries of California.* 4 vols. and an index. San Francisco, 1908-16, the index which covered vols. II-IV being published in the latter year.

These volumes of Father Engelhardt contain the general history of the missions, with many facsimiles of autographs and views and portraits. Father Engelhardt was later engaged in writing up the local history of each mission, most of which accounts were published before he died in 1934. Previous to coming to California he wrote a short account of the missions of California.

Escalona Aguero, Gaspar de. *Gazophilativm Regivm Pervbicvm* . . . Madrid, 1647.

Another edition appeared in 1675.

Although this work has a Latin title it also contains a Spanish part.

Fernández de Navarrete, Martín. *Bibliotheca marítima Española, obra póstuma.* Madrid, 1851. 2 vols.

This work was begun by Navarrete, possibly as early as 1789, but the author died before he finished it and the work was finally published by his son. As a record of valuable manuscripts to be found in the archives in Spain it still remains of the greatest significance, quite a few of the most important having disappeared since his day.

——*Relacion del viage hecho por las goletas Sutil y Mexicana en el año de 1792.* Madrid, 1802. Title, 7 leaves of indexes, clxviii, 185 pp., folding table between pp. 167 and 168, and a folio atlas with title and leaf of explanation of the plates, 17 in number. An appendix appeared in 1806.

The pages numbered in Roman letters constitute the famous introduction written by Navarrete, comprising a history of exploration on the west coast and northwest coast of America.

Fernández de Oviedo y Valdés, Gonzalo. *Historia general y natural de las Indias, islas y tierra-firme del Mar Oceano.* Madrid, 1851-55. 4 vols.

A small part of this work had been previously printed in 1535 and 1557, and great difficulty was experienced in getting together the manuscript of the remainder. As it is, the work was not finished, there being a number of chapter headings inserted for chapters never filled out; and besides Oviedo promised another volume to bring up to 1550 the history of New Spain. His account of that country ends about 1540 or 1541. The book is an immense storehouse of facts recited without much order or plan. What is needed is an index, for unless one has read the entire work it is not possible to be certain that it does not contain an account of some particular occurrence.

Fernández Duro, Cesáreo. *Don Diego de Peñalosa y su descubrimiento del reino de Quivira. Informe presentado a la Real Academia de la Historia.* Madrid, 1882.

Field, Thomas W. *An essay towards an Indian bibliography.* New York 1873.

This valuable work, made interesting by the extensive notes which Mr. Field has appended to a number of his descriptions, has proved a fertile field for enterprising booksellers. I do not know how many hundreds of times his remarks about Herrera have been printed.

Figueroa, Antonio de la Rosa. *Bezerro general, menologico y chronologico de todos los religiosos que . . . ha avido en esta Sta. Provincia del Sto. Evangelio desde su fundacion hasta el preste. año de 1764 y de todos los Prelados assi ñros. M. Rdos. P.P. Comissars. como Rdos. P.P. Provinciales que la han governado, dispuesto . . .*

A manuscript in the Ramírez sale, no. 315, of the first part only down to about 1700, the second part being missing. This manuscript was bought by Quaritch and is now in the Ayer collection in the Newberry library, Chicago.

Florencia, Francisco de, and Oviedo, J. A. de. *Menologio de los varones mas señalados en perfeccion religiosa de la provincia de la Compañia de Jesús de la Nueva España, escrita por el padre Francisco de Florencia . . . nuevamente añadido . . . por P. Juan Antonio de Oviedo.* [Mexico, 1747.] 4°, title, 3 preliminary leaves and 228 pages.

Frejes, Francisco. *Historia breve de la conquista de los estados independientes del Imperio Mexicano.* Guadalajara, 1823.

This is the first edition of this famous book, of which only a few copies are known. It was reprinted in Mexico in 1839, and in Guadalajara in 1878.

French, B. F. *Historical collections of Louisiana.* New York, 1846-75. 7 vols.

Part I contains the documents referring to La Salle's last expedition.

Friccius, Valentinus. *Indianischer religionstadt der gantzen newen Welt.* Ingoldstadt, 1588. 8°, title and 15 preliminary leaves, 200 pp.

This is a translation of a part of Gonzaga, and also contains extracts from Valades.

Gallatin, A. *Ancient Semi-civilization of New Mexico, Rio Gila, and its vicinity.* American Ethnological Society, *Transactions,* II. New York, 1848.

Galvão, Antonio. *Tratado . . . e assi de todos os descobrimentos antigos e modernos . . .* [Lisbon, 1563.] Another edition in Lisbon, 1731.

García, Genaro, editor. *Historia de Nueva León.* Mexico, 1909.

García Icazbalceta, Joaquín. *Documentos historicos de Mexico manuscritos de la colección del Señor don Joaquín García Icazbalceta.* Mexico, 1903-1907. 5 vols.

This series was published by Luis García Pimentel after the death of his father, Joaquín García Icazbalceta.

Vol. I contains the *Memoriales de Fray Toribio de Motolinía,* which in many respects is different from the *Historia de los Indios* published in the *Colección de Documentos.* The other volumes contain matters of no interest to this work.

——*Nueva Colección de documentos para la historia de Mexico.* Mexico, 1886-1892. 5 vols.

Published by Icazbalceta, largely from documents in his possession, and especially valuable for the letters, memorials, etc., of the early Franciscan missionaries.

Gonzaga, Francisco. *De origine seraphicae religionis Frãciscanae eiusque progressibus . . .* Romae, 1587.

Folio, engraved title, 2 unnumbered leaves of preliminaries, 1363[1] pages and 10 unnumbered leaves, 104 plates in the pagination.

González Barcia, Andrés. *Ensayo cronológico para la historia general de la Florida.* Madrid, 1723. See no. 84.

——*Epítome de la Bibliotheca, oriental y occidental, náutica y geográfica de Don Antonio de Léon Pinelo . . . añadido, y enmendado nuevamente, en que se contienen los escritores de las Indias orientales y occidentales . . .* Madrid, Francisco Martinez Abad, 1737-38, 3 vols. folio. Title, 20 leaves, 561 pages, and 53 unnumbered leaves; title leaf, pages 561-1191, appendix 1192 to M.CCXXXVIII; title leaf, pages 1200 to 1729, plus 133 pages of index.

This monumental work contains so much that is useful together with so much that is worthless and incorrect that it has ceased to be anything more than a place to hunt for titles or dates of printing of books which can no longer be found. The arrangement also is extremely bad, making reference to it a work of great uncertainty. Nevertheless for a long time it was the only bibliography of Spanish Americana from which a collector could obtain any information.

——*Historiadores primitivos de las Indias occidentales* . . . Madrid, 1749. 3 vols.

Although this work bears the date of 1749 on the title-page, most if not all of the pieces were printed previously, but it is probable that it was not put on the market and sold until 1749, after Barcia's death. Medina, no. 3499, of his *Biblioteca Hispano Americana,* says that early in the 19th century 1,300 copies of this were turned out as waste paper in Madrid, including 21 on large paper, which he thought were probably all of the large paper copies that had been printed, as he says that none are now known. I have, however, seen somewhere a reference to a copy on large paper. Sixteen pieces in all appeared in this collection, to which was prefixed a title and a leaf of index to the 3 vols. The *Relación* of Oviedo appears in all the copies which I have seen, without the title-page, although the text begins on what is page 3, indicating that a title-page was published or was intended to be published. The collection is not so rare as it was once supposed to be.

González de Torres, Fr. Eusebio. *Chronica seraphica.* En Madrid, en la imprenta de la viuda de Juan Infanzon. 4 vols. folio. Vol. I, 1719, 580 pp.; vol. II, 1725, 598 pp.; vol. III, 1729, 564 pp.; vol. IV, 1737, 392 pp.

This is a continuation of Cornejo.

Griffin, A. P. C. *A list of books on the Philippine Islands in the Library of Congress . . . with a chronological list of maps by P. Lee Phillips.* Washington, 1903.

Hakluyt, Richard. *The principall navigations, voiages and discoveries of the English nation.* London, 1589. A final and enlarged edition was published in London, 1598 [1599]-1600, in 3 vols. and called *The principal navigations, voyages, traffiques and discoveries of the English nation.*

The most available edition is that of Maclehose, Glasgow, 1903, in 12 vols. This retains the pagination of the original.

Hammond, George P. *Don Juan de Oñate and the founding of New Mexico.* Santa Fe, 1927.

——, and Rey, Agapito. *Expedition into New Mexico made by Antonio de Espejo, 1582-1583, as revealed in the journal of Diego Pérez de Luxán, a member of the party.* Los Angeles, The Quivira Society, vol. I, 1929.

——, and Rey, Agapito. *The Gallegos relation of the Rodríguez expedition to New Mexico.* Santa Fe, 1927.

——, and Rey, Agapito. *Obregón's history of 16th century explorations in western America.* Los Angeles, 1928.

This translation was made from a photostatic copy of the original in the Archives of the Indies in Seville. Before the appearance of this edition, Father Mariano Cuevas edited the manuscript, with some omissions, for the Secretaría de Educación Pública in Mexico, which published the work in 1924 as *Historia de los descubrimientos antiguos y modernos de la Nueva España.*

Haroldus, Fr. Franciscus. *Epitome annalium ordinis minorem.* Rome, 1662. Folio, 2 vols. Title, 5 leaves and 1585 pages; 990 pages.

Herrera, Antonio de. *Historia general del mundo.* Vol. I, Madrid, 1601, Valladolid, 1606; II, Valladolid, 1606; III, Madrid, 1612.

Hodge, F. W. *Bibliography of Fray Alonso de Benavides.* Vol. III, no. 1, of *Indian Notes and Monographs* of the Museum of the American Indian. New York, 1919.

This is an amplification of Dr. Hodge's notes to Mrs. E. E. Ayer's edition of Benavides' *Memorial* with a supplementary account of a manuscript memorial and other documents of Benavides of 1634 recently found in the Propaganda archives at Rome.

——, editor. *Handbook of American Indians north of Mexico.* Washington, 1907-10. 2 vols.

——*History of Hawikuh, New Mexico, one of the so-called cities of Cíbola.* Los Angeles, 1937.

Icazbalceta. See García Icazbalceta.

John Carter Brown library. *Biblioteca Americana. Catalogue of books relating to North and South America. With notes by John Russell Bartlett.* Various editions of this were published; perhaps the best known is one in 4 vols., Providence, 1871-75. A second edition was issued in 1882.

——*Catalogue of the.* Providence, 1919-31. 5 vols.

Laet, J. de. *Nieuwe Wereldt ofte Beschrijvinghe van West-Indien, . . .* Leyden, 1625. Folio. First French edition, 1640, Leyden.

This work contains many extracts from Spanish writers on New Mexico, California, etc.

Land of Sunshine. Los Angeles, June, 1894-December, 1901, 15 vols.

Charles F. Lummis while editing this magazine published in it translations of various important Spanish books and pamphlets relating to California and New Mexico, notably the Benavides *Memorial,* the *Verdadera Relacion* and *Segunda Relacion* of Estevan de Perea, the *Estracto de Noticias,* and the *Diario Historico* of Costansó.

Lasor A Varea, Alphonsus. *Universus terrarum orbis scriptorum calamo delineatus.* Patavii, 1713. 2 vols. folio.

The first 60 pages of the work consist of an index of authors cited in the book. The author's name was Savonarola.

Leclerc, Charles. *Bibliotheca Americana. Catalogue raisonné.* Paris, 1867.

This is an auction-sale catalogue of 1647 items, with descriptions, and, in most cases, collations by the well-known bibliographer, Leclerc. He describes many books of great interest and rarity.

——*Bibliotheca Americana.* Paris, 1878. Supplement no. 1, November, 1881; supplement no. 2, 1887.

These are sale catalogues of the house of Maisonneuve et Cie. and are extremely valuable for the descriptions and the collations which are as a rule correct. It may be noted that in the collations, where not otherwise mentioned, the preliminaries do not contain the title. This method is productive of great confusion. Where the number of leaves or pages is stated without reference to the title, the title is included.

León, Dr. Nicolás. *Instituto Bibliografico Mexicano del siglo XVIII, Boletín.* Mexico, 1902-1908. 9 parts issued. This contains Dr. León's *Bibliografia Mexicana* in nos. 1, 4, 5, 7 and 8.

León [Pinelo], Antonio de. *Epítome de la Biblioteca, oriental i occidental náutica i geográfica.* Madrid, Juan González, 1629. 4°, engraved title, 43 preliminary leaves, 186 pages, plus xii of appendix and 1 unnumbered leaf.

This is the first American bibliography and in many respects is better than some published after it.

See González Barcia for second edition.

——*Tablas cronológicas de los reales consejos supremos de la camara de las indias occidentales.* Madrid, 1892.

Lettres édifiantes et curieuses, écrites des missions étrangères par quelques missionaires de la Compagnie de Jesus. Paris, 1703-1776. 34 vols. usually in 32 for the reason that vols. 1-3 are bound together. 28 vols. were issued up to 1758, when the work was suspended until 1773, 6 vols. being published between 1773 and 1776. Some of the vols. were reprinted in 1707 and again in 1713, 1724, etc. A new edition was published in Paris, 1780-1783, in 26 vols. and an additional volume containing the maps and folding plates. In this the material is the same as in the original but systematically arranged. Later editions were issued in 1810-11 and in 1838. An edition was published in Italian in Milan, 1825-29, in 18 vols. 8°.

List of works relating to Mexico. Bulletin of the New York Public library, October, November, and December, 1909.

The New York Public library has a remarkable collection of works relating to the discovery period, including what is perhaps the largest collection of the works of López de Gómara to be found in any library, and these works are duly described in this Bulletin. For the later period the collection is not so complete.

Lockman, John. *Travels of the Jesuits.* London, 1743. 2 vols. Second edition, 1762.

López de Velasco, Juan. *Geografía y descripción universal de las Indias. Recopilada por el cosmógrafo-cronista, Juan López de Velasco desde el año de 1571 al de 1574, publicada por primera vez en el Boletín de la Sociedad Geográfica de Madrid. Con adiciones é ilustraciones, por Don Justo Zaragoza.* Madrid, 1894. xiii, 808 pages, also very large folding map. Small 4°.

Lowery, Woodbury. *The Spanish settlements within the present limits of the United States, 1513-61.* New York, 1901.

Mr. Lowery was chiefly interested in the early history of Florida, but he devotes chapters to the discovery of California, the expedition of Cabeza de Vaca, and the expeditions of Coronado and Marcos de Niza. The appendix to vol. I contains some notes on the credibility of the stories of Cabeza de Vaca and Marcos de Niza.

Maas, P. Otto. *Viajes de misioneros Franciscanos a la conquista del Nuevo Mexico.* Documentos del Archivo General de Indias [Sevilla]. Sevilla, 1915.

A very interesting collection containing large extracts from the diary of Father Garcés and a reproduction of the map of his journey from the original in the archives. About half the volume contains interesting documents concerning Texas.

Malo de Luque, Eduardo [i. e., El Duque de Almodóvar]. *Historia política de los establecimientos ultramarinos de las naciones europeas.* Tomo I. En Madrid. Por D. Antonio de Sancha. Año de M.DCC.LXXXIV. 8°. 5 vols. Folding maps and tables. Vol. I: Frontispiece, prologue, and contents, xvi, 405 pp.; II: Prologue, contents, and errata, xii, 109 pp.; III: Prologue, contents and errata xii, 336 pp., appendix 68 pp.; IV: Prologue and contents xv, 607 pp.; V: Prologue, contents and errata xiv, 384 pp., additional 138 pp.

Translated with some additions from Raynal's *Histoire philosophique et politique des établissements et du commerce dans les deux Indes.* Geneva, 1780.

Maneiri [or Maneirus], J. A. *De vitis aliquot mexicanorum aliorumque qui sive virtute, sive litteris Mexici imprimis floruerunt.* Bononiae, ex Typ. Laelii a Vulpe, 1791. De Vita Antonii Lopezii Portilli, 1791. Also in Bonn. 8°, vol. I, 410 pp.; vol. II, 412 pp.; vol. III, 324 pp. plus 54 (2) pages of the Life of Portillo.

Manje, Juan Matheo. *Luz de tierra incógnita en la América septentrional y diario de las exploraciones en Sonora.* Part I in MS. is in the Biblioteca Nacional of Mexico. Part II was printed in *Documentos para la historia de Mexico,* series IV, vol. I, pages 226-402. Both have since been printed by the Secretaría de Gobernación of Mexico, 1926.

Mapoteca de América. Madrid. Hijos de J. A. García, 1899.

Marcellino da Civezza. *Saggio di bibliografia geografica storica etnografica Sanfrancescana.* Prato, 1879. Large 8°, XIV, 698 pp.

An exceedingly valuable contribution to the bibliography of the Franciscan order.

——*Storia universale delle missioni francescane del Fr. Marcellino da Civezza, M. O. della Provincia di Genova.* Rome, Prato, Firenze, 1857-1895. 11 vols. and 2 appendices. Vol. VII is in 4 parts.

Material of southwestern interest is contained in vol. VI, p. 634, an account of Juan de Padilla; pp. 682 *et seq.*, Marcos de Niza; vol. VII, part 2, p. 400 *et seq.*, Coronado, Chamuscado, Oñate, and Espejo; p. 472, Benavides; p. 574, Mendieta; p. 630, Motolinía; vol. VIII, p. 116, Sonora from 1540; p. 216, extracts from Sotomayor's book on the history of the College of Guadalupe.

Margry, Pierre. *Découvertes et établissements des Français dans l'ouest et dans le sud de l'Amérique septentrionale, 1614-1698. Mémoires et documents inédits.* Paris, 1879-88. 6 vols.

——*Relations et mémoires inédits pour servir à l'histoire de la France dans les pays d'outre mer.* Paris, 1867.

Contains Tonty's Memoire of 1693.

Mariano, R. P. *Gloriosus Franciscus Redivivus.* Ingolstadt, 1625. Folio, 2 engraved titles, 26 leaves of preliminaries, 852 pages, 6 leaves, and 26 plates.

Medina, José Toribio. *La imprenta en Manila.* First part, 1896. *Adiciones y amplicaciones,* 1904.

——*La imprenta en Mexico, 1539-1831.* Santiago, 1907-12. 8 vols.

This monumental work of Medina has for everyday purposes superseded all previous bibliographies as far as Mexican imprints are concerned. For the modern American historical student the work is marred by the inclusion of a vast number of religious works of a purely ephemeral character. The result of this is to swell the bulk of the book unduly without adding anything whatever of practical value. Señor Medina aimed to make a complete list of Mexican imprints, a perfectly impracticable task, but certainly credit must be given to him for near success.

——*Biblioteca Hispano Americana.* Santiago de Chile, 1898-1902. 7 vols.

Mendieta, Gerónimo. *Historia ecclesiastica Indiana.* Mexico, 1870.

This work was printed by Joaquín García Icazbalceta from a copy of the manuscript in the British museum.

Mota Padilla, Matías de la. *Historia de la conquista de la provincia de la Nueva-Galicia.* Guadalajara: . . . 1856. 3 vols. small 8°. 410; 310; 412 pages.

The first 53 pages of vol. I contain the half-title, title, and the preliminaries, consisting of a petition, *pareceres,* and prologue of the author placed in proper form for publication. The work was intended for publication, and it is not known why this did not come to pass. Several copies of the work exist in manuscript. Mota Padilla was not a friar and wrote largely from the lay standpoint, and the book consequently makes much more interesting reading than the chronicles of the friars, filled as they usually are with accounts of imaginary miraculous performances.

A new edition of this work has been issued in one volume, large 8°.

Motolinía [i. e., Fr. Toribio de Benavente]. *Historia de los Indios de la Nueva España.* *Icazbalceta's Documentos historicos,* I. *Documentos . . . de España,* LIII, 297-524. Lord Kingsborough's *Antiquities of Mexico,* vol. IX (incomplete). The above versions are different. The references are to the text of Icazbalceta.

Murr, Christoph Gottlieb von. *Nachrichten von verschiedenen ländern des Spanischen Amerika.* Halle, 1809-11.

This contains two accounts of the latter days of the Jesuits in California: *Nachrichten Von Californien,* by Wenzel Link, pp. 402-512, and *Reisebeschreibung aus Californien durch das gebiet von Mexico nach Europa,* 1767, pp. 413-30 of vol. I, by Franz Benno Ducrue. It also contains Father Och's *Reise in Sonora,* pp. 72-76.

Obregón, Baltasar. *See* Hammond, George P.

Ochoa, Eugenio de. *Catálogo razonado de los manuscritos españoles existentes en la Biblioteca Real de Paris.* Paris, 1844. 4°, vii, 703 pages.

Oviedo, Juan Antonio. *Elogios de muchos hermanos coadjutores de la Compañia de Jesus que en las quatro partes del mundo han florecido con grandes créditos de santidad.* Mexico, Viuda de J. B. de Hogal, 1755. 2 vols. 4°. Title and 7 leaves of preliminaries, 512 pp.; vol. II, 612 pp., 5 leaves.

Pacheco y Cárdenas. See *Colección de documentos inéditos relativos. . .*

Palau y Dulcet, Antonio. *Manual del librero Hispano-Americano.* Barcelona, 1923-27. 7 vols.

Pardo de Tavera, H. *Biblioteca Filipina.* Washington, 1903.

Pérez Pastor, Cristóbal. *Bibliografia Madrileña.* Madrid, 1891, 1906, 1907. 3 vols. folio.

This is one of the finest bibliographies that was ever published. Besides a full description of the titles and careful collations it contains, for all the important books, a description of the preliminaries, and frequently a reprint of some of the most important of these, and critical notes regarding the various editions. In the appendices much valuable material has been printed regarding the authors of books cited in the bibliography, which Señor Pérez Pastor discovered in the archives. The author examined with care the books of the Hermandad de los impresores de Madrid, an institution somewhat similar to Stationers' Hall in London, and from them he has extracted much valuable information.

——*La Imprenta en Medina del Campo.* Madrid, 1895.

Under no. 100, López de Gómara, will be found a description of the second edition of his work with a reprint of the preliminaries and the documents from the archives of 1554 relative to the attempt to collect the printed copies. Under no. 230, González de Mendoza, 1595 edition, is reprinted the dedication and some extracts, and pages 272-296, the famous *Invectiva* of the *Soldado de Cáceres* and the answer by Mendoza.

Pichardo, José Antonio. *Quivira.* [circa 1810.]

A manuscript formerly in my possession.

Portillo, Esteban L. *Apuntes para la historia antigua de Coahuila y Texas.* Saltillo, 1888. 482 pp., 1 leaf.

Purchas, Samuel. *Hakluytus posthumus or Purchas his Pilgrimes.* London, 1625-26. 5 vols.

Maclehose's edition published in Glasgow, 1905, in 20 vols. is the most available, retaining the pagination of the original.

Putnam, Ruth. *California: The Name.* University of California Press, Berkeley, 1917.

This pamphlet contains a reproduction of the Diego Gutiérrez map, 1562, from a copy in the Library of Congress. This is stated to be the first map in which the name California is applied.

Ramírez, José Fernando. *Bibliotheca Mexicana or a catalogue of the library of rare books and important manuscripts relating to Mexico and other parts of Spanish America, formed by the late Señor Don José Fernando Ramírez.* Sold at auction by Messrs. Puttick and Simpson, London, 1880.

In the introduction it is stated that after the death of Señor Ramírez his heirs allowed Alfredo Chavero to select the works relating to Mexico which form the first part of this sale. Chavero sold the bulk of the collection to Fernández del Castillo, who owned it when it was dispersed in London. A large number of the most important items passed into the hands of various American collectors. Many of the manuscripts are in the Bancroft collection at the University of California and in that of Edward E. Ayer of Chicago.

Ramusio, G. B. *Delle Navigationi et Viaggi.* Venetia, 1550, 1559, 1556. 3 vols.

The third volume contains the American section and was reprinted in 1565 and 1606. Only the 1606 edition contains any additional material, and that only of some voyages to the northeast.

Recueil de Voyages au Nord, contenant divers memoires tres-utiles au commerce et à la navigation. Amsterdam, J. F. Bernard, 1715-38. 10 vols. 12°.

Vol. III published in 1715 contains the California material, including the *Informe* of Picolo and a reprint of Father Verbiest's book originally printed in Paris in 1685. It also contains two letters from Monsieur Delisle to Cassini, one concerning the mouth of the Mississippi river and the other entitled "Touchant la Californie" devoted to the question as to whether California was or was not an island. Both letters relate to the map which had been sent to Paris by the Duque de Escalona, namely the Kino map, afterward published by Nicolás der Fer in 1700. Vol. V contains a reprint of Tonti's book under the title of *Relation de la Louisiane et du Mississippi*. There were two editions of vol. III and some of the others.

Retana, W. E. *Aparato bibliográfico de la historia general de Filipinas deducido de la colección que posee en Barcelona la Compañia General de Tabacos de dichas islas.* Por W. E. Retana. Madrid, 1906. 3 vols.

Retana describes 27 editions of González de Mendoza. The collection described and now belonging to the Philippine government in Manila contained Retana's own collection.

Richman, Irving B. *California under Spain and Mexico, 1535-1847*. Boston & New York, 1911.

The notes to this book contain a very elaborate list of sources, with special mention of the various manuscripts which Richman consulted in writing the book.

Rivière, E. M. *Corrections et additions a la bibliothèque de la Compagnie de Jesus.* Toulouse, 1911.

Robertson, James Alexander. *List of documents in the Spanish Archives relating to the history of the United States which had been printed or of which transcripts have been preserved in American libraries.* Washington, 1910.

It appears to me that the plan of this work is exactly the reverse of what it should have been. What is needed is a list of documents in American libraries relating to the history of the United States from Spanish sources, whether they are originals or transcripts.

Sabin, Joseph. *A dictionary of books relating to America, from its discovery to the present time.* New York, 1868-1936, Volumes I-XXIX.

This is the greatest of all American bibliographies, and in one sense it will never be superseded, as it is hardly likely that another general bibliography will be made. For some time Dr. Wilberforce Eames was at work on Sabin's slips to complete it and edited several of the volumes. Dr. Eames himself is the author of some of the special bibliographies in the published volumes, and other special subjects were treated by amateurs who were well-versed in special branches. Sabin began to publish the work shortly after the Civil war, and books covering that period assume an undue prominence in the work. He also copied from Ternaux, Beristain, and others, large numbers of titles without collations, many of which were fictitious or had incorrect dates assigned to them.

Sánchez, Juan M. *Bibliografia Aragonesa del siglo XVI.* Madrid, 1913-14. 2 vols.

Sancto Antonio, Fr. Juan. *Bibliotheca Universa Franciscana, sive alumnorum trium Ordinum S. P. S. Francisci, . . .Matriti: Ex Typographia Causae V. Matris de Agreda. Anno 1731* [1733.] Folio, title, 19 preliminary leaves, 527 pp. plus 19 leaves; title, 5 preliminary leaves, 492 pp. plus 12 leaves; title, 5 preliminary leaves, 164 pp., 49 plus 4 plus 28 plus 5 plus 51 of index plus 45 leaves.

Sanning de Nissa, P. Bernardo. *Der chronichen der drei orden des S. Franciscus seraphicus theil welche serfasst und beschen. . . .* Prague, 1689. 8 vols. folio.

Sauer, Carl. *The road to Cíbola.* Ibero-Americana: 3. Berkeley, 1932.

Shea, John Gilmary. *The Catholic church in colonial days.* New York, 1886.

——*The expedition of Don Diego Dionisio de Peñalosa. . . from Santa Fé to the river Mischipi and Quivira in 1662, as described by Father Nicholas de Freytas, O.S.F.* New York, 1882.

The original text from a copy made by Buckingham Smith from another copy in the Depósito Hidrográfico in Madrid, together with a translation.

Shepherd, William R. *Guide to the materials for the history of the United States in Spanish Archives.* Washington, 1907.

This, the first work published by the Carnegie Institution in its investigation of the Spanish archives, has been largely superseded by later publications; nevertheless it is of considerable value.

Smith, Buckingham. *Colección de varios documentos para la historia de la Florida y tierras adyacentes.* Tomo 1 [all published] Londres [Madrid, 1857]. 4°, title, 3 leaves of preliminaries, 208 pp. and portrait of Ferdinand V.

This contains 37 documents relating to Florida, Sonora, and California, which Mr. Smith had copied from the archives in Spain while he was secretary of legation. He accumulated a large additional store of copies, which no doubt he intended also to publish but was prevented from doing so by his return to the United States in 1858. Mr. Smith's theory was that it was only permissible to print documents where the proofs could be compared with the originals. The New York Historical Society owns most of his unpublished material.

Sommervogel, Carlos. *Bibliothèque de la Compagnie de Jesus.* Brussels, 1890-1909. 10 vols.

A new edition of de Backer.

Sotomayor, José Francisco. *Historia del apostólico colegio de nuestra señora de Guadalupe de Zacatecas desde su fundacion hasta nuestros dias.* Zacatecas, 1874. 667, v pages, including frontispiece.

Sotwell, Nathaniel. *Bibliotheca Scriptorum Societatis Jesu, opus inchoatum a R.P. Petro Ribadeneira. . . .* Romae, 1676. Folio.

Stevens, Henry. *Historical Nuggets, Biblioteca Americana or a descriptive account of my collection of rare books relating to America.* London, 1862. 2 vols. and 2 parts of what was intended to be the third volume, these being published in 1885.

This is a small book but contains notices of very many of the rarest books relating to Spanish America, with complete titles and careful collations.

Stöcklein, Joseph. *Der Neue Welt-Bott allerhand so lehr-als geist-reiche brief schrifften und reis-beschreibungen welche von denen Missionariis der Gesellschafft Jesu aus beyden Indien und andern über meer gelegenen ländern seit An. 1642. biss auf das Jahr 1726.* Augsburg und Wein, 1726-1785. 5 vols. folio.

This work of Joseph Stöcklein not only contains translations from the *Lettres Edifiantes,* but also a large number of letters addressed to religious houses and individuals in Germany by the German missionaries, and constitutes the grand source of the history of Jesuit missions up to 1758. P. Auguste Carayon in his *Bibliographie historique de la Compagnie de Jesus,* Paris, 1864, in the appendix gives a detailed list of the letters printed in this collection arranged under numbers of which the total amounts to 723. What relates to California and Sonora is mostly contained in the first part. It will be found under the following numbers: 29, 32, 33, 53, 55, 56, 71, 72 (the last two from vol. v of the *Lettres Edifiantes),* 171, 173 (Picolo's letter of December 18, 1716), 212, 448 (Father Consag), 543.

Tabula geographica totius Seraphici Ordinis FF. Minorum Sancti Francisci, sub Generali Ministro Rmo Patre in Christo P. Fr. Josepho Ximenez de Samaniego. Monachii, 1680. 8°, title, and 59 pp.

Tanner, P. Matthias. *Societas Jesu usque ad Sanguinis et vitae profusionem militans, in Europa, Africa, Asia et America.* Prague, 1675.

This was translated into German as *Die Gesellschaft Jesu,* Prague, 1683. This contains some additional text and 9 more plates than the Latin edition.

Taylor, Alexander S. *Bibliographa Californica.* Published in the Sacramento Daily Union, June 25, 1863, and some supplements.

Alexander S. Taylor was a prolific writer in the newspapers on the early history of California and the California Indians. He also was a diligent searcher for manuscript material relating to the early history and collected, mostly from the old mission libraries, an extensive lot of manuscripts, which I understand are now in the possession of the Archbishop in San Francisco. Taylor's bibliography is marred by lack of precision in giving the titles of books, many of which, no doubt, he gives from hearsay and not from actual inspection.

Tello, Fray Antonio. *Libro segundo de la Cronica Miscelánea, en que se trata de la conquista espiritual y temporal de la santa provincia de Xalisco en el nuevo reino de la Galicia y Nueva Vizcaya y descubrimiento del Nuevo Mexico.* Guadalajara, 1891.

About 1888 this manuscript was discovered by Dr. León in Celaya. Previously some twenty chapters in fragmentary form had been brought together by Icazbalceta and published by him in vol. II of his *Colección de Documentos para la Historia de Mexico,* 1866. Mota Padilla states that it was written about 1650 or 1651, and Icazbalceta that at this period Father Tello was about 86 years of age. Even if this should turn out to be a mistake it is evident that Father Tello obtained a great deal of his information from living persons who had been actors in the great drama of the conquest of New Galicia. The book is the source from which the subsequent writers, Beaumont and Mota Padilla, have taken a large portion of their works. Father Tello has only written the annals down to 1619, those from 1620-1650 being added by another person.

Ternaux, H. *Bibliothèque Américaine, ou Catalogue des ouvrages relatifs a l'Amérique, qui ont paru depuis sa découverte jusqu'a l'an 1700.* Paris, 1837.

A great deal of historical interest attaches to this catalogue, as it was the one with which the principal early American collectors worked, and it is still today not devoid of interest. Ternaux did not by any means have all the books listed in this catalogue, but he had a great many of the rarest ones. The rest of the titles were taken from various sources, the Spanish ones mostly from Nicolás Antonio and Barcia. His own collection was sold at auction in Leipzig or Paris in 1836, under the name of Raetzel. Many of his rarest books are now in the Lenox collection in the New York Public library.

Ternaux-Compans. *Voyages, relations et mémoires originaux, pour servir a l'histoire de la découverte de l'Amérique.* Paris, 1837-40.

This set is variously said to contain 19, 20, or 21 volumes, no. 20 being *Recueil de Pieces sur la Floride,* and no. 21 *Recueil de Documents sur les posesiones españoles dans l'Amérique.*

Texas State Historical Association, Quarterly of. Austin, Texas, 1898 to date. Title changed to *Southwestern Historical Quarterly,* July, 1912.

This contains a large number of articles on New Mexico and Texas, and a few on California. Dr. H. E. Bolton was a frequent contributor to this journal.

Torres Lanzas, Pedro. *Relación descriptiva de los Mapas, Planos, &, de México y Floridas existentes en el Archivo General de Indias.* Sevilla, 1900. 2 vols.

This little work of Torres Lanzas contains numerous descriptions of early maps, mostly manuscript, of what were then the frontier provinces.

Torrubia, Fr. Joseph. *Chronica de la seraphica religion del glorioso patriarca San Francisco de Assis. . . .* Roma, 1756. Folio, 496 pages, plus xliv of appendix.

This is a continuation of the works of Cornejo and González, the three constituting the standard chronicle of the order.

Twitchell, Ralph E. *The leading facts of New Mexican history.* Cedar Rapids, Iowa, 1911. 2 vols.

Mr. Twitchell, who lived in New Mexico, wrote this from well-known books and such documents as he could find in the archives of New Mexico. It is profusely illustrated with portraits and facsimiles.

——*The Spanish archives of New Mexico.* The Torch Press, Cedar Rapids, Iowa, 1914. 2 vols.

Vol. I is a calendar with some facsimiles of documents existing at the present time in the archives at Santa Fe, these being chiefly those of the original archives which relate to land claims. Vol. II is a calendar with illustrations, portraits, and some facsimiles of signatures of documents now in the Museum of New Mexico.

I made a rough examination of the printed documents in this collection while they were in Washington and found very few which relate specifically to New Mexico. They consist almost entirely of decrees, *cédulas,* and royal orders issued by the Spanish government, either in Spain or Mexico.

Uriarte, José Eugenio de. *Catálogo razonado de obras anónimas y seudónimas de autores de la Compañia de Jesús.* Madrid, 1904-16. 5 vols.

Velasco, Juan. *Histoire du royaume de Quito.* Vols. VIII-IX, Second Series Ternaux-Compans.

Translated from a Spanish original, present location unknown. Velasco was a Jesuit, expelled in 1767 from Quito, who went to Italy and there compiled this work.

Vindel, Pedro. *Biblioteca filipina catalogo sistematica.* Madrid, 1904.

This catalogue was made by Retana.

Wading, Lucas. *Annales minorum seu trium ordinem a S. Francisco.* Editio secunda. . . . Josephi Mariae Fonseca Ab Ebora. Rome, 1731-1860. 24 vols. folio.

Apparently the first edition of this book was issued in Lyons, 1625-1654, but the edition most commonly known is that published in Rome, 1731-1745, in 16 vols. folio (to which were added 7 vols. of *Sillabus universus* by Marcio de Anema).

Wagner, Henry R. "Fr. Marcos de Niza." *New Mexico Historical Review,* April, 1934.

——"Some imaginary California geography." *Proceedings,* American Antiquarian Society, April, 1926.

——*Spanish voyages to the northwest coast of America in the sixteenth century.* San Francisco, 1929.

Winship, George Parker. *The Coronado expedition, 1540-1542.* Fourteenth annual report of the Bureau of Ethnology. Washington, 1896.

Winsor, Justin, editor. *Narrative and critical history of America.* Boston, 1886-89. 8 vols.

Vol. II, *Ancient Florida,* by John G. Shea; *Cortés and his Companions,* by Winsor; *Discoveries on the Pacific Coast,* Winsor; *Early Explorations in New Mexico,* by H. W. Haynes, pp. 473-504. Vol. VIII contains a very much condensed account of the later history of Mexico and its northern provinces, mostly taken from Bancroft.

Wytfliet, C. *Descriptionis ptolemaicae augmentum.* Lovanii, 1597. 4°, title, 3 preliminary leaves, 191, 1 pp., including 19 maps. Dovay, 1605, first French translation.

This is the first distinctly American atlas, and the text contains an account of the discovery, geography, natural history, and ethnology of the New World. The second part contains the maps interspersed with explanatory text. The maps of interest to us are no. 1—Orbis Terrarum, a copy of Mercator's map of 1584; no. 12—New Spain; no. 13—New Granada and California; no. 14—Anian and Quivira; no. 15—Conibas. There are two issues of the original, one with errata of six lines on the verso of 191, and the other without.

INDEX